Dope in the Age of Innocence

First published in 2010 by
Liberties Press
Guinness Enterprise Centre | Taylor's Lane | Dublin 8
Tel: +353 (1) 415 1224
www.libertiespress.com | info@libertiespress.com

Distributed in the United States by
Dufour Editions | PO Box 7 | Chester Springs | Pennsylvania | 19425

and in Australia by
James Bennett Pty Limited | InBooks | 3 Narabang Way
Belrose NSW 2085

Trade enquiries to Gill & Macmillan Distribution
Hume Avenue | Park West | Dublin 12
Tel: +353 (1) 500 9534 | Fax: +353 (1) 500 9595
www.gillmacmillan.ie

ISBN: 978-1-907593-01-7
2 4 6 8 10 9 7 5 3 1

A CIP record for this title is available from the British Library.

Cover design by Sin É Design
Internal design by Liberties Press
Maps by Matthew Enright
Printed by ScandBook

The publishers gratefully acknowledge financial support from the Arts Council.

Dope in the Age of Innocence

Damien Enright

LIB
ERT
IES

*To Glen Eddy, RIP, my loyal compañero; to Chris Smith,
who was my saviour; to Hannah, the pilgrim soul; to Matt, for
the maps; to Marie, forever queen of my heart*

The faintest ink outlives the longest memory
Chinese proverb

Contents

—That time is past,
And all its aching joys are now no more,
And all its dizzy raptures. Not for this
Faint I, nor mourn nor murmur, other gifts
Have followed ; for such loss, I would believe,
Abundant recompence. For I have learned
To look on nature, not as in the hour
Of thoughtless youth ; but hearing oftentimes
The still, sad music of humanity,
Nor harsh nor grating, though of ample power
To chasten and subdue. And I have felt
A presence that disturbs me with the joy
Of elevated thoughts ; a sense sublime
Of something far more deeply interfused,
Whose dwelling is the light of setting suns,
And the round ocean and the living air,
And the blue sky, and in the mind of man;
A motion and a spirit, that impels
All thinking things, all objects of all thought,
And rolls through all things.

from William Wordsworth, 'Lines Composed a Few Miles Above Tintern Abbey, On Revisiting the Banks of the Wye During a Tour, July 13, 1798'

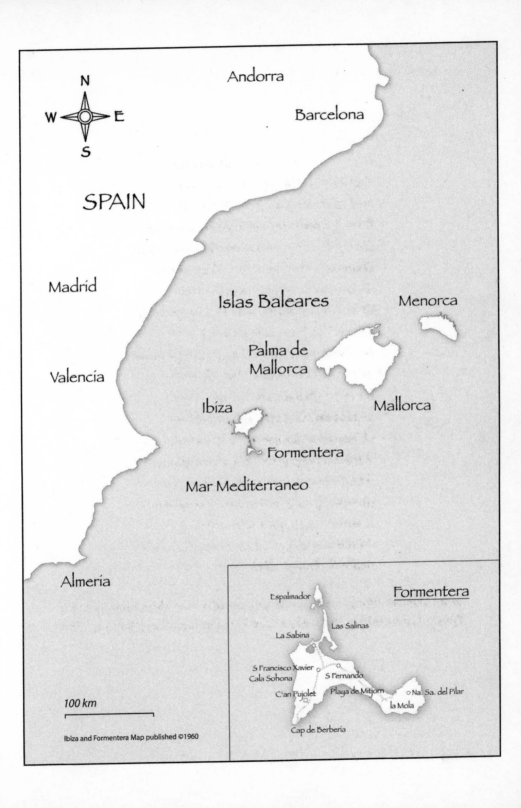

N
W E
S

Andorra

Barcelona

SPAIN

Madrid

Islas Baleares

Menorca

Valencia

Palma de
Mallorca

Ibiza

Mallorca

Formentera

Mar Mediterraneo

Almeria

100 km

Ibiza and Formentera Map published ©1960

Formentera

Espalmador

Las Salinas

La Sabina

S Francisco Xavier
Cala Sohona

S Fernando

C'an Pujolet

Playa de Mitjorn

Na. Sa. del Pilar

la Mola

Cap de Berberia

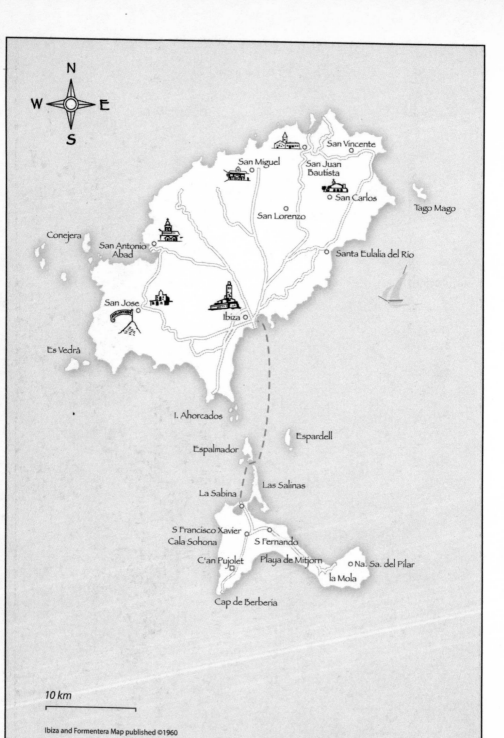

N
W   E
S

San Vincente

San Miguel

San Juan
Bautista

San Carlos

Tago Mago

San Lorenzo

Conejera

San Antonio
Abad

Santa Eulalia del Rio

San Jose

Ibiza

Es Vedrà

I. Ahorcados

Espardell

Espalmador

Las Salinas

La Sabina

S Francisco Xavier
Cala Sohona

S Fernando

C'an Pujolet

Playa de Mitjorn

Na. Sa. del Pilar

la Mola

Cap de Berberia

10 km

Ibiza and Formentera Map published ©1960

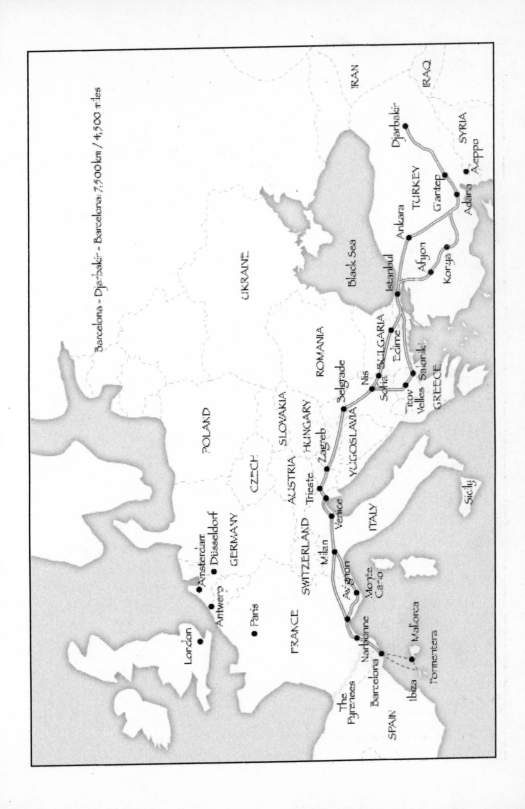

To Follow Knowledge

Chapter 1

THAT MORNING, WHEN WE LEFT for London, I rose in the dark and went into the big kitchen where the double doors were open to let in the pre-dawn light. I found Hanna squatting by the embers of last night's fire in the big hearth set into the gable wall. A lighted candle stood on a stone beside her, and she was pouring boiling water from a blackened saucepan into a jug, making me coffee. I pulled on my old Cuban-heeled boots and stood in the doorway for a minute, looking out at the sky still filled with stars, and the dark line of the sea below them. On the camino, by the gate, I saw cigarette tips glowing in the darkness: Rick and Carlo, waiting; maybe they'd been up all night. At the fire, Hanna held out a cup of coffee and a plate with bread and sardines, but I was too excited to eat and, besides, we had a nine-kilometre walk to La Sabina where we'd catch the daily boat to Ibiza, the first leg of our journey to the north. It was September 1964.

After I downed the coffee, Hanna took the candle and I followed her into the bedroom where Aoife was sleeping on a mattress, her rag doll on the pillow beside her. I kissed her lightly on the forehead and we looked at her together, our tiny daughter. We smiled at one another for a moment before we returned to the main room. There, I scooped a mug of water from the bucket by the door, picked up my bag and bedroll and turned to Hanna. She came and leant against me, so warm and soft and small within the shift she wore. When I kissed her, my lips were still wet. I said goodbye.

I had made no promises of when I'd be back. Much as I would have liked, in that tender moment, to make them, I didn't. I loved her, but what we had together wasn't yet enough. She hoped that, in time, it might be, and I did too. Meanwhile, who knew what this journey held? I had to be free, but I wouldn't deepen the wound with promises, if a wounding, sooner or later, there would have to be.

On the *camino*, I made out Rick's shape by his hat, and moonlight glinted on Carlo's spectacles. The *camino* was broken, but there was light now from the moon, and off to the east the sky was brightening.

We passed through San Francisco Xavier without talking. It was still and silent, like a border village in a black-and-white cowboy film, the big, white church throwing a shadow over the main square of pitted bedrock, and the few squat houses that comprised the village cut out in moonlight and shadow. Then, onward, on a better *camino* leading to the road which ran the length of Formentera, twenty kilometres from Salinas in the north, past San Fernando – which had electricity, a *pensión* and a bar – to the Mola, a big table-land at the south-eastern end.

The road was wider but not much better surfaced than the cart tracks and *caminos*. The only traffic that used it was the old island bus, which went to the boat mornings and evenings, and Longini's battered jeep. Longini had been the only foreigner on Formentera for years. A one-time Louisiana lawyer, he lived with his wife, reputed to be an heiress, smoking dope and spending his time reading and killing flies on his veranda, which was screened with mosquito netting: he had a strange fixation about flying insects of any kind. The only other long-term foreigner was Briefcase Hans, a German who had a steel plate in his head which caught the sun, and who could be seen occasionally in a suit boarding the Ibiza boat, a briefcase in hand. He lived on a *finca* surrounded by trees and thorn bushes with *Eingang Verboten* and *Entrada Prohibida* signs on stakes to keep out intruders.

As for the rest of us, we were the newcomers, coming and going, staying as long as we could, sincere seekers after knowledge or simply a kind of freedom, attracted by the remoteness of the island and the cheap farmhouses to rent. None of us were more than thirty years old and there were rarely more than a dozen of us, a band of dropouts of various nationalities, united by our use of marijuana and LSD. We were forerunners of a culture soon to sweep the coffee shops and colleges of Europe but it was secretive then; if you smoked grass you didn't talk about it even amongst the expats in Ibiza, the island of hedonism and liberty. Dope-smokers were different, with a language and code of their own.

Hanna was English. I was the only Irish citizen around. Three years before, when I was living on Ibiza with Nancy, my ex-wife, I'd sometimes cross to Formentera. I'd spend a night or two in San Fernando at the *pénsion* Fonda Pepe just to get away from Ibiza and the bad trip that was happening with Nancy – and to try to write poetry, which was what I'd come to those islands to do. I no longer tried; in the light of the new reality, it seemed wrong to arrest life and reflect, to leave the Here-and-Now and get entangled in words which were so unsatisfactory for communication anyway.

LSD had changed my mind about a lot of things, although we had taken it only once, Hanna and I. Afterwards, we had left Ibiza and gone to Formentera to live out the reality we had seen. That first time, we had only twelve pounds cash and hadn't been able to stay long. Forced to go back to London, we had fiercely held on to the vision we had seen, worked hard, saved and returned with enough money to last us for maybe a year. Our hope was that we might habituate ourselves to a new way of thinking, a perception outside the twentieth century values so destructive and dangerous for us and our children. Hanna and I humbly, passionately and naively hoped for redemption from the culture that countenanced war and nuclear showdowns, from all we had ever learned. And we loved Formentera, the peace there, the friends and the simplicity of life.

But the plan had gone wrong. Out of the heat-haze hanging over the island one June day, my old friend Mel, an American I'd known in Ibiza and in London, came limping down the *camino* with all sorts of rubies and ropes, as he called them, on his arms and on his legs as a result of months spent in Tangier shooting Maxatone Fort which, as he said, would make the dead sit up and appear to many. It was, in fact, pure amphetamine, meant to revive people who'd had heart attacks and was certainly not advisable for long-term recreational use.

Hanna and I knew nothing of the vocabulary of junkies and we were shocked to see the state Mel was in. Hanna cooked broth at first, because he could eat nothing else, and we looked after him and listened to his endless, motor-mouth rap about how Maxatone got you there, out beyond grass or acid or Romilar or anything else. All bullshit. It was plain to see from the state of Mel's body, never mind the state of his brain, just where Maxatone took one. But he was my friend and, so, we took care of him. As soon as the sores on his legs healed and he could walk a bit, he began to talk about going to London to do Travellers Cheque scams, but he had no money. He put it to us that we owed it to him as friends to lend him three hundred dollars to buy cheques which he would then say he had lost and on which he'd claim a refund, thus to double his money and pay us back.

Of course, this emotional manipulation was typical junkie behaviour but we didn't know it; we didn't know any junkies then. The thing was, what little money we had wasn't just to sustain ourselves and Aoife – I also had to come up with five hundred pesetas every month to give to Nancy in Ibiza for the support of my twin sons. But what could we do? As Hanna said, if the love we spoke of meant anything, we had to help Mel. I agreed. He'd kicked his habit and I knew that, short of the scams going wrong, he'd repay us. So we gave him one hundred pounds – equivalent to three hundred dollars – which he promised to return to us as soon as he had made his pile.

Now, three months later, we had received a letter from him saying he was in London and had the money for us. I was doubly glad: for all his junkie jive-talk, Mel was an honourable man and I'd been right about him: he hadn't let us down. He said he'd get around to delivering it as soon as he could but, meantime, he'd mail it to us or it was there to collect if I decided to come north. He'd done the scams and they'd proved easy – why didn't I do one myself?

It was a temptation. We were on our last few hundred pesetas; beyond that, all we had left was the fare money to get us back to London. From the one hundred pounds Mel said he'd send, I already owed Nancy the last month's money for the boys and there was another month due.

Since Mel had left, we'd supplemented our remaining cash by collecting snails to sell. The small, black *caracoles* lived on the stone walls and could be found at night by lamplight, but we had no lamps and couldn't have afforded batteries, so we collected them in the first light of dawn. Hanna would work with Aoife slung on her back like a papoose; it was a novel idea at the time. Most days we'd fill a bucket, especially if it was a dewy morning. Then I'd take them to Las Salinas on my friend Bruno's bike, riding over the rocky *caminos* to the main road and then down the dusty highway to the pier where the ferryman would take them to a restaurant in Ibiza and bring me back fifty pesetas the next day.

However, the snail season was now over and there was no other way of making money on the island. Bruno offered to share his food with us as long as it lasted, and that was fine but it wasn't going to support the boys on Ibiza. It looked like we should use our remaining cash to get us back to London, to rent a room there and start saving all over again. Cutting short our time on the island would be a bitter disappointment for Hanna. The dream was slipping away and I was to blame; Mel was my friend, not hers. I felt I should do something to save us: I should be her hero, ready to risk my freedom for my family.

By going to London and making the scams work, I could double our hundred pounds. Better still, I thought, if the first scam worked I could do another and twice double it, and we'd be secure for six more months on Formentera. I'd be able to give Nancy what I owed her and more, and bring some useful things back to the islands, a carbon lamp so that Hanna could paint at night, educational toys and stuff for Aoife and the boys, a few books I wanted – and maybe I could even buy another old car because I didn't figure the one we'd left parked in Barcelona five months before would do much more than get me, Carlo and Rick to England before it expired.

I talked to Hanna about this plan. I didn't really discuss it: I was going to do it anyway, whatever she said. She didn't like the risk that I might get busted and not make it back, but she saw the logic. And, as I told her, scamming a couple of hundred quid from American Express didn't seem like a crime; nobody would be hurt even if shareholders lost half a cent each on their dividends. The stash I'd make would mean the world to us. She could see I was set on it and she accepted that I would go.

Because working the scam needed two people, I began to ask around if anybody would be interested in coming north with me. Nobody had much money. When word got around about my scheme, two guys came independently to our house out on the Cap de Berbería, the Barbary Cape, to talk it over with me and learn the score.

One was Carlo, a gentle, easy-going artist from California who, it turned out, had nerves of steel. The second was Rick, an intense ex-jailbird from Detroit on his first ever trip out of America, trying to get enlightened and to find a good life, swearing never to go back to crime. Of course what I was proposing was crime but, as Rick said, it was different from 'knockin' over gas-stations' which he used to do as a kid in Detroit until the cops threw him in the slammer. He was thirty, older than most of us in Formentera. Carlo and I were the same age, twenty-four.

Carlo had weak eyes and wore smoked-glass spectacles. He had a Zapata moustache and a thin gold earring – neither of which were worn by men then, except maybe by gypsies. He was sallow-skinned; his mother was Maltese. He wore jeans, a lumberjack shirt with a faded T-shirt underneath, and he had a piece of frayed pink cord hanging from his neck, a Buddhist symbol. In a certain light, the moustache and his straight gaze made him look like Wyatt Earp or some other gun-slinging marshal of the Old West.

Rick, in contrast, looked like a bum. He wore a beat-up straw hat, breaking up at the edges. His face was naturally pale and dark-jowled; he looked a little cadaverous, with his deep-set, brown eyes. The hat wasn't any sort of affectation; his hair was thinning and greying and he wore it to keep off the sun. The rest of his outfit – a canvas jacket and baggy, once-white trousers – looked like he'd slept in it but not just overnight, maybe for weeks. However, he was careful to keep himself clean, as much as one could on an island where there were no showers or even bathrooms in the houses, and one washed in the yard by hauling buckets of water up out of the well and pouring them over oneself in the bright morning sunlight.

It was still dark when we reached the main road that morning, passing a wake-up joint between us. The island bus clanked by, raising dust, its tail lights disappearing down the road towards Salinas pier and its small beacon, which we could already see in the distance. We caught up with a figure walking ahead and, as we passed, he greeted me. It was George Andrews, an American beat poet whom I'd met in San Fernando one day when we were both sheltering from the rain. He had a reputation amongst the Americans and Rick and Carlo seemed impressed that he should greet me so warmly. I was a little chuffed at that.

As dawn came up, glorious, out of the sea, we passed the salt pools of Las Salinas, a hundred black-framed pictures each reflecting a different patch of sky. Beyond them, a mountain of fresh sea salt stood like a crystal pyramid shimmering in the first light of the sun. We were pink, me, Carlo and Rick, the light reflecting on our skin as we headed for the boat – pink us, the about-to-be desperadoes, high out of our minds under the Technicolor, widescreen, panorama-vision sky.

On the wooden benches on the open deck of the Ibiza boat, the Formentera women sat in their ankle-length black dresses, headscarves and long pigtails, holding handkerchiefs against their faces for what reason I didn't know. Some wore straw sombreros on top of the scarves, and they had baskets of produce and trussed chickens at their feet. My *compañeros* and I found seats at the stern and settled in, pulling our jackets around us against the morning chill, feeling it now after the heat of the walking. Sometimes, pigs and livestock would be winched on deck and, once, even Longini's jeep, set athwart, going to Ibiza for repairs.

As the boat cleared the pier and turned towards the sea, Espalmador, the small island beyond the harbour mouth, caught the sun for a minute and glowed like an ember. The track of the sun on the sea seemed to light our way.

Rick lay back, his hat pulled over his eyes like a sleeping cowboy. Carlo sat with his arms wrapped around himself, staring at a trussed chicken on the floor. For me, there wasn't a moment to be lost; I wanted to drink all this in, make it a part of me, the dawn rising over the sea, the departure, the moving-on. Beneath us, the old timbers creaked and the deck pitched and rose as we met the fresh sea, crystals of spray in the sun, choirs on the wind. How blest I was to be there, my good companions with me! Through ardent eyes, I watched the curve of the earth I lived on turn once more towards the sun.

Over the prow, Ibiza rose and fell like a giant green goddess floating on the distant sea. Ibiza had changed me. It had been an island of destiny and education. It wasn't finished with me yet, but I didn't know that then.

Off to the west, between sea and sky, a small plane flew in an empty sky.

Aerolíneas Aviaco was painted on the fuselage; Ibiza had an airport now but few planes yet crossed her skies. Now, as our boat drew near the port, dawn was catching the tops of the high walls that surrounded the Old Town, the fortress built on the hill above the sea. Ibiza had been Carthaginian, Roman and Hispanic. In its time, it had been raided and raped by corsairs and freebooters from all over the Mediterranean. The most recent colonisers – artists, would-be artists, drifters, mystery-men and ne'er-do-wells – had found the island by chance in the early '60s, as I had. Small in number at first, most were near penniless. They sought what they called freedom, meaning little or no interference from the locals while enjoying a combination of cheap rents, low-cost booze and casual sex, meantime surviving on cash begged or borrowed from home. Inevitably, the word got out and, now, in 1964, Ibiza was attracting expatriates with money, even movie stars and the like.

The boat passed the breakwater and entered the harbour. The engine cut, the white wake sank. We stood up to go. 'I'm starving!' said Rick, beside me, his voice raw. 'Me, too!' said Carlo, 'I could eat that fuckin' chicken!' The chicken clucked and looked indignant. We laughed.

The town was still asleep. We went to the *kiosco* on the dock, the only place open and, there, we breakfasted on sweet, hot *ensemadas* and *café con leche* with an inch or more of condensed milk in a goo at the bottom of the glass.

In his letter telling me he had the money, Mel had said that if he didn't hear from me within three weeks, he'd send it by money order care of the *Lista de Correos* in Ibiza. Junkies could be flaky, I knew. When Mel had left us he was clean but, nevertheless, I worried that he might have somehow blown the lot by the time I met him, or jumped the gun and posted it before time. If it was travelling south as we were travelling north, it'd be a disaster. We'd arrive in England with no capital for the scams, no survival-money and no money to get us back to Formentera.

We'd pooled our bread for the trip north. After putting in for their boat fares and share of the gas, Carlo and Rick had only a few hundred pesetas extra to contribute. I had about the same. I'd left Hanna with what remained of our cash; it was enough to cover rent and keep her and Aoife for a month. If things went wrong for me, she'd have to find her own way back to England.

I had four hundred pesetas to give Nancy for the boys. I'd be meeting her in Ibiza; I knew where to find her. The boat to Barcelona wouldn't be leaving until eight in the evening, so Rick, Carlo and I had the whole day to kill. I hoped to spend it with the kids.

The sunlight crept slowly down the Old Town walls as we sat in the grey morning, waiting for it to reach us. Above us, the huge walls meeting at the corner were like the prow of a giant ship ploughing into the cluttered houses of the Peña. Further along the curve of the bay, the 'new' town – the town outside the walls – climbed in white-painted terraces from the sea. The paint was flaking: Ibiza was run down in those days. The islanders had been on the Republican side in the Civil War and, even now, twenty-five years later, Franco was still exacting his revenge. While nearby Nationalist Majorca was allowed to develop tourism, Ibiza was a neglected backwater, an *isla non grata*. Shipbuilding, which had once flourished, had been stopped – but the Ibicencos did their best to circumvent the law by building new boats on old keels. Island lore had it that there were eight different kinds of police in Ibiza besides the feared Guardia Civil in their shiny, lavatory-pan helmets. But there were cops to watch cops everywhere in Franco's Spain.

We'd have dearly liked *carajillos* – small coffee-and-cognac 'wheelbarrows' – for a further wake-up but we couldn't afford it. We'd have to watch every cent. We'd drive night and day to save on hotel money and only eat stuff we'd put together ourselves. Instead, we went down to the water and smoked another joint, a thin one; we didn't have much dope either. It was kief, chopped grass and tobacco from the Rif Mountains, although I had a small piece of Moroccan hash, rare at the time.

We left our bags at the *kiosco* and headed for the Post Office where Carlo found a letter from his mother with ten bucks inside. We whooped when he pulled it from the envelope, a crisp, new bill. We'd change it in France; we had enough pesetas to get us through Spain. There was no mail for me but I asked if there was a bag going to Formentera. The postmaster knew me from before and took a look. Amongst the half-dozen letters inside was one from my mother. It contained no cash but had a lot of news from home, how the house had been repainted, how they'd let the housemaid go – and also news about my younger brother, in college, and my sister who, apparently, was 'a fright with the boys'. There was a single page from my father, a senior civil servant's epistle to his errant son, affectionate but brief, a page of neat, copperplate handwriting signed 'Your Loving Dad'. Like my mother, he said he remembered me in his prayers. It was amazing they hadn't despaired of me. At eighteen, I'd announced that I was dropping out of medical school, and, at nineteen, that I was in the company of an English woman in a hospital in Germany. This was Nancy. We'd had a major road accident as we were hitch-hiking to India. Seven months later, not long after my twentieth birthday, I wrote to say that I was soon to become a father and wanted to marry Nancy because we were in love.

After the Correos, Rick, Carlo and I walked across the Vara de Rey, Ibiza's main drag, to the Montesol Café. The expats gathered there every morning after checking the post for remittances and, after a coffee, began their drinking for the day. I knew Nancy would be around; where there was a social buzz she'd always be at the heart of it. I didn't blame her; when we'd been together, we'd been the same. In fact, perhaps one reason she was happier when I left Ibiza after our break-up was because she no longer had to share the limelight – not that there weren't plenty of noisier and larger-than-life personalities to compete with both of us in Ibiza at the time.

The package tourists hadn't yet appeared in Ibiza town. On arrival at the airport, they were immediately bussed to San Antonio Abad, the first Ibiza resort, where the one or two hotels and restaurants charged them five times the going rate for everything. Once there, they rarely ventured beyond. The locals spoke no English, the taxis charged a fortune and they'd no more think of taking a country bus than going up the Congo on *The African Queen*. So, Ibiza town remained the preserve of the penniless elite and the opulent arrivistes who came to lotus-eat and get stoned or to kick their habits.

That morning, when I walked across to the Montesol, all the usual characters were there, sitting about in their faded rainments, hair to the nape of their necks, their long-handled Ibiza baskets stuffed with dog-eared newspapers, cartons of cheap Spanish cigarettes and bottles of booze. Some had arrived on rickety bikes from the country, a few with dogs in tow. The women wore eye-liner and eye-shadow, loose dresses and long hair. Some had bouffant hairstyles still semi-intact after months away from the salons in New York or Paris or wherever they'd originally been styled.

There was much chatter and buzz around the tables sprawling over the pavement outside the Montesol and the Alhambra, its sister café. In the background were the usual sounds of handclaps used to summon waiters, sporadic roars of contradiction or howls of laughter as writers and would-be writers exchanged ritual abuse and the oohs-and-aahs of the gossip club as they swopped the latest scandals and lore. Carlo, Rick and I found a table and sat down. Several of the old crowd greeted me; we knew one another because there had been so few of us at the start. I went and said hello but didn't absent myself from my Formentera friends for too long. They weren't part of this scene – in fact Rick despised it, while Carlo simply watched it, bemused. As for me, I'd suddenly seen the superficiality and self-destructiveness of this society the year before when I'd first brought Hanna to the islands and we had been given our first acid trip; it was why we'd left and gone to Formentera. I knew it was all bullshit, ego and hot air but who was I to turn my back on my elders and betters, and the old camaraderie? They might have been drinking themselves into oblivion but that was their business, and some amongst them were old friends.

I'd met Hanna in London when I went there after Nancy and I had split up. She'd moved in with me before I was quite ready, but I had little option; she was vulnerable after the break-up of her marriage and I didn't want to be the author of more rejection, more pain. I was screwed up myself, full of longing for Ibiza, my lost world. Sixteen months later, Aoife was born. I thought that if I took Hanna to Ibiza, all my uncertainties about our relationship might be forgotten and I could commit myself fully to her and the precious child we'd made. We saved money and arrived with enough funds for two months. Then the LSD, and it changed everything. The bombast and self-regard of the Ibiza bohemians seemed shallow and artificial, their assumption that to be creative one had to drink or drug oneself to death à la Van Gogh, Charlie Parker or Dylan Thomas a stupid and outdated conceit. The LSD took me back to elementals; it swept the slate clean. It was the same for Hanna. We wanted a chance to start afresh in the world we'd seen, free from dialectic, as free as possible of material needs, putting other values first, such as love for one another and the planet we lived on. I would wipe the past and its broken dreams and I would love Hanna from now on. We migrated to Formentera a couple of days later. We found a few others of like mind on the island, Bruno and so on.

At the edge of the Montesol crowd, I noticed Nick Phillips. He was stoned on acid, dancing about the *rambla* in front of cars and touching their bonnets – there was little traffic and it was moving slowly that sunny morning in September 1964. Nick was a bright guy, a Cambridge graduate in Oriental studies. Carlo knew him and when he sat down at the bole of a tree, he and Rick went over to say hello – but Nick was too busy playing with a piece of string to notice them, so they returned. I suggested they should go and score us some Centramina to keep us awake when we were driving. I told them where to find the *farmacia* and off they went.

Soon after, Nancy came limping down the pavement. She looked great with her long black hair, and white teeth shining in her suntanned face. The Spaniards called her *La Morena*, although she was Dorset born and bred, an English rose.

Although it was almost three years since we'd parted, I felt a pang, like a wound aching when the limb is gone. It was a pang short-lived, however. As she had said once, '. . . *that was in another country; and besides, the wench is dead . . .*' She was right; where I'd fallen in love with her was, indeed, another country, like the past is another country and, there, she was someone else. Perhaps she never was that 'wench' at all; maybe I'd invented her. I watched her waving her hands, her long fingers, gossiping, laughing. I had lost my mind for her; it was hard to believe it now.

I noticed that she moved a little better and I was glad to see that; these days, most people wouldn't notice the gimp. She had taken an awful hit in the accident in Germany, both her thighs broken when the engine was pushed back into the truck on top of her; she had been trapped for an hour, with sulphuric acid from the battery dripping on to her thighs. I'd been lucky; the acid had somehow splashed into my eyes but I was OK again within a week. The men – the driver, his mate and I – had all survived almost unscathed; it was poor Nancy, the beautiful young girl, who had taken the brunt of it. And, then, in the hospital, where she spent three months, she found that she was pregnant.

Now, at the Montesol, she was on the point of sitting down with a group of friends when she saw me. They were squealing endearments and kissing one another on the cheeks – more Ibiza bullshit – when I caught her eye. I want to talk to you, she signalled, and I signalled back, ditto, me, too. I rose and went over to her. She introduced me to the company, an Americans-in-Europe-looking couple, and we went back to my table to have a private chat.

'*Gimme money, that's what I want!*' she sang, as soon as we sat down. I gave her the four hundred pesetas; I was a hundred short for the month but she ignored it. I explained that I was going to London, that I was going to make some real bread, that I'd give her a couple of months in advance when I got back which should be in a fortnight or so. I guess she figured I was planning something illegal when she heard that – how else could I raise money so fast? 'Don't get busted,' she said, 'We don't want the kids visiting you in jail!' I assured her I wouldn't. Privately, I knew that with certainty; I wasn't in the business of getting busted. I'd always think ahead; I'd always have my escape route planned. I didn't tell her this; we were cordial but not into confidences. When I simply said don't worry, she replied, 'Famous last words . . .'

The kids weren't with her: they'd be along in a minute and she thought it was a good idea for me to take them out for the day. I could drop them with her at the Bahia Restaurant, on the port, before I took the Barcelona boat. Then she said she had to go back to her friends, which was cool by me; we didn't have a lot to talk about anyway. She left me with a week-old *International Herald Tribune*. I was settling down to read it when, suddenly, wham! I was jumped upon by one small boy from the front and another from behind; before I knew it, I was covered in small boys with sticky lollipops. What were we going to do for the day? they cried; would we go catch a mullet off the pier, like last time? I proposed we went to Talamanca beach for the afternoon.

At about one o'clock, we caught the small boat which plied across the bay to the headland of Talamanca beyond which was a long sand beach. We'd often gone there before. Sometimes I'd cycle the five kilometres around the bay-shore, one of the kids on the crossbar and one on the back, or borrow a motorbike and carry them by turns, one on the petrol tank and one on the pillion. It was fun to see the lizards skitter across the dusty road out of our path, and the kids squealed in delight at bumps. We'd stop at a country *tienda* and buy a can of sardines and three *bocadillos* for a picnic. We'd always look at the fish in the roadside ditches; the locals raised some sort of carp, it seemed. But today I had no bike or motorbike so we'd take the ferry, albeit it would cost eight pesetas for the round trip.

The only other passengers were a local woman and her two kids. The boys and I sat in the stern, my arms draped over their skinny shoulders. They snuggled into me, and I felt good. It was as if, somewhere, a camera clicked and took a picture: 'A father and his wriggly sons, the Talamanca boat, September '64.' Maybe it was the acid that made me see moments frozen like that sometimes, the pulling-back from the scene, a clock-stopped second that would remain sharp forever. But such moments happen to everyone, acid or not, I guess.

Talamanca beach edged a promontory of dried-out land with a few old *fincas* here and there, flat-roofed like the Formentera houses, white and thick-walled, with a wide central door and few windows, these barred and unglazed, with shutters that opened to let in light. Once, I met a man there who asked me if I knew anyone who would buy his house, which stood by the sea. He wanted twelve hundred dollars for it, this being the sum he would have to show to gain entry to America. He said that to go to the United States was his dream. I told him I wasn't sure he wasn't better off in Ibiza, but he clearly thought I was a fool. As far as buying the house, I didn't have twenty bucks, let alone twelve hundred; anyway, I thought foreigners buying up houses would ruin the islands and owning things would only tie you down.

At the beach, there was a gathering of locals and their relatives from elsewhere cooking up paella in a pan as big as a cartwheel over an open fire. The boys and I jumped in the sea immediately when we arrived. They insisted we played our usual game where I'd submerge, one of them would stand with a foot on each of my shoulders and I'd rise like Neptune from the depths and throw them from my great height of five foot eight high into the air and they'd dive into the sea. We did this for a while and then, when we came out, I swung them, one after the other, around and around by their arms until I got dizzy and collapsed on the sand. Then they went off to play with a dog and got involved with some of the locals' kids – they spoke Ibicenco like natives and were totally at home with these new friends.

Sitting at the top of the beach, I began to write a letter to Hanna, telling her how much I liked Carlo and Rick and how well the three of us were getting on together. I smoked a small joint; some people said one could bond better with children and better enter their world when one was high but I didn't really believe that – in fact, I'd seen a lot of people get irritable with children when they were high or go into bullshit games – with the kids obviously humouring them while thinking what arseholes they were. But, that afternoon I was laid back and the joint was sort of a holiday.

Before long, the boys arrived with a paper cup of wine and a paper plate of steaming paella, compliments of the folks at the fire. I toasted them from a distance and ate gratefully. Now, I wouldn't have to spend money on dinner later. When they sent one of their children over to ask if I'd have a second helping, I said, '*Como no y muchas gracias . . .*', and a second plate and a slice of melon arrived. I was eating enough to keep me going for two days. Things were looking good; I was already the richer!

At six o'clock, we caught the boat back to Ibiza town. When we docked, I kissed the kids goodbye and told them I hoped to see them in a couple of weeks. They ran across the concrete apron of the port, jumped down into the sunken, unpaved street beyond and ran across that to the Bahia. There, their mother sat, having dinner with friends; she waved to me. They were great, Col and Kilian; each different, each the same. They were so identical, people couldn't tell the difference, and they had fun with that. They were full of life and joy, and love for both Nancy and me. They warmed my heart and when I was with them I felt that even the eventual heartbreak of Nancy was worth it because if I'd never met her, I wouldn't have them.

I had time to kill before meeting Rick and Carlo and decided to walk up to the Old Town. I always enjoyed rambling around there alone, and if the sunset was good, it would be spectacular from the walls facing west over the sea. I'd watched it rise; now I'd watch it set. It would round off this perfect day.

Near where the ramp entered the Old Town walls, I ran into an old friend, Chris Longley, waiting outside the vet's office with his dog, a beautiful

Podenco hound, descended from the hunting dogs long ago brought to the islands by the Carthaginians. Podencos looked like small antelopes, and their ancestors were pictured on Egyptian tombs. Chris was English, and he and I had been friends back in 1960 when we were the two youngest members of the Ibiza crowd – Nancy was two years older than me. These days we rarely met – I'd moved to Formentera and he'd taken to living out of town in an old *finca* on the road to San José, painting his pictures and getting by on the meagre fees he earned from occasional proof-reading for a Paris publisher. The reason he was in Ibiza that evening was because his neighbours had spotted his Podenco bitch mating with a renegade male, a known sheep-killer, and they wanted him to have her aborted for fear the pups would turn out like the father. He didn't want to do that, he said, and hoped the vet would talk sense to the farmers who were his neighbours and friends. The kennel clubs hadn't yet recognised Podencos as a pure breed but word was out and the sale of a few of pups might well bring Chris enough money for a year.

I kept him company until the vet showed up. I waxed lyrical about the Formentera scene and said he should move over. Not for him, he smiled. He smoked a little dope and he had nothing against psychedelics, or the idea that they might open the mind; he just didn't think it was that easy. When the vet came, we parted warmly and he asked me to get him some tubes of oil paint in London; he'd pay me when I got back. I went up the ramp that led into the Old Town and through the high-walled, cobble-stoned passageway overlooked by a row of Roman statues standing in their niches, grass growing out of their necks where their sculpted heads had once been.

Up in the Villa Alt, as the Ibicencs called it, local women, mostly in black, were cooking meals outside the small, crowded houses, and the lanes were full of smoke and the smell of fish and burning charcoal. From the walls, I watched the sun sink into the sea, with Formentera off to the south-west, the high plateau of the Mola catching the last of the light. Over there, I thought, Hanna would be cooking on the fire under the big chimney and trying to get Aoife to eat her supper rather than feeding it to the dog.

It was beginning to get dark when I arrived back on the waterfront. I ambled along the unpaved street below the concrete apron that ringed the port to the Domino Bar, and found Carlo and Rick sitting on rickety chairs in the dust outside.

The Domino had a single, naked bulb over the door, and the name scrawled on the whitewashed wall in black paint. It was the only foreign-run bar in the town. It had been there from 1960, the cradle for the kind of speakeasy madness that was to make Ibiza a legend a decade before the foam discos and rave parties arrived. It was run by Alain Bleu – Domino Al – a French Canadian; Dieter, a German; and Clive, an Englishman. They'd gone partners to rent the place which was actually the cellar of the house above. Owing to Dieter's connections, it had possibly the best collection of modern jazz records in Europe.

At night, the door of the Domino was like a hole blasted in the wall by sound. Out of it, into the silent night, poured the wildest, freest, most innovative music most of us had ever heard. The musicians made it up as it went along; and the same could be said of the listeners. Shouting and swearing and drunk on its rhythms, they too were making it up as they went along.

Three steps took one down from the dirt street facing the port and the fishing boats and led into the long, narrow, lime-washed catacomb that was the bar. The bar top was to the right and to the left, on a raised step, were open stalls, each with a concrete table and benches covered in cushions. Being a cellar, the Domino was below sea level, and the reason for the step was that at high tides the sea would flood in via the 'john', which was in the corner to the right of the door. It was an ancient Turkish-style toilet: a ceramic bowl set into the floor with a couple of foot-shaped plinths. It would have been one hell of a shock to be squatting when the sea suddenly heaved up from below.

In the Domino I was greeted as an old friend, valued client and fully paid-up debtor. When we were together, Nancy and I had drunk there on a tab which I'd eventually paid off. I told Dieter I was headed for London and he asked me to buy him the LP of John Coltrane's *A Love Supreme* and a couple of other LPs that had just hit the shops. He gave me an English fiver to cover it, more than they'd cost. That was useful; we could spend the fiver if we got stuck and buy the LPs later from the scam money. I went out with a *cognac con sifón y helo* in hand. It was the cheapest drink in the bar – the soda water was free from glass siphons on the counter, ice came with the glass and the Veterano cognac was two and a half pesetas for a big shot.

Rick and Carlo had already collected our gear from the *kiosco* and as I joined them, I could hear the long wail of the Barcelona boat's siren as it turned the headland into the bay. The first chair I sat on fell over —the dirt street was uneven – so I picked it up and straddled it and told my friends about the unexpected bonus of Dieter's *dinero*. Short of the car breaking down, we'd be OK now. We had enough bread for the fares to Barcelona, for the gas to Calais or whichever port in France, for the ferry to England and the gas to London and, once there, I knew people and we'd be alright.

The boat pulled in, the old Trasmediterranea Line's *JJ Sister*, and passengers began to disembark. It was a sort of custom for foreign residents to watch who was coming off the twice-weekly boat and by this time we'd been joined outside the Domino by various expats. Lise de Graaf, my Dutch friend, a painter, was amongst them, a little drunk.

'Hey, Irishman, what's happening?' he greeted me loudly and sat down. I told him that I was off to London to make some bread. 'You're a crazy fucker, D,' he said. 'Better live on snails in Formentera than porridge in a London jail!'

As the boat pulled in, a woman standing on deck was looking towards us. She was a foreigner, probably an American, and pretty even from a hundred yards away. Soon she was coming down the gangplank, carrying a child. Behind her came the husband, lugging a big suitcase and leading a little girl. 'Hey!' said Cliff Cruzet and 'Hey!' said Tall Eddie, two of the would-be studs around town.

'Why don't you two fuck yourselves?' Lise suggested sourly. His young wife, fresh and blooming as a Friesian meadow, was, even now, sitting with old Steelbaum, the one-time famous American writer whom, the whole world knew, she'd been screwing for months.

'Hey, Lise, she'll do it if she wants to do it,' said Eddie, grinning. 'She'll do what she wants to do . . .'

When they reached the street, the woman's husband went back up the gangplank and fetched another couple of suitcases while she waited. Then she started walking towards us. Clearly, she'd seen that we were foreigners. Most of us knew what she'd ask; we'd asked the same questions ourselves when we'd first arrived, using inquiries to make friends – where could we get a hotel, where could we rent a house, how much did this and that cost, what was the scene like anyway?

Eddie and Cliff were immediately on her case. In Ibiza, not many marriages lasted for long. Mine had been a casualty; now Lise's. With cheap booze, no rules and money in the post, there was no need to get up in the morning or sleep in the same bed at night. Like Eddie said, you did what you wanted to do. Anyone who said otherwise didn't belong in the crowd – they should go to some middle-class place like Majorca or Minorca, where the expatriates played bridge and had dinner parties. No dinner parties in Ibiza, poker but not bridge, raw jazz, not guitar recitals. Wandering wives were supported by others in the name of Simone de Beauvoir and the liberation of women – Eddie and Cruzet applauded them too. Husbands that demurred found themselves pilloried as members of a universal male hierarchy that had conspired to keep their wives' latent sexuality suppressed back there in Slough, Buckinghamshire or Nowhere, Nebraska. They themselves didn't have much opportunity for philandering even if they had the stomach for it; there were ten men to every woman, and the single guys were the ones who scored. If they weren't careful, they'd be labelled as Victorian pains-in-the-ass, spoilsports and bad company. In Ibiza, women were free!

And so, some of us saw in this lovely, young American woman another familial disaster, and in her awkward, friendly husband, buying drinks for everyone, another heap of heartbreak. I feared for them, and for the children in their pushchairs looking wide-eyed at the crowd.

Chapter 2

WE MADE IT ONTO THE boat and dumped our sleeping gear on some padded seats downstairs. There was no panic for seats; there were few people on the boat that night and all of them seemed to have the bread to pay for berths or cabins. It was as though we had the entire cavernous innards of the ship to ourselves. Carlo began to roll up a jay and I offered him my Moroccan but we'd have had to burn it, which would've raised a smell and, besides, like Rick said, it would be better to smoke the kief while we had it and keep the Maroc as a last resort when we were running out. We talked about how it was an American, One-Eyed Mose, who'd taught the Moroccans how to make hash by shaking flower heads on a nylon stocking and sieving the pollen through and pressing it into hash. By and by we laid out our bedrolls, mine a sort of blanket, Rick's a sleeping bag, Carlo's a piece of poncho, and went up on deck to have a smoke.

Afterwards, they went on downstairs again, and I stood by the rail smoking the roach alone and watching Ibiza disappear behind me, thinking of the time after the bust-up with Nancy when I'd left with a broken heart. I was then going into exile and leaving the fabulous Domino behind me and all the people I knew, leaving it to her and going northward into certain exile in London. Bad Jack Hand had told me that if I was taking a piece of dope with me I should go through Andorra, and I did so, with half an ounce of kief stuffed down my sock. I found myself snowed in up there in the Pyrenean village for two days and, when a thaw came, I hitch-hiked with a mountain farmer in a Deux Chevaux van who took me a certain distance to a crossroads where he left me in the white emptiness. While I waited an hour for another car to pass, I saw wolves.

That going north in 1961 after Nancy and I split up was a heavy experience. I was twenty-one years old, out of my head with grief and confusion, still thinking that if I went away and gave her space she would come back to me. At least that was what she'd half-promised and so I seized on the illusion. I went home; to my parents' house, where I hadn't been for two years.

At home, I admitted the failure of my marriage, a marriage they had never wanted. But, seeing that I was a wreck and in great pain, they never said that, but did their best to cure me and bring me back to myself. My father said that maybe I should come home altogether and stop my wandering, that he could help me get a secure job in the civil service, that I could best provide for my children if I returned to Ireland and that maybe, in time, Nancy would join me. My mother took me to the cinema to see *East of Eden* and said I looked like James Dean and wouldn't all the girls love me and if Nancy didn't, it was her loss, and there were other fish in the sea – a strange thing to say considering there was no divorce in Ireland. My father even said he'd provide for the children if I went back to medical school and when I qualified I could take over the practice of his friend, the local GP, who was childless. But there was no way I could stay in that small town, in that priest-ridden country, in that parochialism. I apologised and left the nest again within two weeks. Resigned, they gave me ten pounds for my fare and ten to send to Nancy for the children. I think they were in despair.

Back in London, I rented a cheap room in Earls Court, smelling of age and previous occupancy. I began to teach, getting private tutorial work through an old-established educational trust that dealt with preparatory and public schools. I had no qualifications except the year's experience I'd gained at a run-down prep school in Slough, where I'd taken a job after the twins were born because we had no money and needed a decent place to live. A free house and small wages came with the job.

Nancy had been unhappy there from the start. One day, we were fancy-free, she a drop-out from the University of London and I a drop-out from medical school, heading for India and adventure. Next day, she was the mother of twins, living the life of a junior schoolteacher's wife in Slough. It was Nancy's disaffection that led us to leave England, not that I ever had plans to stay in Slough; it was a temporary measure to put a roof over our heads and food on the table while the kids were young. The job had turned out well; I enjoyed teaching and was good at it. I was popular with the kids, who ranged from seven to thirteen years old. As the school, Hampton House, deteriorated even further during my year there, I ended up teaching not only English and Geography, which I had signed up for, but English History (of which, being Irish, I had a novel version), Maths and Games. I umpired cricket matches but, being Irish, wasn't entirely conversant with the conventions. The tradition of being a clothes-horse for the bowlers' and fielders' pullovers came as a surprise. Umpiring against Eton, I gave our school eight bowls to their six – inadvertently, but more than once. When our bowler cried 'Howzat!' after the ball hit the stumps, I said, 'It looks alright to me . . .' It was no wonder I was popular with the boys.

Now, this new kind of teaching, travelling around London from private pupil to private pupil, suited me well, and I put my heart into it; at least when I was busy, Nancy wasn't on my mind. I especially liked working with the younger kids – I knew enough to teach up to the level of the 13-plus exam, but no higher – because sometimes they had learning difficulties and one could really change their lives and expand their opportunities. The pay wasn't bad, a guinea for two hours, and I could send Nancy money orders for the boys' upkeep. Also, I was able to save a little with the view of returning to Ibiza after a few months in the hope that Nancy, whose lover had left the island, would be more approachable and that my world might somehow come back together.

As soon as I woke each morning, I would think of her and it would seem that without her my life would never be right again. A huge weight pressed down on me, making it almost difficult to breathe. During the months of grief in Ibiza, when I'd tried every way of winning her back but seemed to be driving her farther away, I had lost myself in labyrinths of introspection. A voice started talking in my head, a thing that took up residence there and wouldn't shut the fuck up. It was like an incubus possessing me. It followed me, commenting on my loss, and I thought I would never escape from it again.

When I talked to friends, it was as if I was listening to someone else talking, someone who was not me. I dared not talk about what was in my heart: when I tried to, they seemed to move away. My life was not lived, but acted. I had lost myself. I attempted to be normal but failed; I cringed at the hollowness of my words, the dying fall, the awkward silence of the listeners. I blamed myself afterwards. By trying too hard I was driving them away.

I had always been outgoing and confident; now, I became unsure, afraid. I saw death staring from faces all over London. I was haunted by the fear that I'd forget what my world had been like, what it was *meant* to be like and that, one day, I mightn't even notice the difference and accept the muted tones as if it could be no other way. '*Do not go gentle into that good night*' I told myself, in the words of the poem – '*Rage, rage, against the dying of the light.*'

A few friends tried to jolly me back into reality; I was grateful but I was beyond hearing, entombed in my grief. In my mind, death bells tolled. In the chapels, mouths opened, babble issued. In the pubs, newspapers held conversations with newspapers; in the sad London bedsits, machines fucked machines. 'Do not create abrupt silences!' the voice shrieked, 'Converse politely, according to convention. If you have dead, bring them out at night, before you sleep. If you are a leper, hide it. If the shadow is upon you, conceal it. Prepare a face to meet the faces that you meet . . .'

Stop – Go – Halt – Insert – Push: words proliferate and invade the mind at every turning. It's a mind full of words, a reality of syllables, a city of messages, of instructions. A Wayside Pulpit. Dogs must not foul the pavement. The house Alice Meynell lived in . . . It is a day the colour of brown Thames water. As every day. The sunset, like a sateen tablecloth brought back from China, hangs at the end of the street.

I met a girl one night in an Earls Court pub – a willowy creature, soft of flesh, red-haired, and lonely – and, somehow, she came back to my room and we lay on the bed. I was grateful as, indeed, I have always been grateful for the attentions of women. She was compliant, willing, but when I went to put my hard-on into her, the incubus told me it would fail. It told me in Nancy's words that I had failed, that sex was much better with her lover. My penis softened and wouldn't stand. I was distraught. The girl sat up, shamed and offended. When I tried to apologise, she wouldn't answer. She pulled on her clothes and left.

Sex had never been the main attraction between me and Nancy. For me, love alone had been the spur and the aphrodisiac and, as far as I was concerned, my love was all my passion and I never thought it might not be like that for her. Sheer inexperience was to blame. And yet, I had had some experience.

When I was eleven years old, a young housemaid took to climbing, fully dressed, into my bed every time my parents were out for the evening. At first, she said it was because she was cold and wanted to get warm in the big, cold house; then she said she was too warm, and began to take bits of her clothes off. She directed my hand to her, and took my pencil-thin dick in her hand. Soon she rolled me onto her, and eased it into her. When I ejaculated and pulled out, we saw, where my foreskin had been, an angry bulb like a burst gut and, in panic, thought I was mortally wounded, that I'd die or have to go to the doctor and my parents would find out. She knelt beside me on the bed and I lay on my back as she tried with her fingertips and fingernails to coax the skin back over the still stiff penis-head; and, at last, she succeeded. I felt pale and sick but almost daily afterwards she plagued me to come to her room, or to let her come into mine. In the back seat of the car, she would unbutton my short trousers under cover of a blanket while we sat between my younger brother and younger sister and my father drove us to the seaside, talking to my mother in the front.

Sometimes the pressure was too great for me, her constant demands, but I couldn't tell my parents and so she and I lived in another world within that respectable Catholic house in a small Irish town. When I went away to boarding school, she left my parents' employment and took a job near the school. She would harass me to spend my monthly 'exeat' Sunday with her, the only day we were allowed to leave the school grounds. She would take me to the cinema, remove her knickers and plunge my hand between her thighs. Once, she hid in bushes in a lane along which the boys of the school were paraded to a rugby match and pulled me into the bushes as I passed. Once, she brought me to the house where she worked and, having introduced me to the other housemaid, took me into the nursery and laid us down in a children's cot. She was mad, of course; perhaps she had been abused at home. I remember the day her father first brought her to our house, to ask if she might get a job so that she could train for 'service'. My father said at the dinner table that she came from a family of fourteen, whom the father, a small farmer, couldn't afford to feed, so we took her on, although we already had a maid.

She was a slim girl in her dark maid's frock, only a few years older than me, not bad-looking, with bobbed hair; she looked a little like the French actress Leslie Caron. During all the years, we never once kissed or talked of mutual affection.

When I was eighteen, in medical school, I met a working-class girl at a Dublin dance-hall, and we made love once or twice a week in my rented room until I left college that summer and never returned. Kathleen was a lovely, warm-hearted girl; she chewed gum and rode a bicycle with turned-down handlebars. I had no money to take her out more than once a week, so I would make a fire in the grate of my small room and we'd turn off the electric light and sit beside the fire and she'd sing. She had a lovely voice and knew all the songs of the time. At around ten o'clock, I'd stand and stretch. I'd say I was tired and go and lie on the narrow bed against the wall. Minutes later, she'd come over. I never saw her flesh. It didn't matter. The touch of her body against mine was titillation enough.

But from such adolescent encounters, I learned nothing about the art of satisfying a woman. Kathleen had been a virgin, so I needed little expertise to arouse her. With Nancy, therefore, I thought that I had little to do to make her happy but simply perform the act, but of course that wasn't enough. Later I learned, first from Hanna, then from other women. Everything I know about sex, I learned from women.

The exile in London was death for me. After Nancy, I was sexually, as well as socially, disabled; in any case, the English are not easy people to open one's heart to.

After a few months, I'd saved the money to go back to Ibiza. I brought presents for Nancy and the kids. The kids were overjoyed to see me, and hugged me and hung from me, as if they'd never let me go. Nancy was polite but cold. When I pressed the question, she told me she now had another lover, the new barman at the Domino. 'Don't take it personally, old chap!', an elderly British yachtsman told me, 'Half the English women that come to Spain sleep with a Spanish barman!' It wasn't like that with Nancy, I told him. Also, Ignacio was a decent guy, quiet and unassuming. For many Ibicenco men, foreign women were unapproachable objects of desire. Ignacio was brave, given the local view that foreign women were easy. In any case, he was replaced before long.

For three weeks, my heart bled as I watched Nancy every night in the Domino – there was nowhere else to go – sitting at the end of the bar, queen of the scene now, greeting friends, knocking back her *Cuba Libres* with a cigarette poised in her hand. She looked so full of life, full of joy. And I was full of pain, made the worse for watching her.

Sometimes I went to Peggy Leibler's place afterwards, a house over the beach at Figueretas where there were only a dozen or so houses then. When her balcony doors were open, we could hear the sound of the sea. I'd go there with Rainer, my Canadian artist and jazz drummer friend, and we, and others, would lie about on cushions on the floor in the room lit only by firelight, listening to the waves of great jazz music sweep over us as the surf broke gently on the sand below.

Peggy was from Chicago, a jazzman's woman; she was her own woman too, having long since split from the notorious Bad Jack Hand, with whom she, and his brother Philly, had started a jazz club, the Jamboree, in Barcelona in the late fifties, and crossed to Ibiza when they were on the run from creditors and disgruntled colleagues. Jack and Philly were left-over in Europe after taking advantage of the GI Bill. Out of money, they hung on, living on their wits and occasional bank robberies, jazzmen with guns. Wanted in Belgium and Holland, they had fled to Spain. They, and old Longini, were the founder members of the Ibiza scene sometime around 1958/59. Jack Hand later – and inadvertently – was responsible for a murder during a robbery in Barcelona, and went to jail. Coincidentally, one of two women living with him at the time – and who was with him when the murder happened – was a Scottish girl, Joan Briden, with whom I had hitchhiked south from Glasgow to London in 1959. The night we arrived in London, we went to a pub and, in that pub, on that fatal night, I met the lovely Nancy.

Nancy was celebrating the end-of-term with other students from her college. She was in wild form, as was I. Our eyes met at the crowded bar and, a few minutes later, she accused me, with an outraged shriek, of having stolen her drink. I hadn't —but it was a great excuse to bandy wit, and we both had a surfeit of wit to bandy. I was overwhelmed when she said she would come home with me for coffee; my feet were hardly touching the ground as we walked hand in hand. She was the loveliest and brightest thing I'd ever met and how was a boy from the Irish sticks so lucky as to be even gazed upon by the likes of her?

Joan, my platonic friend, had also found a partner, an Irish pal of mine, the only Irishman I knew in London, an architectural student working there for the summer. When we'd arrived in London earlier that day, we'd rented a single room between us to save money. Owing to our platonic status, we'd split the divan mattress from the base and put it on the floor. Joan and Derry slept on it and Nancy and I on the base, a foot above and two feet away from them. We made love and they did too and then, full of drink and laughter, fell asleep.

Next day, Nancy took me to her student flat and played me records of Dylan Thomas reading his own poetry, and Jussi Björling singing Puccini. I was slayed. I had never heard such beauty. I had always loved poetry but Dylan reading Dylan, and Richard Burton reading Dylan, were incomparable. She was my bohemian girl, fully paid up, a student with a library of books and LP records who knew things about literature that I didn't know, who was funny and dramatic and, like a dream-woman, had come out of nowhere and had chosen me. She stole my heart away.

I had peeked into fabled bohemian pubs in London when I'd come over for student summer work during my last years in school, but I hadn't dared enter the exotic milieu of women who looked like Juliette Greco and drank pints and smoked roll-ups as they stood talking in paint-smeared jeans to men with beards and intense eyes. I'd met an arty crowd in Glasgow when, after leaving medical school earlier that summer, I'd gone there hoping to further a brief romance with a young Irish nurse, my friend's sister, who'd quickly and firmly rejected me in favour of young doctors now that she had a choice. I'd met students at Glasgow Art School and found them approachable and friendly. Their background, like mine, was mainly Celtic and Catholic and, at home, they had the same conservatism to rebel against. In Glasgow, there was no work so I spent hours in the libraries trying to educate myself, reading Heidegger, Kierkegaard and Sartre, writers I'd never heard of at school. In the La Causette Coffee Bar, where my friends and I sat around being intellectuals and talking about Existentialism, I met Joan and, one day, set off with her to hitchhike south to my appointment with Nancy and destiny. Before leaving, I'd taken an entrance exam for the Glasgow School of Dramatic Art, rather as I had taken the entrance exam to medical school in Dublin – in Dublin, I had used it as an excuse to my parents to let me stay on in the city; in Glasgow, I was persuaded by a friend who was taking the exam himself. As in the previous case, I found, to my amazement, that I had passed – I discovered this months later in Germany, sitting beside Nancy's hospital bed, when a letter arrived, forwarded by my parents.

Soon after Nancy and I had met, we had made plans for travel. We worked overtime to save money, she in Foyle's Bookshop, I as a daredevil house painter perched on the roof of the BBC building in Portman Square. We would work our way across Europe, grape-picking in France and taking whatever jobs we could find as we went. We would go to India, we would go around the world if possible or, at least, travel until the money ran out and we were forced home. One night, we went to the pub in Berkeley Square where her previous lover had sometimes taken her – she had had one, and swore she couldn't get pregnant because she hadn't with him. There, we met, by chance, a famous BBC radio presenter who took to us and gave us ten pounds, an enormous amount of money, to further our travels. We were good together, Nancy and I. We were in love, and we were full of life and wit and energy; we made a great team.

We set off for France, slept in a bunker behind Dover beach, and took the ferry to Calais next day. When we got off the boat, there was already a line of hitchhikers on the road, young, clean-shaven students, some with lederhosen, Valderee-Valderah rucksacks and shorts. Nancy and I dragged our bedrolls and tattered haversack to the end of the line and proceeded to hitch the cars as they came off the boat.

Cars passed and cars passed. Then a car stopped and picked us up. It had passed the line of fresh-faced competitors and chosen us. Why? we asked. We looked more interesting, the couple told us. Well, I guess we did. Nancy wore a pair of knee-high Victorian lace up boots we'd found in an attic; she was dressed in black, and had long black hair. I had an embryonic beard and hair to the nape of my neck, a pair of old jeans and an open-neck shirt. That night, we got to south of Paris, where we slept in a barn.

Two days later, heading for Switzerland, where she had a friend who thought he could get us bookshop jobs, we climbed out of a car we'd hitch-hiked somewhere in south Germany and Nancy went for a pee in the bushes. It was mid-afternoon, a very hot July day, and trucks were passing every few minutes. When I heard her call out that she was on her way to rejoin me, I stuck out my thumb and waved it at a truck – which had, in fact, already passed us. The driver must have spotted me in the wing-mirror. He stopped. We ran, Nancy and I, laughing and hollering, to climb aboard.

The driver's mate stood out to let us climb in, Nancy first, next to the driver, me next, and the driver's mate by the passenger door. We spoke for a few minutes – bad German, bad English – and none of us remembered what happened after that. The truck driver had been on the road for fifteen hours. Soon after we climbed aboard, he hit a bridge. Neither Sally nor I could recollect the moments before. We were later told that the driver had fallen asleep. Did we all sleep, him, his mate, the two of us? Or did those of us who were awake, and saw the truck swerve fatally, simply blank out the horror afterwards?

I woke in a blurred daze with Nancy screaming beside me and the truck tilted to my right. Through the smoke and the steam and the blur in my eyes, I saw that she was trapped and everything around her was hot and steaming. Beside me, the driver's mate was throwing open the door and jumping out (he broke his ankle doing so). The driver, on Nancy's other side, had his door open and was standing out and pulling at her, frantically. Half-blind, I tried to push her towards him. The truck was leaning to one side, pinioned on the narrow, metal bridge rail and leaning dangerously over a culvert ten feet below us. When the firemen arrived, they saw that this was the only side from which they could reach Nancy, so they bridged it with planks and cut her free with oxyacetylene torches. It was more than an hour before she was released from under the engine and the battery which had been pushed back into her lap.

From the start, the German motorists who arrived on the scene were valiant. A wedding party stopped and the men, in their dress suits and white shirts, tried to pull the stuffing and the springs from under Nancy to lower her and get her out that way. Meanwhile, other men, some of them both fat and elderly, ran up and down the slope from the culvert stream bearing water in their hats and pouring it over Nancy's lap to try to cool the engine block which they thought was the main cause of her pain. In fact, it was probably the battery acid, and they were indeed helping by dissolving it.

Meantime, I stumbled about, distressed and anxious beyond measure, almost blind, acid having somehow splashed in my eyes. An ambulance stood by and we were taken to the *krankenhaus* in a town near the Swiss border. It was a small, clean, efficient hospital. My eyes were treated over the course of a few days, and they recovered. My clothes and heavy shoes, which had been impregnated with acid, literally fell off me in ragged pieces.

A young German woman who spoke perfect English came to the hospital to help us and she offered me a room in her house and got me a job with a local supermarket chain. Every morning, at dawn, I unloaded railway freight carriages full of tomatoes from Italy. I visited Nancy every evening. My German boss and workmates were kind; they let me off early and gave me fruit and cakes to bring to her. The accident had been reported in the paper, and many local people came to visit us – indeed so many that the private ward was like a party, with never-say-die Nancy laughing and chattering in the middle. In the end, the hospital authorities said we could have no more than four guests in the room at one time.

The woman who was my kind hostess was married to a German air force pilot stationed far away who rarely came home. She made dinner for me each night after I finished work and we would drink beer together and talk. One weekend, when her teenage son was away, she left the door to her bedroom open and called me as I passed and asked me to sit on the bed and talk for a while longer; music was playing on the bedside radio. Only afterwards did I realise that it was an invitation. She was thirty and attractive, but I was madly in love with Nancy and very innocent. By failing to respond – it would have been no different had I understood her intentions – I invoked her enmity, I believe.

Each day, a doctor came to Nancy's ward and spooned the dead flesh out of her thighs, calling it *chokolade*. She missed her period, and we put it down to stress. They put silver pins down her bones and her legs hung in traction for two months, healing. She missed another period. A doctor confirmed that she was pregnant and, after we'd weathered the shock, we were full of joy.

At last, the time came when she could walk and we could leave. Her parents arrived from England. They clearly disapproved of me; who could blame them for deciding that I'd led their daughter astray? A German insurance man came to make a settlement but, on being informed by my hostess that we should receive no compensation for loss of wages because I'd told her we had no regular employment in England, reduced our payment so that we ended up with the equivalent of four hundred pounds. It was a lot of money – equal to forty weeks or so of the average wage – but not much considering the pain and the permanent damage to Nancy. However, she and I knew nothing about compensation and were amazed to receive anything at all.

Back in London, we rented a bedsitting room but, as the months passed, we decided we should find a more salubrious home to bring our child to. Many landlords refused us as soon as they saw that Nancy was expecting a baby, but at last we found a nice one-bedroom attic apartment in a house belonging to a 'genteel' Irish couple in West Kensington. The husband worked in the city, carried a rolled umbrella and wore a bowler hat.

Nancy regularly went to the Princess Beatrice hospital beside the Brompton Road cemetery for check-ups. A few months later, I headed north to Glasgow to retrieve things I had left behind. I arrived back in London at midnight next day, an obliging lorry driver having taken me straight to my door. When I entered the flat, Nancy was sitting on a plastic washing up bowl in the living room, joking with me about the fact that she was leaking and couldn't stop. She said she thought it might be the breaking of the waters, and we resolved to go to the hospital the next day.

On the way to the hospital by bus, we passed a cinema in Fulham that was showing a good movie, so we got off and watched it. We arrived at the hospital at about six. The docs took a look at Nancy and said they wanted to keep her in overnight: would I get her nightdress and toothbrush and come back with them at visiting time at seven o'clock?

I jumped on the bus again, and collected her things. When I returned to the hospital forty minutes later, I went to Admissions and asked for Nancy's ward. I was told the doctor wanted to see me. My stomach turned over. I conceived the worst possible fears: there were complications; the child would be born dead; Nancy was at death's door; she had already died in childbirth. I walked into the doctor's room. He looked up from behind his desk. 'Sit down,' he said, and offered me a cigarette. I took it and lit it impatiently; I just wanted to hear what he had to say. 'Is she alright?' I asked, full of trepidation. 'Oh, yes,' he said, smiling broadly, 'And congratulations. You're the father of twins!'

The news was a bombshell. Twins had never been mentioned. This was before the age of scans, just as it was before the age of contraception, except by condom or complicated devices. Dazed, I went into the ward, to find Nancy in bed, looking beautiful and tired, smiling, telling me she was high on the pethadine they'd given her after the babies were born. The twins were in incubators. They weighed just 3.5lbs and 3lbs. Born at seven and a half months, they had to be carefully cared for if they were to survive. Nancy told me that the doctor who delivered them had wanted to give her the post-natal injection after Colin, the larger and first, but the midwife had told him to wait, suspecting a twin, and then Kilian shot out into her hands. They looked tiny in the incubators. We had to quickly choose names.

I gave the ward sister Nancy's parents' number; it was better I didn't ring them myself. I went home to the flat in West Kensington. I had almost no one to tell about the birth; the few friends we had in London weren't on the phone. I rang my parents, in Ireland, from a phone box; we had no phone in the flat. My father answered. There was a long silence. Then, 'Have them baptised,' he told me, and hung up. Unique amongst the middle-class kids I had grown up with, I was in England, like an emigrant, living with an English woman, and the father of two children at only twenty years old. I imagine that he and my mother dodged questions about me from relations and friends for years. But what did I care? I might never go back to so-called 'holy Ireland'. Career, respectability and status had no meaning for me.

After making the call, I left the phone box and walked home. I remember the evening: it was about eight o'clock and the sky was red, the city quiet. I felt exhilarated, in a sacred state, walking a few feet off the ground. Something wonderful had happened. I had left Nancy happy, and she was well. I was a father of two boys, and they were well. The future was full of excitement. I had no worries; no anxiety; no fear. We, Nancy and I together, could manage anything.

As I went up the stairs to our attic flat, the lace-curtain Irish landlady came out of her first-floor drawing room and asked me how my wife was. I told her the good tidings. Oh, I must come down and have a glass of sherry with her and her husband, she said. I went to our flat, feeling its emptiness without Nancy, whiled away five minutes, and went downstairs. In the drawing room, her husband, the city gent – and a man definitely under the thumb of his wife – stood by the mantelpiece and poured sherry. We exchanged pleasantries and news of the birth and, after the single drink, I went back upstairs.

I was there no longer than ten minutes when I heard the letterbox scrape open and went out to find an envelope on the mat. Our landlady had decided that the flat was too small now that there would be two children, and we were given until the end of the week to leave.

Finding another flat, with two small children, wasn't easy. An Irish friend had a garage which was warm and dry and he and I moved a bed in there so that Nancy and I had somewhere to stay when she came out of hospital a few days later. Luckily, the kids were kept in the hospital, in intensive care. We tried all the noticeboards for rooms or flats. We went to see the kids every evening, and every few hours I delivered Nancy's milk to the hospital, taking a bus from wherever we were at the time. I remember her getting up to go to the loo in a dark cinema and coming back with a small, warm bottle of milk which she had 'expressed'. I left the cinema, caught a bus to the hospital, and was back after missing only half an hour of the flick.

At last, we struck lucky with a room in Earls Court where the landlord, a Nigerian, had no objection to children. It was a large, double, first-floor room, with a balcony, a gas stove and sink in one corner and a shared bathroom down the hall. The children came out of hospital. They had to be fed every four hours, and being so tiny, they each took two hours to feed so that, for one of us alone, it would been a round-the-clock job. We split the task. I invented a sort of sling, made from an orange box with the front and back replaced by woollen scarves tacked to the frame. With it, one could feed them both at the same time. Meanwhile, they could feel one's body warmth against their backs and one could burp them without taking them out of the contraption. Necessity was the wet-nurse of invention.

Chapter 3

AFTER A FEW MONTHS IN our one-room pad, we had to find somewhere better to live. An English friend, ex-public school, had found a job teaching at a prep school. He had no qualifications, no degree, no teacher training – a decent accent and manners were enough. Prep schools were desperate for staff, employing all sorts of oddballs. They paid a pittance, but a free house often went with the job. My friend put me in touch with Gabbitas Thring, Educational Consultants of Sackville Street, W1, and that was how I went to Slough and became a teacher, unqualified but willing to learn.

Besides the free house, there was a salary of eight pounds a week, barely enough to live on. The thought of owning a car never even crossed our minds; besides, neither of us could drive. We moved into the house, a twenty-year-old teacher without an hour's experience, his two kids and the children's mother, to whom he wasn't married. At first, we had no furniture except a bed, and hung sheets over the windows as curtains. Each morning, I dressed in my one-and-only collar and tie, jacket and trousers, and went off to teach. Hampton House was an eccentric school – the elderly Mrs. Boding, in a wheelchair, was the owner; the staff comprised a bearded, irascible old man who regularly caned the kids, and a couple of fresh-faced young teachers like myself.

I enjoyed the teaching, and was popular. I kept control without resorting to violence. I was designated sports master and, although I had no idea of how to teach the subject, enjoyed racing about the field with the boys, being able to keep up with, or outrun, even the fastest thirteen-year-old. I gloried in energy, high as a kite on the rush. I told Mrs. Boding that I knew little about cricket. 'Oh, I'm sure you'll manage!' she said, 'You won't let us down.' She was well aware of her new sports master's shortcomings, but where could she find qualified staff for eight pounds a week?

In Slough, with the help of friends, we painted the inside of the house and recycled old furniture, found on skips. Our friends had been students at Chelsea Art School – an Irish painter and his rich English wife; an English girl, also rich, and her boyfriend, Harry – an ex-wrestler and jazz musician — and a rarefied intellectual and writer from Guernsey and his 'county' girl.

When I was twenty-one in the October of that year, we got married in the Catholic Church in Slough. A few months before the twins were born, I'd asked my father for permission to marry and he'd agreed but, belatedly, had consulted his brother, a priest, who had warned him against it, so he withdrew permission when we were, literally, on our way to the church. I resolved to marry Nancy as soon as I turned twenty-one and would no longer have to ask for permission. Although I styled myself an agnostic at the time, I married in a Catholic church for my parents' sake. Sometime in the early 1980s, long after we'd divorced, a church lawyer wrote me to say he'd discovered I'd married a pagan – Nancy, nominally a Protestant, had apparently never been baptised – and offered me a papal annulment. I have the letter still. My then neighbours, Canary Island villagers, loved the story but insisted that the annulment was arranged only because I was secretly related to the Black Nobility in the Vatican and was probably a friend of Prince Rainier of Monaco and Princess Grace.

Our half-dozen friends constituted the entire guest list. We didn't bother to tell our parents; mine already thought I'd been kidnapped by an English floozy (which the priests warned was the fate of many fresh young Irish boys emigrating to England) while hers thought she'd been hoodwinked by an Irish rogue. We returned to our house, with bottles of cider, for a party. Our wedding presents were a frying pan, a lampshade and a vase but we laughed, drank our cider, and listened to Harry's modern jazz LPs, which we didn't understand. There were no drugs then. We'd heard of marijuana – something smoked by jazz musicians, mainly black, but it wasn't part of our world. Once, I read a story in an *Evergreen Review* where the writer listed his drug schedule, ensuring that every phase of his day was chemically supported or enhanced. I found it fascinating.

I often read poetry, and wrote some, too. I was very content, very fulfilled. I loved it with Nancy – the house, Slough, Stoke Poges, Eton by the river. In the long summer evenings, I would lie in the garden, underneath the apple trees, and write. I wrote some sonnets, Petrarchan and Elizabethan, love poems for Nancy. They took me many hours but I'm sure she must have known the results were amateurish.

Elderly folk in the park would stop to look at me walking along with an identical twin on each shoulder. 'What a good boy you are, taking your little brothers for a walk,' they'd twitter. I enjoyed telling them they'd got it wrong. They thought we were wonderful, me, Nancy and our children. I suppose we were, although I didn't realise it. We had no money to spare; one day we had to turn back on a planned outing to London because the bank wouldn't give us an overdraft of one pound. But I was still in heaven. However, Nancy suddenly began to be depressed.

I didn't know why. I asked her again and again but she said she couldn't explain it. I would arrive home from the school at four o'clock on sunny afternoons and find her and the children in bed, asleep. It was difficult for me to be so full of joy and she so full of care. I'd ask her would you like to do this, would you like to do that, what if we did this . . .? Nothing would make her happy. I think the trouble was that she didn't like the life she found had happened to her: a prep school master's wife, two kids, a satellite town. Then, I had an idea. Maybe, I could find a job abroad.

For some reason, I thought we'd like to go to an island. At Slough Public Library, I pored over atlases, noting every island in the temperate or tropical zones. I discovered exotic places – an atoll in the Pacific where everybody, from mayor to police chief, was called Williams and they were all genetically wall-eyed. I found an uninhabited island off New Zealand that had once been settled by mutineers on a sailing ship and their Tahitian wives. I found UN Protectorates, and British Protectorates. I'd bring home details of the Cook Islands, St Helena, Bonaire, Réunion, the Kermadec Group, exotic places with strange-sounding names, and I'd write off to the authorities in my best copperplate, seeking work as a teacher. I was eventually offered a job in the Gilbert and Ellice Islands, a British dependency in the Pacific, and this seemed OK until they sent us a wardrobe list stipulating that officers should bring three pairs of 'dress' shorts and their ladies should have three evening gowns. Nancy and I found this pretty hilarious, Englishmen in dress shorts out in the midday sun.

At last, I came around to the Mediterranean islands, and the Balearics looked good. There was a song at the time, '*Just off the coast of Spain, There is a lovers' lane, And they call it Majorca, isle of love . . .*' The lyrics were schmaltzy and saccharine but it occurred to me that the island might be nice, so I enquired about living there at the Spanish embassy and was introduced to a diplomat, a Señor Bueno, a native of the island. At the time, it was highly original for a foreigner to think of living in the Balearics and I must have intrigued or charmed him, what with my young family and adventurous ideas. He invited me to his home where he and his German wife gave me wine and told me all about Majorca, and that the cost of living was half the price of England. Our London avant-garde friends thought I was crazy to consider taking Nancy and the two young children 'out there'. Did they think we were going to Borneo or darkest Africa? It made us laugh.

Since Majorca was Spanish-speaking, there was no hope of teaching work and we had no savings. The only hope was that I could persuade my father to finance us for a year; I'd tell him I wanted to learn Spanish so that I could get a 'proper' teaching job. I'd do it, too; I'd always loved Spanish words and Spanish place-names; they were replete with romance. He agreed to give me two hundred and fifty pounds. Whoopee! I could rescue my Nancy from the Slough of Despond. We were on our way!

I went first to find a house to rent; we couldn't afford to spend a week in hotel rooms while we searched. When summer holidays came, we vacated Slough, leaving our gear with friends, and Nancy and the boys went off to stay with her parents. I took a train to Paris, changed at the Gare du Nord and took a connection to Barcelona. From there, I caught an overnight ferry to Majorca. I arrived in Palma de Mallorca, quickly decided the city wasn't for us and headed off to explore other towns. On a country bus, I met an

American girl, and she invited me to her home, a lovely house where she and her husband lived, with a salt-water pool on the edge of the blue sea. I'd never been anywhere like it. They were young and she was beautiful; they were like a mythical couple, straight out of Scott Fitzgerald. They told me about Deya, where a few writers had gathered around Robert Graves, the poet, and there was a small expatriate scene. A few days later, I went there. I ran into an Irish writer and his wife who drank like camels and fought like tinkers. It was a lovely place but the people there seemed to do nothing but drink and belabour one another; it seemed to be the literary thing to do.

I went south to Puerto de Andraix, a charming fishing village where I found a cheap house, right on the sea. However, before paying advance rent, there was one more place to explore, the island of Ibiza, where my young American friends had told me they'd heard some foreigners lived and there was a crazy scene. I returned to Palma and took a ferry to Ibiza. I arrived in the evening, and saw a motley crowd of foreigners drinking and carousing at some battered tables outside a bar. I went over and talked to them, asked them where I might find a cheap hotel. *Sit down!* they cried, *Have a drink! Where're you comin' from? Where're you goin'? Tell us your story. Are you passin' through? Are you here to stay?* I told them my story, part of it; they seemed to like it; everyone chipped in. Being Irish was exotic; I was the only Irishman among the polyglot crew. An American called Brunswick – Brunswick the Legend-Maker, I later called him: he dubbed me 'The Irish Poet' – challenged me to a game of 'Stretch' in the dust beside the tables. He had a large, rusty bayonet, and we took turns throwing it at each other's feet, making us 'stretch' our feet ever wider, until I fell over. He said it was a game GIs had played during the Korean War.

I checked into a *pensión* for half of what I'd paid in Majorca and had a meal at a restaurant, which was dirt cheap too. Then, back to the Domino for more drinking. I got to bed at maybe 2 AM. In the morning, I met an Englishman staying at the same *pensión*.

Vern was a wanderer. He was a couple of years older than me, a good-looking guy with blond hair and a small blond beard. We took to one another immediately. We explored the town, which he knew no better than I did. Sometime in mid-morning, we sat at a café near the fish market, a roofed area supported by pillars situated below the ramp leading up to the Old Town. He asked me if I'd ever smoked marijuana, and I said no. He took me down a quiet alley, under the walls, filled a little pipe from a leather pouch, and handed it to me. 'Inhale deeply,' he said, 'and hold the smoke as long as you can before you let it go.' I inhaled too quickly and exploded into a fit of coughing. Patiently he tutored me, showing me how he did it himself. I got the idea, and I got high . . . very high.

Everything he and I said was suddenly hilarious. So also were the antics of cats and dogs, the way people looked, the way they walked, the way the fishwives handled the fish in the glistening ice. Colours were more vivid than I'd ever seen colours before. That night, the music in the Domino Bar entered my head and filled it so that there was no other sound. The following day, we rented a motorbike and drove around the dusty villages of the island, the back roads, the *caminos* of ancient Spain, unchanged by time. Women in sombreros hoed in the fields, their long dresses hitched up to reveal petticoats of all colours. The men were grizzled, wore berets and drove patient mules that pulled wooden ploughs. My heart was full of it. The names alone seduced me: Santa Eulalia del Río, San Juan Obispo, Vedra and Vedranella. I loved this Spain.

But in this Spain, on this enchanted isle with its Domino nights and lazy days, I'd get no work done and it was my secret vow to spend the year productively, learning how to write good poetry, and learning Spanish too. So I opted to return to Majorca and Puerto de Andraix where I could work uninterrupted; I could see, from the quiet respectability of the town, that there were none the likes of Brunswick and the nightly Domino denizens there.

Vern said he'd take the ferry with me to Majorca because he'd never been there. That was OK by me, except maybe Nancy wouldn't be too happy if she arrived to find a stranger living with us. However, he didn't think he'd stay long. We arrived and moved in, and I soon met some of the local expatriates. I was invited to a cocktail party – and put on my single good shirt and trousers, and went. There, I met the expat community who turned out to be, almost all, British ex-colonial officials or army, much older than me, retired and settled in Spain because there, as opposed to in Britain, they could still afford servants. The men wore shiny shoes, long stockings and pressed shorts, and brayed under the horse-brasses and copper kettles they'd brought with them from the Home Counties. They drank their beer from pewter mugs while, in asides, the women seemed intensely interested in me. One of them – not bad-looking but all of forty – whispered that I must come and see her garden when her 'hubby' was out sailing. She stuck her wet tongue in my ear. One cocktail party with the Puerto set was enough for me. I fled as soon as I decently could. I met Vern on the way home, returning from the bar with a bottle of wine. We uncorked it, smoked a couple of pipes by the sea and ended up lying in the middle of the dusty road, laughing our heads off at the stars.

Nancy arrived by plane from England with our offspring, now eighteen months old; the luggage, a trunk of books and effects, was to follow by ship. She didn't mind Vern being there. We sat on the balcony at night, in this new world, and smoked kief, and drank wine, and told each other stories and looked out at the glittering sea. Vern's yarns were good, as good as our own, and Nancy and I were no mean yarn-spinners. I told her about the ex-colonials and their pressed shorts and the woman who had stuck her tongue in my ear. The realisation quickly dawned on us that we would be misfits in this cosy colonial society. We told her about Ibiza, Vern and I, about nights in the Domino Bar. She was dying to go. I decided that if we lived outside the town and didn't get too involved in the Domino scene, I could still teach myself Spanish and learn to write poetry. The fact that the islanders spoke a dialect of Catalan, rather than Spanish, didn't bother me.

Again, I went ahead to find us a house. I left Vern with Nancy, a pretty dumb move but an indication of my innocence, my belief in the trust between friends and that Nancy felt about me as I did about her. I crossed to Ibiza and found a house at the Casas Baratas, meaning cheap houses. It was a fine house for a thousand pesetas a month – eight pounds sterling at the time. The year's rent would be ninety-six out of the two hundred or so quid we still had left after shelling out for our fares and the Majorca experience. I telegrammed Nancy and told her to come. She arrived, with Vern carrying one of the children, a few days later. She walked down the gangplank, took a look at the white town rising against the blue sky, the huge walls, the old cathedral, the motley gang disporting themselves at the tables outside the

Domino, and fell in love with it instantly, just as I had done.

It was our destiny, Ibiza. It was so familiar; we both thought we'd been there in some previous life: the smells of the charcoal cooking fires outside the houses of the Peña, the smell of the drains in summer, the quality of the light. It was all, somehow, familiar. It was liberty, it was license. It was kindred spirits from half the countries of Europe, although there were then no more than thirty of us on the island. It was beyond our wildest dreams.

Things went wrong quickly, though. We were there no more than ten days when Nancy told me she was having an affair with Vern, who had moved into a room in the Old Town. I was knocked sideways by the revelation but I didn't really take in what it meant. My attitude seemed to be: OK, it's honest of you to tell me, I respect that. Now, let's just act as if it had never happened – it's no big deal. This was fond hopes and wishful thinking. I was considering only the physical and that Vern had taken nothing important, really – he'd made love to her, and so what? But for her it was more – perhaps for self-respecting women, affairs have to be more; there's a need to make them more because otherwise guilt would spoil it. So I soon discovered that he had indeed taken something important; I had lost Nancy's heart or, at least, he had begun the process of my losing it. This realisation was like a physical wounding, and it panicked my mind. I had thought that she was telling me they'd simply had sex together and she was sorry and that it was over. But it wasn't. When I realised this, the earth seemed to fall from under me and I began to go slowly, but surely, mad.

When I accused her of betrayal, she threw back in my face a betrayal of my own. One night, in London, when she was visiting her parents, a friend and I had met two girls in a café where one of them, called Cosette, was a waitress. We went to a pub and afterwards ended up at their flat. When my pal and the other girl began some serious snogging, Cosette and I went into the bedroom and got into some heavy petting on the bed. When Nancy returned to London, I told her about my wild night on the town and about the girl. She made light of it, 'Cosette!' she mocked, 'She sounds like a French tart's daughter! *Voulez-vous Cosette avec moi?*' As usual Nancy was very funny, and knew her literature too.

At the time, I had no inkling that it had hurt her deeply, as she now insisted it had. 'Don't complain to me about infidelity!', she spat. 'You started it!' I argued that the hour I'd spent with the girl was meaningless, a stupid, half-drunken peccadillo. I'd had no interest in her; I'd never seen her again. I was happy to forget her scene with Vern if only she'd end it. I'd been honest with her, just as she'd been honest with me. We were very 'modern', Nancy and I. But, when it comes down to it, the heart is old-fashioned.

The first happy days, when I'd taken her on the back seat of the bike and she pulled the double pushchair with the laughing twins behind us as we cycled home from our morning visit to the post office and the Montesol, were now over. They had been an illusion all along. I now realised that on those very afternoons when I sat in the Bodega, a small, quiet bar, and wrote my stupid poetry for love and art, she was in our house making love to Vern.

A sort of madness came on me and I accelerated it by filling my every waking hour with trying to think of ways and means to get her back. She said the affair would soon be over, so I reluctantly agreed not to object to her meeting Vern 'a few last times'. Then, one afternoon, she told me he was leaving on the following day. He would take the Valencia boat; he was heading to North Africa and then Greece. That evening, she persuaded me that she should meet him once more before he left. She faithfully promised she would be back by midnight. She didn't return until three in the morning. For weeks, I had been dwelling on her betrayal and her false promises, for there had been other promises, all of them broken. For weeks, I had got lost in the maze of my mind; this not helped by the cognac, Benzedrine and kief I'd been imbibing almost nightly at the Domino and, for her part, not helped by her heavy drinking and smoking dope and love-making with Vern.

Lost in the maze of my mind, one day, I would decide that I should refuse to accept the arrangement, tell her I was laying out no more money, that we should pack our bags and leave Ibiza; the next, I would decide that such bully-boy tactics would alienate her forever and, indeed, she'd warned me that this would be the case. I would reconsider; I would decide I should stay away from her, have patience, grin and bear it, let it work itself out. Then I would think, '*But if I do that, she'll think I don't care, that I don't really love her and that will drive her further into his arms . . .*'

I was a confused young man, in grief and pain. The dream was collapsing around me. I was bitter too; she was sailing forth, full of herself, puffed up by the attention, by her notoriety, while I was the loser, the sad sack, the cuckold, the pathetic bastard. Before she'd arrived, I'd told my Domino friends about my lovely wife, about my loving family. Now, she had made a public fool of me. There was no place to hide on Ibiza; if one wanted society – and, gregarious as I was, I was never more in need of it than now – there was only one bar, the Domino, and one meeting place in the day, the Montesol and Alhambra, side by side. All pain was public; there was no escape.

And so, on the night before Vern was to leave, when I waited at home by the fire in Casas Baratas while she went to meet him 'for two hours, only for two hours, just to say goodbye' and did not return in three hours, or in four, or five, I finally flipped and, leaving the window of the kids' bedroom open so the woman who lived in the shack next door could hear them if they woke, I went out to look for her, the pictures conjured up in my mind by my intake of dope and wine sweeping over me in an insane sea of bitterness.

I walked to the new houses being built at Es Vive and there imagined I heard snatches of voices and music from somewhere and thought she might be at a party but the houses all seemed to be shut up and asleep. It began to rain and I took shelter in a big concrete pipe on a building site and watched the rain grow heavier and turn the red earth to blood. I moaned with pain but it was alright; there was nobody to hear. I found my way home and sat by the dying fire, getting crazier and crazier with my imaginings and the memory of her lies.

When she finally returned, and the children still lay fast asleep in their bedroom alongside, I screamed at her and with some extraordinary strength tore the iron fire surround set in the floor out of its moorings and smashed it down on the hearth tiles. She begged me to stop, crying out that she was sorry, that she hadn't noticed the time passing, that it was her last few hours with Vern: he would be leaving the island next day and she wouldn't see him again, she promised.

I stood by the dead hearth, my arms by my sides, my mind reeling. She sat on a chair nearby, sobbing, her face in her hands. Her sobs were the only sounds. The room was full of desolation. What had we done? What had we done?

Near dawn, we lay, fully clothed, on the bed, both miserable, in worlds apart. I was trembling still; my thoughts were in a blur, like after the road accident in Germany. If I could bridge the gap: what had happened earlier didn't matter now. Vern was leaving: it would all be alright. I reached out and took her hand. I squeezed it tightly. She didn't pull it away. It seemed to me a sort of reconciliation: her hand clasped tightly in mine, I shook with relief. After the storm, the calm; all anger spent, all bitterness exhausted.

The next morning we talked. I knew that, after Vern, it couldn't be the same between us straight away. It would need time, and I was ready for that. But within hours I found that I had again been lied to. Vern hadn't left. Inadvertently, I came upon them, sitting together in a quiet place in the Peña. When he saw me, he turned and walked quickly away. I confronted her; she said she couldn't help herself, she had had to see him. She thought she was in love with him and couldn't let him disappear forever from her life. I told her he was a wanderer, not a stayer, but she didn't believe that. That evening I went to Vern's room and told him that if he wasn't off the island on the next boat, I'd throw him in the fucking sea and he could swim to Spain. He left next day, not through fear of me but because Vern was a travellin' man and he was leaving anyway. I was sorry for her, in her disappointment. The days passed, but she would not come back to me again.

Now *I* was the demon; *I* had driven him away. Bullshit, of course; he was bigger and probably stronger than I was, although I would have fought him with conviction. But that would have been no deterrent if he'd really wanted to stay on Ibiza and continue screwing Nancy, for that is what he was doing, screwing his friend's wife; never mind the grief to him, the dissolution of a family, for that is what happened, his hard-on stole his honour, a common thing with men. Vern was the beginning; Nancy and I never recovered. It would have happened anyway, I think. It wasn't Vern's fault. It wasn't Nancy's. She'd fallen out of love with me and there was no cure.

I didn't realise it right away; I didn't accept it. We continued to live together; we came to the Domino each night, leaving the boys' window open so that Juanita, next door, could hear them if they woke. We ate together sometimes; sometimes she ate with friends and I ate alone. We sat with different groups in the bar. At night, I would walk down the pier with Rainer and smoke a joint; we would go to Peggy's at Figueretas, or to his house, where he'd play the drums. She would stay on in the bar, and cycle home out the unlit road with a Dutch woman. We did not sleep together; we did not make love. When I tried to talk about my feelings, she didn't want to hear.

Suddenly turning on me, she told me that that night of my madness, as we lay on the bed, I had squeezed her hand so tightly that she thought it would break. Scared out of her wits, she hadn't dared move or tell me to stop.

I was dismayed that I could have done such a thing and not been aware of it. I believe that in my distress, I had indeed lost my senses, had suffered a sort of nervous breakdown and more than a year passed before I was right again. The shakes, the sweating, the blurring of vision, the supernormal strength all indicate this. No wonder she was frightened – although not for anything would I have hurt her. Even in the white heat of anger I hadn't done so and, by then, my anger was spent and she would have had nothing to fear if she had pulled her hand away. But now, hearing that she had been too afraid, I was ashamed of myself and full of regret.

There was no hope for me now in Ibiza. Every night, I had to watch her enjoy the attention of men around her, enjoy the limelight while, heart-sore and fucked-up, I sat in the dark. We were running out of money, despite having tabs in the Domino. Everybody had tabs; everyone was waiting for the remittance cheque, the royalty cheque, the birthday cheque to come in the post. Al, Clive and Dieter understood the delays, had great patience and charged no interest. Nancy's bar bill was even bigger than mine, not because she drank more but because my drinks were cheaper.

As things fell apart, we sold the books we'd brought from Slough, a suitcase-full, to a rich and unpleasant old Englishman who didn't give us much for them. Nancy said she thought he was hoping to fuck her, for a price. When she told me this, I wanted to go back, take the books from him and stuff his lousy few thousand pesetas down his throat. How dare the bastard think that because she'd had one affair, she would be easy!

As the money further waned, I played poker on Friday nights: American games of Seven-card Stud, High-Low and Roll Over Beethoven. My mother had taught me to play as a child and, through divine intervention or her prayers, I won roughly a thousand pesetas every week, just about enough to keep us going. 'Lucky in love, unlucky in cards' is an old saying and maybe the opposite is also true. One of the company, Les Mee, US Navy Captain retired, a bearded, Hemingway look-alike sailor, said I should play professionally and, indeed, a year later in London, I briefly tried, accompanying my friend James Whittaker to West End gaming clubs. I lost every time. Hanna lent me half her wages and that went too. Playing against Nick the Greek and the like, I was a lamb to the slaughter.

The same Les Mee and his wife had a yacht in the harbour and he would take couples to 'international waters' – actually the mouth of the bay – and marry them by the official powers invested in him and I'd write them a 'marriage certificate' in copperplate or Chancery hand and earn four hundred pesetas for it. But still, inexorably, our money ran out.

I decided to go back to London. I could no longer support us and, besides, Nancy said she needed space. I harboured some desperate hope that if I left for a few months, got work and sent her money for the children, I would prove my unfailing love and she might favour me once more when I returned. I was still deranged, as I said.

Back in London, the three terms I'd spent in Slough turned out to be useful; the educational trust found me jobs as a private tutor. Years later, I was to become top 'tute' in London, introduced by one family to the next, teaching the sons and daughters of kings, prime ministers, international movie and pop stars and ex-dictators-on-the-run how to pass entrance exams for exclusive London schools or to get out of academic trouble. I didn't let it interfere with my lifestyle, with the clothes I wore or the company I kept. Concerned parents seemed only too happy to welcome me into the drawing rooms of the finest homes in London, where, in my ignorance – it wasn't arrogance, just the fashion of the time – I blew the smoke of my Gitane cigarettes all over their children while their butlers brought me tea. The kids, junior and senior, liked me, and I liked them. We met in a world I took care to keep quite separate from their parents and their schoolmasters, and so we succeeded together where they had previously failed. Some wise person once said that what we do as a sideline often turns out to be our real talent. At the time, I was chasing tutoring jobs wherever they were. I would travel any distance and take on any subject or situation. I was into making the maximum of money in the minimum of time. I was in the city purely to make bread and I bull-shitted my way into work and learnt as I went. I was able to send Nancy regular money and, three months later, I returned to Ibiza, hoping we could get back together again. It turned out to be a false hope.

Now, as I stood at the rail on the deck of the old *JJ Sister*, with my *compañeros* below decks getting ready to sleep, I shook off the ghosts of Ibiza past and watched the lights of the town disappear as I had back then when I was going into exile. Except now, I had good friends with me; good friends on Formentera; a good woman waiting for my return. And she *was* a good woman; already, absence was making my heart grow fonder. Rick had laughed earlier, outside the Domino, when he'd seen me take the letter I'd written to her from my pocket to add a line. He said I'd never leave her, whatever I thought. He had a sort of affection for Hanna, although it wasn't long since he'd met us. Maybe he thought I was unappreciative. Rick didn't have much luck with women himself, it seemed, but then he certainly didn't go out of his way to attract them.

There, standing alone at the rail, I didn't feel like descending to the salon, into a closed world. I always tried to be on deck when boats were departing or arriving. Memories faded into the distance and all that had happened in the place I was leaving, good or bad, was over – or watching the lights of the new place rise out of the sea, I could almost hear the whispers of promise from the shore. Then, as now, I left at night, and watched the self-same squid boats bob in the bow wave of the ship, the brilliant phosphorus lamps on their sterns dancing like fireflies in the darkness of the sea. The beam of the lighthouse on Talamanca head still swept over us every count of nine and then it, too, was gone.

I went down below, to the noises and creaks of the ship, the dull thuds of engines, the slaps of water. Carlo was still awake, reading *Siddharta*. Rick, for once without his hat, was fast asleep.

Chapter 4

IN THE MORNING, WE DISEMBARKED in Barcelona and went to find the old British registered car I'd left parked in a side street in the Barrio Chino beside the gypsy quarter. There she stood, a six-cylinder Ford, looking sad and begrimed with city dust, the fine grains that twinkle with motes of carbon from exhaust pipes. A bust window, which I'd put back in place with wedges of cardboard, was wide open; it looked like somebody might have been sleeping in the back seat. That didn't matter but what did was that all the tyres were flat, and two of them, for sure, were perished, the wheels sitting on the rims. After asking around, I found a small garage where the guy said he could get us second-hand tyres and tubes for small bread but it couldn't be done before the next day. We opted for that and thought we'd sleep in the car overnight but, after counting our pennies, decided we could afford a fleapit hotel in Calle de la Ancha, where, at night, the watchmen came with their long staffs and bunches of keys to let you in, after you whistled to summon them. We whiled away the day looking at the port and the extraordinary Gaudi cathedral which, after a joint, was even more extraordinary.

After crashing out for an hour at the hotel, we found a cheap place to eat and then went over to the Plaza Real where we came upon a magical scene. We'd already noticed gangs of uniformed American sailors walking the *ramblas*, often arm in arm and ten abreast, singing and shouting and plainly drunk and having a good time. The American fleet was in; it happened once a month or so. The Plaza Real is a small, ancient square with a fountain in the middle and surrounded by colonnades or covered walkways with bars sprawling into the street and the doorways of cheap hotels between them, with dark steps leading to the rooms above. That night, it was like a scene from *Carmen* by way of *Madame Butterfly*, white-uniformed sailors with their dinky hats drinking and whooping it up at the tables, and all the whores in Barcelona, in slinky skirts and smoking cigarettes, standing in the doorways or leaning against the pillars of the colonnades, or hanging out of the balconies overhead calling 'Hey, Sailor!', and young sailors, cheered on by their friends going to them and being conducted upstairs and arriving back all red and blushing, with the girls advancing to take the hands of their friends to pull them from their chairs, to urge them and entice them and seduce them with their lissom figures, long hair and smiling Spanish eyes. Some of the ladies were old enough to be those matelot's mothers but for all their garish makeup, sagging breasts and generous thighs, were favoured above the young girls. One such woman was up and down stairs every ten or fifteen minutes, with a regular queue awaiting her attentions. And there we sat in the subtropic night watching these vignettes, Carlo and Rick, the quiet, alternative Americans and I, the Irishman who, like them, had never seen anything like this before.

One girl, slim and dark-eyed, almost tubercular-looking, took my attention and, in the reverie of the dope and the noise and the colour, I wove dreams around why she was there, in that warm Mediterranean night selling herself to sailors, taking their hands, leading them upstairs, some of them boys no older than herself. And coming back down for more.

My romantic dreams had always been for waifs with dark eyes and sallow skin, but neither Nancy nor Hanna fitted that description. Somewhere in my mind as a child I had become fixated with the image of a sort of Anne Frank, a Jewish girl or gypsy from Middle Europe who played the violin, someone one could love, ethereal and doomed. This young Spanish prostitute looked to me like that. I wished I could have met her – not for sex, but for the romance of knowing her. I couldn't imagine paying for sex. If I knew a woman was only doing it for the money, it would kill my hard-on dead.

Next day, the car was ready, and we headed out of town. It was good to be moving. Here we were, out on the highways in the middle of the action, like aliens in a space capsule, suddenly part of the speed and clamour, with the wheels hissing on the asphalt beneath us.

We talked as we went. We did nothing but talk. We had no radio in the car and time to kill, driving day and night, talking to keep ourselves awake, the driver with a partner riding shotgun, the other one asleep on the back seat. And then, of course, we were popping speed as well, so as not to doze off at the wheel or to stay awake to keep the driver company.

In mid-morning, after about a hundred miles, steam suddenly rose from the bonnet and we pulled in and found a radiator hose perished, and water all over the block. A small village was visible below us, off the main drag, so we pushed the car a bit and coasted down there, knowing there would be no garage but that there would be a shop where we could score what we needed to get us temporarily back on the road. When I told Rick we needed eggs, mustard and a pair of nylon stockings, he said never mind the groceries, what about the car? In no time, we'd dropped an egg white into the radiator and bandaged the split pipe in a nylon stocking pasted thick with mustard. It held and we limped onward to the town of Orriols, where we bought a radiator hose and fitted it ourselves.

We passed through La Junquera, the big Spanish border post at the Mediterranean end of the Pyrenees and went on into France. Nobody bothered us for driving licences or car insurance, which was just as well because all I had was a so-called 'International Driver's Licence' which I'd scammed from the Royal Automobile Club in London, talking my way out of having to produce a current UK driving permit as was legally required. It was out of date anyway, but I'd fixed that, having some calligraphic skills nurtured at school when I should have been listening to the teachers. Rick and Carlo, like good Americans, did have valid licences, although how Rick ever passed a driving test was beyond me. Personally, I'd never been tested. The one and only legitimate licence I'd ever had was bought over a post office counter in Dublin. It had long since expired, and many tens of thousands of miles had passed beneath my unlicensed wheels.

Hanna and I had bought our first car for twelve quid. I got a half-hour driving lesson from the guy who'd sold it to me and straight away we loaded our luggage and set off with Aoife for a holiday in Cornwall three hundred miles away. We were crazy, of course – she was as bad as I was – but what an amazing thing, to be sitting in our own car! Forty!, we whooped, forty miles an hour, flying downhill with the wind behind us! And then forty-five, and fifty! But then we slowed down because the old engine and we, ourselves, could hardly take the strain. I side-swiped a line of cars in Exeter – luckily this was after midnight and there was nobody about. Reversing into the driveway of the holiday cottage, I hit a stone wall and knocked it down. And that was how I learned to drive.

As I came to think of it, the old Ford I was driving now had cost the same amount: twelve quid. It was a six-cylinder Zephyr, firing on only four, with a column gear shift and a big bench seat across the front where the driver and two passengers could sit side by side. Figuring that she might overheat in traffic jams, we decided to avoid Paris and headed east towards Nîmes before turning north for Dijon and Reims.

France was lovely that autumnal afternoon as we drove up through Provence and we admired it when we stopped to eat *bocadillos* which we'd bought at the shop in the village back in Spain, with a can of sardines decanted into each one. I favoured sardines in olive oil; my American friends preferred theirs in tomato ketchup. We ate, and drank milk, sitting on the side of a by-road looking out over a huge vista where the cornfields swayed below us like in a Van Gogh painting. When I was half-nuts after Nancy, I'd gone to a gallery in Amsterdam where Van Gogh self-portraits lined the walls and he and I had looked at one another, one crazier than the next, his eyes following me as I walked and his face all alive with little squiggles of paint like multicoloured maggots or amoebas moving over the skin surface, all alive, generating their own light.

That was after I had returned to Ibiza in 1961 to see my sons and to try to win back Nancy. It hadn't worked. She'd told me about her and Ignacio, the barman at the Domino. This time, then, it was truly over. I wandered the island for a couple of weeks, unable to accept it, shivering even though it was warm, wrapped in my old sports jacket, a folder full of poems and half-poems under my arm, probably none of them real poems at all. '*Last night she sailed./ I watched her from the walls / all white and beautiful sail out to sea . . .*' This was about Nancy leaving me; she wasn't very white, in fact. I wrote it sitting on the Old Town walls watching the sun sink behind Espalmador and Formentera, which I didn't know well then, although I'd crossed over a few times to spend a night alone at the Fonda Pepe in San Fernando when watching Nancy's romances grew too much. I'd smoke joints and write by candlelight in the bare room; the Fonda had no electric light then. On those nights when a mysterious man sometimes seen around Ibiza had crossed on the boat with me, I'd hear the chatter of a typewriter from the next door room. Aboard the boat, he would always sit in the stern, usually with rolled canvases of paintings and his portable typewriter beside him, smoking those strange Gitane cigarettes that were black tobacco wrapped in maize-coloured paper and you licked the gummed edges and stuck them down yourself. I found out later that he was a French-Egyptian art dealer, the lover and controller of Elmyr de Hory, the little, gay stateless Hungarian who, unbeknownst to us all, was faking Impressionist pictures which were to hang – indeed, still hang – in many of the major galleries of the world. The Egyptian would rent a room in the Fonda, as I did, and do his nefarious business, creating provenances for Elmyr's phoney but brilliant art.

One night, outside Ibiza town, making my way from Figueretas along the rocks, I came upon a party in progress around Elmyr's sea pool with perhaps twenty boys and young men, all entirely naked or in white towels, draped over the rocks or swimming in the sea which was silver with phosphorescence. Food, drink and a towel was offered to me. I ate and drank and swam, the water flowing off my arms like molten silver. I have never seen a sea so dense with phosphorescence as that night; the surface was heavy with it, like a skin. There was music, and I cannot remember exchanging a word with anybody. After swimming, I dressed and continued to the town. The scene was like a dream; it was as if the Romans had returned to Ibiza. I had never known Elmyr had such a beautiful home or such a coterie of boys. Where did they come from? Had they been flown in for the party? I had never seen such decadence, or known it was there.

During the weeks in Ibiza, I rented a small room in the Peña, and wrote

Nancy letter after letter, whole copybooks declaring my love for her and for the children and how we owed it to them to try again because surely there wasn't that much wrong between us. In a reply, she told me that she couldn't come back because she was in love with Ignacio and that he satisfied her in bed as I had never done. She called me Victorian for talking about our responsibility to the children. The fact was, her love for me had died but I had refused to recognise this until now. You can't make someone love you if they don't; they can't make themselves love you if they don't. Love isn't a matter of volition, wishing it won't make it happen. But the bit about little Ignacio being a superior lover hit me like a wet fish in the face. It got through to me, and I made no further overtures for her affections.

I now had no more business in Ibiza. I couldn't make the money to support myself there, let alone my children. I would hitchhike back to London, and find work there again. To take Col and Kilian with me would be impossible. How could a penniless twenty-one-year-old travel with two toddlers – and when I found work, how could I afford to have them cared for? For their sake, it was better to leave them with Nancy, in a proper house, in a good climate, and to send Nancy money for their support. When I would see them again, I didn't know.

I left on a night boat to Barcelona. Once aboard, I met a Dutch chick, Hetty, whom I'd seen around. She asked me if I had any dope and I made us a joint and she said that, since I couldn't afford a cabin and the boat was crowded, I could sleep on the floor of hers. But, after the joint, we somehow ended up in her narrow berth and she set about making love. As with the woman in London, my dick wilted at the last minute. Hetty was very pissed off indeed.

Nevertheless, the next morning she asked if she could come with me as I thumbed my way north because she didn't want to hitchhike alone and she'd pay for hotels on the way. We had two nights in France, sleeping, by mutual consent, in single beds – she didn't want the disappointment and I didn't want the shame. She was a good-looking girl but bedraggled. Somehow, hippies always get the best-looking chicks, maybe because they are generally more interesting than straight guys; they're always heading off, going somewhere, always some adventure.

Hetty de Beer and I split up outside Amsterdam. Our final ride dropped us at a truckers' café where she walked straight to the jukebox and banged on Ray Charles singing 'Hit the road, Jack, and don' you come back no mo' no mo' no mo' no mo' . . .' 'This is for you,' she said.

I had an address of an abandoned house near the Leidseplein where I could stay for nothing. I arrived there pretty well out of bread but, by chance, a black guy I'd known in Ibiza, Bill White, from Philadelphia, was also staying at the house. I was there only twenty-four hours when I found myself pissing razor blades; sex hadn't worked with Hetty but she'd given me the clap. By sheer coincidence, Bill had the clap too, and he was attending a doctor, so I went along with him. I don't know what the doctor thought when Bill introduced me but I didn't care. Anyway, the doctor said it was NSU, non-specific urethritis, no big deal – it mightn't even have been sexually transmitted. I needed an injection a day for three days and the doc said I could pay him on the last shot. Bill and I tried ripping off milk bottles from doorsteps and selling them back to the dairy but they earned only a *quartje* each and one couldn't keep turning up at the same dairy or they'd get suspicious, so we had to walk all over town. When it came to my third shot, I had no money but for the price of a meal, so I hitched south to The Hague and presented myself at the Irish Consulate, asking for repatriation to England. They took my passport as surety that I'd repay the loan and issued me with a travel document. The official who signed it was the consul himself. It turned out he'd been to the same Dublin boarding school I'd attended and was a good guy. Since there was no boat from the Hook to Harwich until the next day, I was very chuffed when, without my even mentioning my difficulty, he invited me to stay at his home that night and rang his wife to say there'd be an extra guest for dinner. Later, we cruised out to the leafy suburbs in his fine, chauffer-piloted Mercedes.

After dinner, he and his wife had to attend a reception, so they left me alone with the au pair, a truly gorgeous young French girl who'd been making eyes at me – I guess it was the suntan, the faded jeans and the bleached-out hair. In any case, romance was out of the question. She didn't know what was wrong with me; maybe she thought I was gay. Yeah, Ireland's answer to Casanova, I was leaving a trail of disgruntled women behind me, for sure!

However, in truth, the NSU was yet another blow to my self-esteem, which was often at a low ebb. The voice in my head was still commenting on everything I said, laughing at me. The pain of losing Nancy was receding, but I was still adrift in the changed personality it had brought about. I was still searching for myself, my old self, but the more I searched and the more I thought about it, the farther it drifted away.

And then, two days after I got back to London, something happened that was to change everything; that would bring some sort of love back into my life. This was Hanna, the woman I was with now, waiting for me in the farmhouse in Formentera while I took my chances doing the scams.

Arriving back in London, the first thing I did was go to a clap clinic and get the third of the three injections; I'd missed two days since the last but the doctor reckoned there would be no problem as a result of the delay. That night I met an old school friend, probably the only Irishman I knew in London, and he had this lovely girl with him whom he'd just met. I was in great form in that pub in Ladbroke Grove; some magic happened and I was full of laughter and traveller's tales, quite eclipsing my poor pal who'd had a pretty dull time in Dublin finishing his degree. When it came to ten o'clock, the girl, Hanna, said she'd have to leave soon to catch her bus to south London. South London? I was going that way and had a borrowed motor scooter and could take her to her door.

I didn't take her to her door; I took her to mine. First we stopped at a tea stall on Battersea Bridge and looked down on the Thames and up at Battersea Power Station, and got romantic. I asked her if she'd like to come to my place for a coffee, on top of the cup of tea. She agreed; some sort of alchemy was working between us. I was staying with Harry and his wife, my old Chelsea Art School friends, who owned a beautiful house on Clapham Common and who had lent me the motor scooter. They were already in bed when we arrived. I took Hanna into the drawing room where, instead of having coffee, we made love on the carpet. It was lit by a street light with a plane tree outside the window moving in the breeze and casting its shadows around us. There was no trouble making love to Hanna. We swam in the leaves, like a sea.

Afterwards, on top of the world, I drove her home on my Vespa and, after making a date to meet her the next evening near where she worked, I returned to my room. Then, the shock: in the jacks, I again found myself gripping the pipe behind the cistern, pissing razor blades. The last shot had come too late; I still had the NSU thing! What was I to do? I had to warn her. She'd told me she was married: what if she made love to her husband that night? I jumped on my bike and shot off across the empty streets of late-night London, back to where I'd delivered her forty minutes before. Luckily, it was she who came to the door when I rang the bell for their room. I told her the bad news; I told her not to screw her husband. I told her how sorry I was. Nothing to worry about, she said; she and her husband were sleeping separately – they had amicably applied for a divorce. Then, knowing that I'd have to get some more injections and that she might need some too, we agreed to meet at the clap clinic at St George's Hospital on Hyde Park Corner the following evening. It turned out that she was in the clear – but that was where the gentle but spirited Hanna and I had our first date.

Driving up through France, my friends and I took to back roads a lot because we liked them better, Rick for one who didn't feel too safe driving with the steering wheel on the wrong side, as he considered it, but we all loved looking at the countryside, and the villages too. The earliest boat to England that we could hope to make would be the next morning, so we had fifteen or sixteen hours to drive the length of France to Calais. If there was no boat from there, we'd head for Boulogne or Dieppe. In the long September afternoon we drove between Avignon and Valence, with the low sun pouring across the fields and the shadows of the tall, roadside poplars slicing the light into golden sections like one of those old piano-wire egg-slicers might slice the yolk of a hard-boiled egg.

All the time we rapped. We heard how Rick had learned everything he knew while doing time when he was 'a lowlife punk' growing up in Detroit. He'd served three years, reduced to two for good behaviour, and swore he was never going back to jail. After he got out, he'd saved some money with a view to travelling the world in search of true enlightenment, rejecting material things; the only reason he was on this expedition, like Carlo and me, was not to get rich or richer but because he'd run out of bread. He wasn't after a fortune; none of us were. Too much money pollutes, and is bad karma. We wanted only to score the equivalent of a few months' wages in Britain, enough to keep us going for a year in Formentera or to continue travelling.

Rick reckoned that, after London, he'd wander for a while. He said he wanted to visit 'the glittering capitals' of Europe. When he'd arrived in Tangier, aboard the legendary hundred-and-ten-dollar Yugoslav cargo-passenger freighter that was advertised in the *Village Voice*, he'd crossed to Algeciras and made his way north. In Granada, a Dutch guy had given him his first LSD. It hadn't been a heavenly experience, as it had been for Hanna and me, but it had opened enough of his mind for him to want to go back again, to see the demons and to pacify them or root them out. He'd smoked dope for a few years: his partner-in-knocking-over-gas-stations was a black guy who'd been heavy into jazz and had turned him on. He believed, as we did, that mind-expanding gear like LSD, Mescalin and Psilocybin mushrooms could take us to places where we could by-pass the implanted circuit boards and catch the current clear.

Carlo had tried peyote, in Mexico. It had made him violently sick and the trip lasted twenty-four hours. Part of the time, he thought he was a dog. Did he cock his leg to piss? we asked. Yeah, he said, he believed he did, and laughed into his mustachio. Carlo was a gas; he was ready for anything. In San Francisco, he'd studied art and turned on to dope one night Ginsberg was reading 'Howl' at City Lights. He was overawed but then started giggling. His friend, who'd taken him there, was mortified but Carlo couldn't stop and, finally, had to leave to a chorus of *ahems-ahems* from a whole lot of serious, and seriously disgruntled, people. He'd come to Europe with his wife and another couple. They'd made it all the way to India in an old truck and hung out there for a while until it broke down and then they took trains and buses across Asia to get back to Spain where'd they started out from. Like Rick, they'd crossed the Atlantic to Tangier and, from there, headed to Algeciras.

Once they were back in Spain, his wife had taken off with the other guy, Carlo's best friend. 'Best friends are the worst!' Rick told us, and when we asked him how he knew, he said that when he was in the joint, dudes who were serving long terms often told him that their wives, outside, had left them, very often for their best friend. What did Rick know about women? I wondered. I'd never heard of him being with one, and yet he admitted to the desire and had an eye for beauty in women. The night before, in the Plaza Real, Carlo and I had ribbed him about going upstairs with one of the young whores whom he'd pointed out was beautiful, but no way would he even think of it. In fact, none of us had ever been with a whore and, what was even more amazing, we'd never heard of, let alone been to, one of those orgies the newspapers seem to think beat people and hipsters were into every night of the year.

Carlo's stories were good, and Rick's, too, and I guess I had a few to tell. Lying in the back of the car when it was my turn to sleep, I'd half-wake to the rumble of the tyres on the cobblestones as we passed through French villages, the street lights glimmering on my eyelids like magic lanterns. For a while, I'd lie and listen to the click-click of the driver's foot on the dimmer-switch on the floor as cars approached and passed, and I could sometimes see, on the roof above, the shadows of Carlo and Rick thrown by the dashboard light or the flare of a match as they lit cigarettes. Their voices were low and muffled, and farther and farther away as I drifted back to sleep.

Later, sitting beside Rick as he drove, he talked and I listened. It seemed to me that Rick was one of the most honest people I had ever met. He had looked into the depths of his soul and had seen his shortcomings. He was weak, he said – that was his trouble. He was always easily led.

We talked about weakness, about my uncertainty over committing myself to Hanna. Rick understood; the weakness of the power of love, he called it. We talked as brothers, open and honest with one another. We talked as the road unfurled, and that common thread of pain and hope that runs through all lives drew us close.

Morning came and I was back in the driving seat, Rick dozing beside me, watching dawn come up in the wing-mirror as we passed through the cold, flat fields of northern France.

When Hanna and I were driving down to Spain in that same old jalopy a few months earlier, I'd gone to sleep for a second at the wheel and dreamt I'd driven right through a house, in the front door and out the back, and snapped awake just in time to keep from going off the road. I pulled in and Hanna – who didn't drive – stayed awake, in the dark car, Aoife asleep in the back, me asleep beside her, so that after half an hour she could wake me up and we could go on.

The wagon was piled high with all we owned and we must've looked like something out of *The Grapes of Wrath*, with Aoife's pushchair, cot and plastic bath on top, like Okies fleeing the Dust Bowl. On the back seat were boxes of tinned goods our friend Mike Darby had 'purloined' from Fortnum & Mason where he'd worked (unusually, for Mike) packing Christmas hampers addressed to Sir Winston Churchill, Sir Laurence Olivier, the Duchess of Kent and the like. Aoife's Moses basket was laid on top, she sleeping soundly on the contraband. Even now, we were still half-living on jugged hare in aspic, goose liver and brandy pâté and stuffed anchovies in jars, which was sort of ironic considering we were living on an island where food was cheap and fresh from the fields or the sea. However, every penny we saved would lengthen our stay.

The thing about my scene with Hanna was that it had all happened too fast; I had warned her that it was not a good idea her moving in with me so soon after we'd met. Yes, I loved her, but I was not *in love* with her. I couldn't be; Nancy was still in my head and it still seemed to me that my life could never be the same but always be spent in shallows and in miseries. I didn't want to bring Hanna into these miseries and neither was I prepared to settle for a relationship that was second best. I thought it was better I stayed free until I either found I loved her as I had loved Nancy, or had found someone else to really love. To live with her as second-best wasn't fair on her, and I knew it. She was lovely to look at, blonde and petite, and she had a soul full of yearning for the good, for the truth, for the happiness she had been denied as a child when she had had no lease of innocence before it was taken from her for ever.

We shared dreams. After seeing Fellini's *La Strada*, and watching Giulietta Masina and Zampano, the evil strongman, travelling from town to town putting on their show, we dreamt of travelling across Europe and all the way to India in a horse-drawn caravan and giving puppet shows to earn our living on the way. Hanna was good with puppets. She had been to art school and had studied ballet but, to earn a living, had had to learn to type. Then, somehow, she, a neat director's secretary, had got involved with a bohemian painter, her husband, and then with a vagabond, me.

When she and her husband vacated their furnished room and she had to find a new home, I took her on my motorcycle – a 200cc motorbike, also lent to me by Harry – to see bedsitting rooms for rent. None were right, she said, and then one night, in that very cold London winter, I heard a knock on the half-windowed door of my basement flat and peered out. There she was, standing in the snow with her suitcase and a blue woollen hat, looking like Little Dorrit. I told her to go away; I told her she couldn't stay with me, that I would only hurt her with my own pain but she stood weeping, and what could I do but let her in, and into my life?

Soon afterwards, she became pregnant; she, like Nancy, having told me it was impossible for her to conceive because she hadn't with her husband, and so we took no precautions. In any case, I used to say then that using a condom was like washing your feet with your socks on. It seemed funny at the time. Afterwards, she got a diaphragm but that didn't work either, as it turned out. Of my seven children, all but one happened by serendipity, but they were all welcome. We talk about 'love children' – mine were all love children, and they were all loved.

So, Hanna came into my life before I was ready for her, but now, with a child coming, I resolved to stay with her and make it work if I could. Both our divorces had come through and we married at a registry office in Chelsea. Our guests and witnesses were a barman from the Queen's Elm pub and three of Hanna's old friends, Cockney Londoners, good people. Afterwards, we had a 'knees-up' in their rented flat in Old Street. Hanna looked beautiful and radiant but she would have known my uncertainty; I sometimes saw it, mirrored in the uncertainty of her smile. Any other man would have given her his heart and soul; I could give her my soul but not my heart. If the occasion demanded, I would have laid down my life for her and our daughter but I couldn't, somehow, make my love migrate. It was still trapped in that unreal past, the loss of 'what could have been'. To have pretended otherwise would have been a con-trick. It would have made it worse for her if and when the day came that I had to leave. She didn't deserve to have her trust destroyed – she had already been too much hurt by those she trusted. So, I avoided lying to her at whatever costs. I was protective of her; it was my duty. Young men were all a bit macho then, especially the nomads on the roads untravelled, living outside society with our women and our kids.

Nancy still haunted me; the days were empty without her and my sons. No sunlit room, no quiet sea, no children's voices. The light seemed dimmed; the days had no substance or resonance. I still woke to the losses, then closed my eyes and ears to them, and tutored all day. I sent Nancy what money I could. She came back to England once, to visit her parents in Dorset, and I rode the hundred or more miles on the motorbike to see the twins. I stayed the night in a grim B&B and, next day, after taking them to a park, headed for home. My bike had no fairing or windscreen and I rode bare-headed, with only woollen gloves, a corduroy jacket, polo neck sweater, and thin working trousers with a pair of Hanna's tights underneath. I froze as stiff as the bike itself, the cold like a metal band around my forehead squeezing ever tighter. In London, where the night streets were glazed with ice, hypothermia rose and washed over me. While waiting for traffic lights to change, I dozed and fell over, the bike on top of me. Luckily, it wasn't a big bike. With the help of a motorist, I picked it up and rode on, and soon was home with Hanna, with her warmth, sitting over the glowing candles of our bedsitter gas fire, drinking cups of sweet tea.

One night, at the Queen's Elm in the Fulham Road, we met Mike Darby, a clubbable rogue a couple of years older than ourselves and the best company one could find, with his twinkling eyes, goatee beard, florid 'kisser' and car-pet-bagger suit. He often slept on our floor when he was short of a few bob, which he was most of the time, having squandered his weekly handout from the Social Security on pints of bitter. He looked like someone permanently on his way to a race-meeting or, rather, on his way *back* from one, having lost his shirt and slept in the suit. A gentleman conman one might call him. His vocation was to entertain, and he did it for the price of a pint, being marvellously adept at moving in on newcomers to the hostelry, as he'd call it. Spotting a mark, he'd shoot us a wink, drift off and, lo and behold, ten minutes later would arrive back with a fresh pint for each of us, compliments of his new-found friend sitting over at the bar.

My Irish painter friend came back to London from Morocco with half a pound of kief and laid an ounce on me. I turned Hanna on, and she liked it. Lovemaking was always good and now it was even better. It was so long since I'd been high, I giggled with her like a novice smoker. I offered to turn Mike on but he'd have none of it. Nobody we knew, except our Irish friend, smoked dope. Dope hadn't yet arrived in London.

Chapter 5

IT WAS MAYBE AFTER I'D been six months with Hanna, a year after the fuck-up with Nancy, that I began to reclaim my mind. I wasn't the same but I was a near approximation. I decided to drive down to Barcelona with the purpose of going to Ibiza to see my kids; with passengers to pay the gas, driving would be the cheapest way. Hanna didn't come. I didn't ask her to and I didn't say when I'd be back. In fact, we gave up our furnished room and she moved to her parents' house; it was like we were splitting up, although for sure I was going to see her again because she was carrying my child. I no longer dreamt of getting back with Nancy; what pining I did wasn't for her but for the person that I had been. But that old self was returning, and I wanted to find out what it would be like to be alone. So going south had a double purpose: to see my sons and to be free for a while.

I had an old Morris, and to help pay the gas I took aboard an English couple, a pale and high-foreheaded nerd called Bernard, and his girlfriend, scatty Kathy, who lived in a whole different world from his. How they came together, who knows. She worked nightclubs while he was doing a doctorate in philosophy at Cambridge. They weren't easy as passengers, Kathy especially, who liked pills, but I was cock-a-hoop to be back on the road and when Kathy, a hard-nosed girl, started to argue about how much they'd agreed to pay me, I stopped the car abruptly and invited them to either pay up right then or get out and walk the last hundred kilometres to Barcelona. In

Barcelona, things warmed again and I decided to tell them about Ibiza – which I had planned not to do – and they couldn't wait to join me on the boat. That was how Bernard and Kathy found Ibiza. They got into smoking kief, and Bernard turned into a very different philosopher. Later, back in London, we all became close friends.

It was great to see Colin and Kilian again and I took them out to the beach or to the country every day. Nancy and I maintained a cold civility; at first, she was apologetic, but I really didn't want to hear any of that shit. She did tell me that back then, on the battlefield, she'd lied about my shortcomings as a lover – great news and thanks, Nancy, but it was a little late, given the numerous women (two) I had slept with and then disappointed as a result of her psychological emasculation. When I asked her if I could have the folio of poems I'd left behind, she said the kids had drawn on them and, not knowing what they were, she'd thrown them out.

When it came time for me to leave and drive back to London and Hanna, I took aboard a crazy guy, Marty Kline, a dropped-out nuclear physicist from New York who looked like Einstein, and his wife, Sylvia, an abdicated Jewish princess. I also took a dog, a Kerry Blue of high pedigree. Not only valuable, it was beloved of an American family that had come to Ibiza on holidays and, upon deciding to stay, wanted to send the dog back to their home in France where their older children and grandchildren were missing it. Hearing I'd be driving through France, they asked me if I'd take it and offered a fee, plus money for its keep on the way. I refused the fee but they insisted, and that was OK by me.

So Marty, Sylvia, me and the dog took the night boat to Barcelona. I carried the animal aboard because it was shaking with fear and it was now my responsibility. I had received a fistful of dollars from the owners who came, tearfully, to see him off.

It was summer and, overnight, Kerry – not his real name – slept on deck with me, Marty and Sylv. In the morning, we shared our *sobrasada* sausage with him. Sylvia wanted to spend the day in Barcelona, and I agreed, so the dog went with us to see the church of the Sagrada Familia, and we took him to the beach. He was a playful hound, and we enjoyed rushing around after him, Marty and I. However, on the street, on a lead, he was a pain in the ass, pulling to get away. He was very strong.

After getting something to eat, we decided to hit the road. It would be good driving at night, with little or no traffic. Marty said that if I got tired, he'd take the wheel. Meantime, he sat up front. Although he wore huge bifocal spectacles, he scanned the map and was a good navigator when he could keep the hair out of his eyes.

As we pulled away from where I was parked just off Cristobal Colón, the dog started to whine. It was freaked by the car. In the back seat with Sylvia, it began to claw at the windows. 'It wants to join the party,' Marty said. Barcelona, that Saturday night, was a vast party and, driving up a wide *rambla* out of the port area, we found ourselves in its midst. The American Sixth Fleet was in again, four battleships of free-spending shore-leave sailors, and the crowds were out, Spanish hustlers and gypsies trying to sell them things, and the assembled citizenry looking on. The pavement-side bars spilled onto the street, and the roadway was an obstacle course of drunken matelots, gypsy serenaders and hip-swinging ladies of the night.

The dog didn't like it at all. He jumped over the seat, landed in my lap and scrabbled at the steering wheel. He was going berserk. 'Stop!' yelled Marty, pointing. 'There's a pharmacy. Get him a tranquilliser!' 'OK,' I agreed, 'Hold him while I get out!' The chemist was *simpático* and I arrived back with a knock-out pill. But when I opened the car door, Marty forgot to hold on to the animal. He shot out, like a demon, flew between my legs and into the crowd. It took me ten seconds to gun the car onto the pavement, where we leapt out and gave chase. Dodging through the night-walkers and sailors, Marty and I wove at high speed after Kerry's expensive, disappearing tail.

At times, we got close to him. We'd come from two directions, arms outstretched, voices soothing, but he'd shoot past. We ran a mile up and down the *ramblas*; we were limber and lean as hounds. 'Kerry, Kerry, Kerry!' we cried. Drunken sailors, in their white outfits, took up the chorus. Holding arms, they formed a human barricade. This made things worse. If Kerry had been freaked out before, the wall of sailors really got to him. The last I saw of him was his tail as he disappeared down an unlit alley into the Barrio Chino. Having lost Marty and Sylv, I followed him alone. It was a run-down place, with vacant lots where fires were burning and shadowy people were sitting about. I walked deeper into the labyrinth but there wasn't a hope of finding the dog. Later, when I told the story to a policeman, he said the gypsies lived there and had probably eaten him. It wasn't true, of course; they'd have seen he was a pedigree hound and sold him on.

So the dog was gone and what could I do? Tell the owners that he'd been barbecued by gypsies in Barcelona? Things were bad enough already; the truth would break their hearts. I sent them a letter from France – a lie. It was a good epitaph but I hope that, even after all this time, they never read this story. I told them how Kerry had become ill, how we had taken him to a vet who assured us he was in no pain and had given him tranquillisers. He'd died that night in Sylvia's arms, and we had buried him under an oak tree near Dijon. I sent them back the money they'd given me; I'd sneaked him aboard the boat and hadn't had to pay his fare.

Later, on that long road north, Marty, Sylvia and I hit Pamplona and, by sheer chance, the famous Fiesta de San Fermin. We got stuck in the crowds and they pulled us out of the car and plied us with wine; in a fairground, we rode in swinging boats, a rope in one hand, a bottle of wine in the other, Marty and I, in competition, sending the boats so high they almost went over the bar as we soared out over the massed revellers below. Later, we rode the chair-o-planes too, grabbing one another's seats as the carousel spun and pushing one another with our feet, so we swung high and wide over the stalls and lights, while the music blared below. Next day, with sore heads, we watched the running of the bulls and the crazy fuckers sprinting ahead of them, touching their horns and jumping the barriers just when they were about to be gored. And we saw a foreigner, who had crossed the barrier to take photos, being hit so hard with his baton by a Guardia Civil that blood poured from his skull like a stream. Yes, he'd warned him twice – but it showed what vicious bastards the Spanish cops could be during Franco's time.

Near Bayonne, the car died and I tried to sell it for scrap to a garage before we abandoned it and hitchhiked on. I can't remember what happened to Marty and Sylvia, but I got to London and, at the first phone box, I rang Hanna at her parents' home. She told me she'd lost our child: she'd had a miscarriage in the third month. She had told nobody. I think it was anxiety about the future that caused it. I said I'd find a room for us and she sobbed at the end of the phone.

The room was in Earls Court – called Kangaroo Valley because so many Aussies doing their trip to the Old Country hung out there. It was typical Kensington bedsitter-land. The room was pleasant and it felt good to be back with Hanna. She got jobs as a temp typist and I chased tutorial work. Since she was a Londoner and had been married to a painter, she knew the bohemian hang-outs; I was no longer a hick standing outside the arty pubs in Chelsea and Soho, looking in. We'd go up west to the French Pub, run by the magnificently moustachioed Gaston in Old Compton Street, headquarters of the Free French during the war. There, Hanna was on nodding acquaintance with luminaries and drink-crazed denizens like Jeffrey Barnard, Lucian Freud and Francis Bacon. Two or three times, I met Patrick Kavanagh, the great Irish poet, and he didn't attack or abuse me as he did many a poetaster, maybe because I was young. Hanna and I drifted to the Caves de France, a drinking club for the in-crowd in the afternoons, and sometimes went to the Colony after the French closed at night.

When we didn't go for a drink, we went to a film. On my little motor-bike, come rain or shine, we'd zip across London, north, south and west to Stella Cinemas where art movies were shown. We saw Kurosawa, Ishikawa, Fellini, Antonioni, Jean-Luc Godard and Polanski.

Next thing, Hanna was pregnant again. The Dutch Cap hadn't worked. At times, we had raging, dangerous rows when I'd tell her don't make demands, '*I never made any promises. You moved in with me to begin with. I didn't ask you to. Don't tell me what I should and shouldn't do!*' It was unfair, she said! I was better with words than her, I could turn anything around, and she would weep bitterly, face buried in her hands, eyes puffy, mascara running, and I would feel the greatest heel on earth. Having resolved to walk out of her life ten minutes earlier, I knew I couldn't. It was impossible to leave her in that state. I would take her and try to comfort her and she'd come into my arms, and I'd look at my face reflected in the mirror on the mantelpiece and wish it could be alright, wish that we didn't have to cause one another such pain. And then we'd go on, as before. The child was coming. It would be a love to share. Maybe it would make the difference.

But in these skirmishes, Hanna could be fierce too. For all her small size, she packed a punch and could swing her shoulder bag like a baseball bat. She clocked me once, out of the blue, when I said something to her as we were walking down the street. I never reciprocated physically. Up came the bag out of nowhere and knocked me sideways. We would row in the street; we had no concern for what anybody might think about us. The battle royal might rage along the pavement, as we crossed the street, as we boarded an underground train. We didn't mind; we were spontaneous. Of course half the world – like Mike back then, like Rick, now sleeping beside me as I drove – would tell me I was mad not to cherish Hanna, who was so beautiful, so loving, and so good. But I was not one to settle for compromises. No way would I lead a life of half-measures. It all had to be the best that ever could be: all or nothing. With what fierce intensity I burned.

Sometimes, on nights we stayed home, Hanna and I would get on the bike around midnight and ride down to the Cromwell Road Air Terminal, five minutes away, for cheap entertainment watching people. Real life was more interesting than television. At the terminal, airline passengers from all over the world checked in for flights and were taken by bus to Heathrow. There was a multi-storey car park, a novelty in London, and we'd gun the bike up the winding ramps. We'd buy a coffee and sit for an hour picking out interesting-looking travellers and guessing their nationality, their professions and where they were going. Then we'd return to our bedsitting room in Earls Court.

One night however, in October 1962, when we turned on our rented black-and-white TV, we saw aerial footage of Soviet warships with missiles like huge, upright cigars approaching Cuba, and heard news of hot-line telephone calls from Kennedy to Khrushchev telling him he'd better turn them around or else. It was the famous showdown at the Cuban Corral. We watched, fascinated, not believing a nuclear holocaust was really going to happen, that someone would stop it, but for a few hours, we, and the world, held our breath. Later, we went down to the Queen's Elm and had a pint and met our flamboyant friend, Mike Darby. 'Let's have one before we go, squire!' he said, winking. Hanna had been on the Ban-the-Bomb marches with her husband, but for me it was all too English, duffel coats and Bertrand Russell. I wasn't into British politics. I preferred to be a dumb, dope-smoking subversive, living in Spain.

Sometimes, after Hanna was asleep, I'd lie thinking about the Domino, what was going on in that parallel universe as I lay in a half-dark London room. In my mind, I'd walk down the steps into the bar, smoky, claustrophobic, and warm. On the stereo, Miles Davis or Cannonball Adderley or Ornette Coleman are blowing their heads off with trumpets, axes and plastic saxes. All around me are my fellow revellers in the alcohol-fumed gloaming, the mystery-men, remittance men, yachtsmen and black sheep, the ex-wives, the ex-husbands; I know them all. Heartbreak Hotel, Brunswick called the Domino. *'Well, since my baby left me, I've found a new place to dwell, It's down at the end of Lonely Street and you drink yourself to hell . . .'* But it wasn't all heartbreak, and those who were there wouldn't have missed it for anything.

Ibiza, the Domino Bar, December 1961. It's a typical deep winter night. Island-itis rages, a type of 'stir-crazy', like inmates get in jail. Through the bar, the punters come and go. Few are sober. Some are hyped on Benzedrine, as well. Many haven't been off the island for a year; they have unpaid bills and no money for a ticket. There have been few newcomers since summer. Most of the couples who arrived then have split up. The majority have, by now, ceased to do one another violence.

There's an electricity in the air. My amigo, Rainer, and I flop ourselves down on either side of one of the concrete tables along the wall. I call for a *cognac con sifón y helo*. Angel brings it. *'Para su cuenta?'* he asks. I smile positively. He already knows the answer: he's just being polite. Rainer tells me he's got a little kief. After dinner at the Bahia, we bop down the breakwater and smoke a joint. The few amongst us who smoke keep the secret to ourselves.

A sharp drag, a cigarette tip palmed, 'Here, take it . . .' He passes it to me. I suck it, hold the smoke deep in my lungs, then exhale slowly. I feel a rush sweep over me. The tropic night, the sea licking the stones. *Speak to me in divers tongues, whisper . . . See, the moonlight on the oil-black water; read, overhead, the semaphore of stars . . .*

Along the harbour front, the Valenciano fleet is moored two abreast, two-masted, mast-lights arrowing over the water as they gently sway, arrows of light shattering into facets as they fall into the depths below. Dark silhouettes of the men on deck are huddled over red fires, over steaming paella pans. The white cubes of houses in the Peña are like ghosts behind them. Above everything rise the gigantic walls.

'Evenin,' William.' says Rainer, as William, Ibiza's first junkie, the son of a famous American pianist, passes, taking his Silver Gibbon, Motherfucker, for a walk.

Back we drift, Rainer and me, chortling and giggling, into the Domino, and slide into a seat. Mingus is on the stereo, *'Ah-um'*. I close my eyes; Rainer's are already closed. When it's over, we grin at one another and call for drinks. Angel obliges. We sit back to watch the night-people pass by.

First up is George Rahn, New York *'intelecsual'*, contributor to the *Village Voice*, author and critic. He sidles over, mouth loose, eyes crossed, gin glass in hand. Same old conversation: 'Why do you smoke that shit? Why do you schmoke that shit? *Hic!* Don't you know it's gonna rot your brains, and so on?'

He grins, rotund, loveable and swaying, as is his usual style at that time of night. Rainer tells him that when Sir Walter Raleigh smoked the peace pipe with the Indians, it was actually full of the best grass but when Sir Walter asked 'Where-the-fuck-can-I-get-morea-this-shit?!' the hip Injuns sold him tobacco. Re-crossing the Atlantic, he smoked some and realised the Injuns had burnt him and he had nothing but a shipload of Virginia weeds. In England, he had no option but to eulogize their sedative and intellectually enhancing properties, and that is how tobacco-smoking was sold. Rainer tells the story well. George giggles like a goosed virgin and staggers onward, mumbling like Mr Magoo.

Enter King Hal, newly arrived protagonist for the-legalisation-of-marijuana, with train. Hal is a tall American executive of middle age. He looks like he's walked in off Wall Street; he still wears his grey flannel suit, and tasteful, if rumpled, tie. The train follows, twenty-five years his junior, two thin girls, dressed all in black with white, death-mask makeup, shrouded kohl eyes. Each, apparently as a result of shipboard accidents, has her arm in white plaster, in a sling. Two jet black men follow, spades in shades.

'Hi, D, hi, GR . . .' Hal murmurs softly, stooping to smile in our eyes while passing. For Hal, we are paid-up members of a conspiracy to turn the world on.

Hal's is a Road-to-Damascus story. At forty nine, he smoked dope for the first time and, instantly converted, walked into the local precinct house, put down two rolled joints in front of the desk-sergeant and said 'Bust me!' The desk sergeant obliged.

The test-case, in which Hal argued that marijuana was a benign influence, cost him his home and his wife, and ended with him serving a year in jail. Soon after he got out, he arrived in Ibiza with his small retinue of acolytes, straight from New York, his avowed object being to start a 'Free School' and teach everybody to swing. One couldn't put the cat down, although it was doubtful anyone in Ibiza needed that sort of tuition.

Now my friend 'The End of Mercy' Steelbaum, still suffering from a hangover acquired with Hemingway in the late 1940s, heaves himself off his barstool and calls down shit and damnation upon all money-mongers, critics and publishers wherever they may be. Jan Cremer, an ex-Rotterdam docker, jailbird and boxer, pushes past him, heading for the street. Cremer is the strong, silent type. A big-selling artist, he's no older than I am. We exchange nods as he passes. He's into motor-cycle boots and leather jackets with zippers, more New York than Ibiza, maybe early Rudi Gernreich style.

Some Valenciano fishermen have come in and the Slick Spick, as Brunswick calls him, has sneaked in with them, the only customer ever to be barred from the Domino. Already he's doing his short flamenco shuffle in the direction of the nearest woman, *Ole!*, with his hand somehow coming in lingering contact with her buttocks. The question is who's going to throw him out first – the dour Scandinavian sailor with his troll woman or the French kid who says he's on his way to join the Foreign Legion and is talking to Hughie's Jacqueline, a *pied noir* from Algiers. He's an obnoxious fucker but Rainer and I can understand him wanting a piece of the action. From where he's looking, the foreign women seem to spread it around, so why not to him?

As he sets off again, this time towards Nancy, sitting with her *Cuba Libre* at the end of the bar, I think maybe I should get between them but I know she can very well look after herself. Anyway, crash, bash! – the big Scandahoovian has thumped the little fucker for getting fresh with his Valkyrie wife. He's pushing him towards the door but two of the Valenciano fishermen have got the wrong idea and are squaring up in defence of their countryman. Now Bligh is on his feet, and Crippled Ed, with his stick. '*Tranquilo, amigos, tranquilo,*' Al-the-Owner is yelling. Angel has come around the counter to grab the groper and escort him outside. 'Free drinks!' yells Al. He puts Ray Charles on the stereo, '*Only one more time . . . !*'

Thing settle down, and I look around me. Brunswick, the Legend Spinner, farther up the bar; Fat George and García; Cap'n Bligh and young Armand, the would-be Legionnaire. George arrives by taxi every morning. The taxi nearly turns over when he stands on the running board to climb out. A loving man; a detached mind. In Ibiza, there is a kind of love, even if there isn't always goodwill. Alcohol is the drug of choice; only ten of us blow dope; Nancy doesn't. Now there's King Hal and the acolytes, new additions to the ten happy heads.

At one of the tables, the Valencianos have started arm-wrestling. Angel calls me over, trying to get me to have a go. Why me? I'm not some outsize bruiser. Ah, *porque* the Valenciano has just beaten that good-looking yacht bum who's talking to Nancy. '*Hey, amigo Angel, ain't nobody's goin' to be impressed by this shit!*' Nevertheless, I slide into the stall. I see Nancy looking towards me. I wink at her to share the sport and shoot her a crooked grin. She pulls deeply on her cigarette and turns away, her dark hair on her back, her brown shoulder against her white dress.

We shake hands, me and the Valenciano, then lock palms. I'm sweating, he's sweating, shared rivers of sweat run down our arms. People are leaning over, crowding. Rainer hisses, 'Now, D, now!'

But not now. After the first struggle, we're at peace, at equilibrium, arms upright, hands gripping like brothers. Only the crowd around us bustles; we're at the still centre of the world. 'Now, D, now!' Rainer urges again. I look towards Nancy but she has left.

Back in the London bedsitting room, I stir before sleeping. I don't want to think of that again.

Chapter 6

IN LONDON, HANNA'S LITTLE BELLY grows rounder and I teach all the hours I can get and stash as much as possible of the money. It's a sort-of escape fund; one day soon, we'll hit the road. Meanwhile, teaching Geography – amongst other subjects – to rich kids, I evolve a system to help them relate latitude and longitude to climate and crops and, ever the entrepreneur, decide I'll write a textbook about it. After many a long afternoon of research in the Reading Room at the British Museum, I find the system is original only to me, which is why I've been teaching it with the enthusiasm of a new-found revelation. This was the case with many of the subjects and texts I thought; I'd never understood or appreciated them at school but did so now and wanted to tell my pupils all about them. So, while I taught with energy and heartfelt conviction, I was no academic. No sweat; I was good at communicating. A communicator was all I wanted to be.

One night, by chance, Hanna and I ran into her ex-husband in the Queen's Elm and we drank a pint or two together. When closing time came, I offered him a ride to his bus stop. Hanna would walk back with Mike Darby and I'd meet them afterwards.

When I'd dropped him off, I remembered that a girl Hanna knew at work wanted some information about Majorca and that her flat was on my way home. I decide to drop in for a minute. The flat was shared by three or four girls, all secretaries. The front door opened into a big living room and, as I crossed it to go to the chick's room, I saw that there were three guys hanging about, smoking, heavy-looking geezers dressed in suits, not the kind of people you'd expect to see in a secretaries' pad in Kensington. I didn't give it any thought but proceeded to the girl's room, told her what she wanted to know, and headed back to the living room and the front door.

As I reached the door, one of the heavies jumped up and blocked my way, spreading his arms wide. Thinking it was pretty funny, I make some sharp crack about 'What, is it Good Friday already?' but the guy doesn't laugh. He says, 'Sit down with the others. You're not leaving.'

I now notice that there are four new people in the room, including one of the girl tenants, and that they're sitting in a row on a sofa and that a heavy silence reigns. Unfazed, I say that yes, I *am* leaving, and go to push past him. For this, I get a smack on the back of the head with a wine bottle that was serving as a candle-holder. But for the straw around the base, my head would have been split open. I crash to the deck, and the team goes to work on me – and very experienced they are too. They kick my face, my head, my back, my balls and every part of me. Then they rush out of the door and down the stairs. I stand up, and – this is a weird thing – grab a tea cup, stagger out onto the landing and hurl it down two flights of stairs after them. They slam the front door and are gone.

Now, having no idea of how damaged I am, I say goodnight to the company and head downstairs to my motorbike to ride home. I make it as far as the pavement when the others come out of the house and stop me. They insist that I can't ride. They want to call an ambulance. I think it's ridiculous – they're English wimps, making a fuss about nothing. I am numb as a potato as I try to wave them away and mount the bike. There is a taxi passing and someone hails it. They tell me I must leave the bike and get into it. They practically throw me aboard.

When I reach Mike Darby's place – Mike, for once, has a place, a borrowed flat – numb and dumb as I am, I find the right bell and ring it. Hanna comes down to let me in. She opens the door, sees me and cries out in horror. As I reach to peck her on the cheek – at least one of them, because I can see four – I catch sight of two of myself in the mirror of a big wardrobe at the end of the hall. My white working shirt is scarlet with blood. There is blood all over my jacket. My face is distorted, my jaw hanging sort of loose. Mike arrives toot-sweet, digs the scene and rushes out to detain the taxi, while Hanna props me up. I *am* sort of woozy, it now occurs to me. Things are moving about in slow motion and their voices seem far away. 'The Princess Beatrice,' Darby tells the taxi-man, 'and don't spare the horses!' The Princess Beatrice Hospital; I haven't been there since the twins were born. I settle back, nestled on my darlin' Hanna's lap, and watch the street lights swirling.

In Emergency, a young intern adjusts my nose, which is lying flat on my face. He does it by pushing it up with his thumbs; it's a temporary job, he says, to make sure I can breathe. He explains that I have concussion, I may have a fractured skull, and I have a broken jaw. And so I am carted off to a ward. I object to this; I don't like hospitals and I resent the loss of wages a hospital stay will entail. Someone shows me a mirror. I look a holy fright: eyes black, nose bent, lips puffy, jaw black and blue.

The first day, I'm unconscious for hours and don't recognise Hanna. The second day, I get out of bed to leave. I run out of steam and fall flat before I even reach the ward door. The third day, having gained strength, I get up, find my clothes, dress myself and head for the street. A nurse apprehends me. The doctor is called and tries to dissuade me, but to no avail. As far as Dumb-Ass D is concerned, this hospital stuff is for sissies; he is The Iron Man. In a couple of days, he'll be as right as rain.

He is right as rain, as it turns out, but for the fact that his jaw was never re-set and ever afterwards clicks like *maracas* when he eats. He has a cross bite because the upper and lower jaws no longer fit together. The hairline fracture in his skull is never fixed. His nose-job remains like a ski-jump for the rest of his earthly. Hail The Iron Man! Youth is wonderful. All things are possible when you're young.

Later, I discover that the heavy crew were there to beat up one of the flat-mate's boyfriends who had welched on a gambling debt. They'd expected him home after the pubs closed but he hadn't come. Pissed off, they vented their aggression on the uppity Irishman, who was in the wrong place at the wrong time. And so, bad timing and a refusal to be pushed around altered his well-formed hooter and added character to his kisser. But sweet little Hanna loved him all the same.

One day, I spot a familiar figure boppin' down Portobello Road with an Ibiza long-handled basket over his shoulder and a radio held to his ear. It is Mel, whom I know from early days in Ibiza, a lanky American who lives for music. He has hair falling over his forehead, a beard all over his face and dark shades; all you can see of his face are his lips and his buck teeth. In the Domino Bar, he'd talk to no one, just stand in the annex at the back, shuffling to the jazz, the wrap-around shades catching the light. It is fortuitous meeting him. He knows nobody in London but has a shoebox of Ketama grass from the Rif Mountains of Morocco and a steady line in inner-consciousness rap. He wants to sell some of the grass to stake him for a few months in England. I have no commercial connections but my friend Bernard knows some university people who'll buy dope.

Evening after evening all that winter, we smoke and rap in Bernard's two-room pad off Westbourne Grove. Shy Bernard, of the high forehead, Kathy, his night-club-hostess girl, ganglin' Mel, born in an army camp in Missouri, Hanna and me, to the dark, velvet background of Mingus music, through the deep London evenings, we talk about everything under the skull, all the agonies, ecstasies, hang-ups, aspirations that we know. I arrive at Bernard's when I've finished teaching and Hanna meets me there after work. Occasional excursions are made into the Outside, into the great out-of-doors, sociological expeditions, a bus to Leicester Square to the movies, straight London observed through stoned eyes. We may stop into a pub for a pint afterwards, but we drink hardly at all.

We talk about existentialism and how we should act in the world, about the Theosophists, Gurdjieff and Ouspensky, about *The Dawn of Magic* and *Chariots of the Gods*. We conclude that there are more things in heaven and earth than we have dreamt of in our philosophics – out the window with Descartes: look to the East. We read *The Phenomenon of Man*, *Magister Ludi*, the *Tao Te Ching*. We consider the possibility that other parts of the mind can be reached where there is another knowledge, where this charade can be seen from afar. But the workings of the stoned mind are also observed, examined and laughed at. Self-consciousness and paranoia are laughed at; they are the pot-head's disease, the price we pay. As old Brunswick in Ibiza memorably put it, 'The long grey wolf of paranoia stalks the pot-head's heels.'

In the smoky, top-floor room with the bed on the floor at one end and windows looking down on the tops of the London plane trees, we'd sit around in the half-dark, with the jazz playing softly, and talk, with total openness, about our loves and fears. Around eight o'clock, Kathy would disappear into the bathroom and shortly emerge in her finery and sit on the bed and do her eyes and put on her false eyelashes and get ready to go out to the clubs. We'd disperse soon afterwards, to meet next evening and take up the theme again. Hanna, who trusted intuitions more than words, wasn't always as enthusiastic as I was about this scene.

Aoife, our daughter, was born in a hospital within the sound of Bow Bells, which should have made her a Cockney but didn't because Hanna and I were only passing through. I was present at the birth, and was amazed at Hanna's courage and good spirits. All went smoothly. Aoife Jane was an easy, companionable child and Hanna breast-fed her for the required time. We were able to go to the cinema less often, although Salim, the Pakistani medical student who lived in the next-door room, was a sterling guy and always willing to keep an ear open for Aoife any night we wanted to go out. Upstairs lived old Mr Skidelski, whose room, the landlady told us, was so full of newspapers that there was no space to move around any more: they stood in columns and pillars and walled in his bed.

On the landing outside, the coin-operated telephone was fixed to the wall and it was from there that I hustled up my tutorial work. The agency would post out notices of parents seeking tutors for their children. I'd grab the mail as soon as it came through the letterbox and, armed with a pocketful of sixpences, skip upstairs to the landing and get to work on the phone. The notice gave details of the job, the address, the kid's age, and any requirements or problems. When there were two phone numbers given, the father's work number and the number of the family home, I'd always ring the family home. There, I'd get to speak to the wife, Mrs This or That, Countess This or That, wife of the Ambassador of This or That, and listen attentively to the problems of the beloved child. After murmuring sympathetically, I would opine that perhaps I could help the little fellow or girl because I had had experience of just that sort of difficulty, or had previously taught that course. I would be happy to meet the child one afternoon after he or she came back from school to see how we got on together and – Goodness me! – I'd just noticed the address (Eaton Square, The Little Boltons, Kensington Palace Gardens) and – what a coincidence! – I was passing that very way this very afternoon with half an hour free between other pupils and perhaps I might drop in? Charmed, the lady would invite me. I would meet the offspring and, for sure, we would get on. When harassed hubby returned from work with a list of damn tutors to interview, his fragrant wife would assure him that all was well; she had already engaged the services of a nice Irishman who got on with young Peregrine or Hortense like a house on fire. And we did get on, too.

With Aoife to look after, Hanna couldn't work any more, but that was OK; I could make enough to keep us and send bread to Nancy, even to save a bit, although we gave up renting the black-and-white TV. Never mind; real life was more interesting. We'd have a bit of dope now and then if an Ibiza friend was passing through and we'd get out to the pub with Mike sometimes or he'd show up with a bottle he'd 'purloined' from somewhere. Come the school holidays of 1963, when there was no teaching work anyway, I scored another old car, a bigger version of the Morris, and we headed for España, this being Hanna's first time, and her first ever visit to Ibiza, of which I'd told her so much and where, inevitably, she'd meet the woman who had broken my heart.

By 1963, there were still no more than thirty or forty resident *estranjeros* on the island, so there would be no avoiding Nancy. The Domino remained the only foreign bar. Nancy was cordial; more than that, I think she was dying to see this new woman I'd gotten, and gushed all over Hanna, as if, poor thing, she'd need someone to take her under her wing in this hip Mediterranean world so new to her. She cooed over Aoife but Hanna would have none of her blandishments. She looked at Nancy with slitted eyes and went cold. I didn't ask her what she thought of Nancy; I knew.

The first night on the island, we slept on someone's roof – I guess because it cost nothing – and woke in the morning cooked by the sun. I found my old friend Andreas, the house-hustler. He lent me a rusty bike to match his and we cycled out to Es Vive where he showed me a breeze-block house looking out on a field of weeds, with Figueretas hill, now with a few more white houses than before, and the beach beyond. We rented it. It was OK and it was cheap; we'd stay as long as the money lasted. Then we'd take the boat, pick up the car, beat it back to England, and earn some more escape money.

When Andreas offered me a cigarette, I said no thanks. I'd learned my lesson about Andreas's fags. One evening in 1960, I found I was out of smokes and had no money, and Andreas gave me his battered packet of Peninsulares. I'd been trying to get a job giving lessons to the kids of a divorcée American lawyer, just arrived, and was still wearing my good shirt. After I'd smoked a couple of Andreas's Peninsulares, I noticed holes in it and realised that sparks were flying off the tip every time I took a drag. The shirt was already beginning to look like a string vest. Peninsulares, like Ideales, were said to be made from the sweepings of the factory floor; they had phosphorus mixed with the crap tobacco to keep them alight. Peninsulares were probably behind many cases of supposed spontaneous combustion.

It was great to be back in Ibiza! However, Hanna had her reservations about some of the people, which made it a little difficult for me. Maybe she was uncertain about would happen between me and her, now I was back, but these people were my friends and while I looked after her, I had to do my own thing too. Also, there was Col and Kilian to think about. They were warm towards Hanna and Aoife. Indeed, they were intrigued by their two-year-old half-sister but nevertheless claimed possession of me. I think they felt I was their father first.

There were new people now but some things hadn't changed. One evening, I met an extraordinary red-haired Jewish American, Melissa D'Arcangelo, wheeling two of her kids across the beach. She told me how, back in Chicago, when her Italian husband was at work, she'd go out and pick up men on the subway and take them home. Her husband was still in Chicago, she said . . . at work. I loved the way she smiled, but it was the old Ibiza syndrome and I wasn't going to be party to it. I'd brought Hanna to the island, and I wasn't going to fuck her around.

The foreign women in Ibiza were exotic, with their suntans and short skirts. I looked beat in my old blue jeans, bleached-out shirts and half-long hair, but Hanna still had her London-secretary, Brigitte Bardot bouffant hairstyle. Her clothes were plain and pretty, no Indian bracelets, ankle bracelets or the like. Hippy gear came in later, in the summers of 1966 and '67, when the Carnaby Street arse-freezers and Beatle jackets went out of style and weekend beatniks began to buy far-out clothes from friends of mine on Portobello Road who made spiritual and commercials journeys to the East.

One morning, a few weeks after we arrived, Hanna and I were sitting outside the Montesol with Aoife in her pushchair when a Dutch chick leant over from the next table and handed me a school copybook. 'This is for you, D,' she says. I know her name is Barbara but I don't know her well, only that she smokes a bit of dope and that she's the wife of Bart Hughes, who was a medical student when I'd met him on Ibiza two years before; he later became famous for boring a Third Eye in his skull. Even now, in 1963, there were still only a handful of dope smokers on Ibiza and we all knew one another, a sort-of dope underground amongst the drinkers. Besides, there were Franco's Secret Police to watch out for – if they were really there; I was never sure myself – so no one smoked dope in the street or in the bar.

I took the copybook and leafed through it. It was a scrapbook of newspaper cuttings about the Cuban Missile Crisis, pictures of Kennedy and Khrushchev and of ships loaded with missiles. I was mystified as to why she'd given it to me and then I came upon two pages glued together with two squares of cardboard in between, each with a large black dot, like an ink blot, at the centre. She smiled at me. 'Twelve hours,' she said. 'Fast for four before you take it,' and she left.

On our way home, I told Hanna I thought the two dots were a new drug I'd heard about, called LSD. I'd read about mescaline and that the writer Aldous Huxley had experimented with it and written about how it opened the mind, but that was all I knew. LSD was like mescaline, I thought. I had no clear idea but I trusted that Barbara, a fellow dopehead, wouldn't put me wrong. So, that evening, we took a trip into the unknown, having first put Aoife peacefully to bed, and prepared food in case we got hungry. I put a piece of cardboard in my mouth and Hanna put one in hers. It stuck to my tongue and I couldn't help thinking that it felt like the Communion wafers I'd taken every Sunday from age seven to seventeen before I went off to university and began to miss mass. Hanna said the same. She'd been partly brought up as a Catholic – her parents changed religions a lot. Not really knowing what it was, other than that it was important, we took it like a sacrament.

We sat a while, waiting for something to happen. Then it began to come on, slowly at first, changes of vision, and we knew we were going out and there would be no coming back for twelve hours. We squeezed one another's hands and nodded; we both felt it. But for glimpses, that was the last time our eyes met through the long night. We were as remote from one another as stars in the sky. Once or twice I looked at her, blurred or dim, or intensely beautiful and shining, not knowing if she saw me, and she, no doubt, also looked at me and thought the same. When our eyes met, we looked away, knowing that we couldn't talk, that we were beyond words, overawed and dumbstruck. We may have reached out and touched once but then forgot we were touching.

All night long, it was like my mind was going through a psychic washing machine, programme after programme flushing through my brain like cataracts, new worlds whizzing in like comets, transporting me at breakneck speed to places with no earth or sky and surges of sound engulfing me in static. There was laughter and tears, happiness and grief, but no anxiety. All sense of time was gone; I fell through gaps in time to worlds before time, where there was no other being but no sense of loneliness either. There was no self; or the self was all and everything. I was lucky, and Hanna was too. We felt no fear, only wonderment and, afterwards, exhaustion.

The places we had been were, for each of us, as real as the world we had left and the world we returned to. When you're there, you're there; there is nowhere else. Detractors will say it is illusion – and it is, just as our everyday perception is illusion, subjective and authored by conditioning. A botanist sees a plant quite differently from the way we do, or as a poet sees it. A geologist sees in a rock a history and events we don't see. I saw, or imagined I saw, in a piece of wood, the atoms that constituted it changing, as they do constantly over time; this was slowed-down time. One might have seen the same thing under a powerful microscope. The atoms are there, and they change: it was no illusion; rather, it was insight. The doors of perception had, for us, been the gates to heaven: they could as easily have been the gates to hell.

There is no fixed and definitive perception of the material world, much less the singular world within each of us: we all see everything differently; we just agree on a convention of perception. But it doesn't mean it's right. And it isn't enough if you want to get to the heart of the matter.

As we began to come down at dawn and started to recognise each other and move little by little towards each other, the conviction struck me like a beam of light that what I had seen was the true and enduring reality and that everything else was man-made bullshit, of which I no longer wanted any part. I could have kissed the earth as the dawn swept over it. The weeds had become wildflowers, the earth sang. Hanna and I stood in the doorway of the unplastered block house like children just born; the air on my face felt as if my skin was new and raw. The houses around us were prisons of concrete, enclosing souls. How sad I felt for them, for us, for me, for her, wandering in this vale of illusion, striving so hard, so lost and trying so hard. This was where it was at; this was where it had always been but I had missed it somewhere on the way. I pitied me, stumbling amongst the ruins, not only for the pain I had brought upon myself from the illusion of Nancy, but for the blindness that daily kept my heart and soul from This. And I mourned not just for me but for my friends, for Nancy and for poor Hanna whom I had made so uncertain, whose unconditional love I found it so hard to accept, as if she wasn't worthy. *Mea culpa, mea culpa*, for every arrogant thought and every bitter word.

The door was open wide, with grey light pouring through. We looked in at Aoife, in the bedroom. She slept in a world of her own, in a cradle of our making. We went outside. I turned to look at Hanna and the colours of the dawn rose and made her face golden and the colours of the flowers seemed to dance in her eyes. She smiled uncertainly, and bit her lip, and her eyes filled with tears. There were tears in mine too, but I held her hand firmly and, hands entwined, we faced the sun and the new day, the first day of the new world, as we thought it to be. We were Man and Woman, born together to this changed reality, complementary beings in a dimension that had always been there, although only now, in these minutes, did we see it. We were part of everything, with no wish to harm or rule or even stir a blade of grass.

We decided to go to Formentera, the island on the horizon. We had just twelve pounds left but we figured we'd make it last out there for a month or even longer; as long as the bread held out, we'd stay. I was ready to leave Ibiza behind, and the Domino Bar crowd with the drinking, dialectic and drama I loved so much, and lead another kind of life from then on. Maybe we'd take acid again sometime, but not soon. It wasn't something we felt we needed to do again, or even to smoke dope. Acid was wearing – the head-pummelling and the pace and intensity of it; it wasn't something you'd take again next day, at least not pure Sandoz acid in the full dose. Later people started taking mini-doses for recreational purposes, to go out and dance or whatever, 'disco doses' – they'd even drink with it. But that wasn't the way we took LSD. It was pure acid then, with no cheap speed added. We fasted and dropped the full dose, 250 micrograms; we weren't into half-measures. I'd caught a glimpse of a world that could be and knew that only our minds, our history, was excluding us from it. I wanted to go there, to live in it, and Hanna wanted that too – '*To follow knowledge like a sinking star, Beyond the utmost bound of human thought . . .*'

Chapter 7

FORMENTERA WAS INDEED ANOTHER WORLD. It was only twelve miles from Ibiza, though it could have been a thousand. We rented an old house west of the Cap de Berbería – where we now lived, a half-ruin, built of adobe clay, with a flat, earth roof. Where the walls were broken, the clay spilled out of the skin of stained whitewash like dried blood. There were no other houses around. We were still in the acid world, hardly talking, not wanting to do anything that might break the spell.

I wrote letters to Simon, Hanna's ex-husband, telling him of our revelation beyond the world of words. I gathered firewood each day and repaired some of the broken walls. Hanna sketched the rocks and trees and made jam out of figs from a gnarled old *higuera* on the land. The water came from a white-domed well in front of the house. Beyond it, the fields were dry but in some there were a few watermelons gone wild. The shore below the house was empty and looked out at the infinity of the sea and sky. The only sign of human presence were the walls dividing the fields, where bedrock broke the earth here and there. At dawn, a mist hung over the land between us and the sea. During the day, the sun beat down so fiercely one could hear the brown grass crackle and the stones split beneath its heat. It was glorious in the evenings. At sunset, we'd sit on the flat roof, holding Aoife. Sometimes, I fancied I could hear the *Concierto de Aranjuez* raining down the sky, or Miles Davis playing his lonely trumpet in *Sketches of Spain*.

Hanna loved Formentera, its profound and other-worldly peace. Her skin went golden brown; she wore wrap-around skirts, made bracelets of pine kernels and sea shells and, despite her bleached, blonde hair, looked like a squaw in the sun. We lived in absolute simplicity. There was no kitchen but an open hearth under a big chimney. Our budget was fifty pesetas a day; this bought us eggs, potatoes, vegetables and *bacalao* from the shop in San Francisco, where it hung in the darkness over the counter, big, grey slabs of salt cod, suspended amongst the bunches of yellow candles hanging by their wicks and the canvas tyre-soled shoes hanging by their laces, everything covered in a fine dust.

Apart from Longini, Lorca and Briefcase Hans, most of the foreigners on Formentera had arrived on the island during the previous year, not having found Ibiza to their liking. They all smoked dope, and one or two had taken acid. They came from all over Europe and North America and lived as we did, in primitive farmhouses amongst the rocky fields. No other couple had a child. Our first friend was Bruno de Galzain, a French painter from a landed background which he had spurned. He looked like Cyrano de Bergerac, having a large nose, but was small and wiry. He was full of a love for beauty and was generous beyond measure. But Hanna and I had little social life in Formentera during that first stay. We didn't seek it. We lived in a sort of bubble, a state of grace. We didn't smoke dope. We were so high anyway, why would we want to smoke?

Once or twice, the boys came over from Ibiza. I collected them on Bruno's bike. We went to the beach, along with Aoife, with whom they played. We explored the forest and they loved getting the fire going at night and watching the huge moths fly around the candles. Hanna was very good with them. It was easy enough for us to enter their world.

When the money ran out, we had to leave the old house and the island. We had managed to stay in the Balearics for three months. We set off back to London and the grey world, the world of illusions and desires, swearing we'd return.

The car, miraculously, made it back to London where we sold it to pay the deposit on rent for a room in the same house as before. Salim, our Pakistani friend, still lived there, but old Mr Skidelski, upstairs, had died and they had had to bring a small truck to take his archive of newspapers to a museum. Right away, I started hustling up teaching jobs. After a couple of weeks' work, I bought a motorbike. Helmet-less, licence-less and insurance-less, I'd whizz all over London, no job too far away, no assignment too daunting. You want me to teach Roman History? I could do it, so long as there was a book. When faced with a Maths problem I'd never seen before, I'd solve it by following textbook examples. I could truthfully say to my pupil, 'Look, it's easy. If I can do it, you can! It works like this . . .' Whole new worlds of learning were opening up for me, for them. And I was learning on other people's time!

As for pay, it was still a guinea for two hours but I had a minor scam going. I charged for travelling time, as if I set out from home and returned after each lesson. This wasn't the case, though: I arranged jobs back-to-back, only five or ten minutes apart, the first maybe in Bayswater, the second in Kensington Gore just a drive across Hyde Park, the third in Knightsbridge down the road from there, and so on. I'm sure the parents were aware of the ruse but they didn't seem to mind. They were all super-rich anyway, and I was making headway with their children where others had failed. I almost doubled my money, like Rick, Carlo and I were hoping to do once we reached London, now only a ferry-ride and a three-hour drive away.

Meanwhile, Kathy told us that she could get Hanna a job working as a hostess in the clubs at night, when I'd be home and could look after Aoife. Hanna agreed. I wasn't sure – she was no good-time girl like Kathy. However, she was brave: it was a chance to make us real money and so she went for an interview at an upmarket place on Piccadilly, passed and was given a chit for a weekly hair-do. She was told what to wear and issued with a dress allowance. When invited by a customer to his table, she would sit with him and get him to order bottles of champagne. Hostesses were instructed to refuse any other drink and the more champers the punter bought, the more bread the hostess made. Then, there were tips. They had to hustle for these because the wages weren't great; there was some sort of hostess fee.

So, each evening, Hanna put on her war-paint and false eyelashes, slipped into one of her two court dresses, and did up her hair. It was bizarre watching her do this in the bed-sit, with the cot behind her and the gas cooker in the

99

corner. She might even slip down her dress front if Aoife suddenly woke up and wanted a hit of her breast before she left. It was even more incongruous to be collecting her at two o'clock each morning on my motorbike so that we could save her taxi fare allowance, her in her fine dress climbing on the pillion, Salim meanwhile listening out for Aoife in case she woke while I was away.

The clubs were expensive and pretended respectability; expense-account executives, gangsters and cabinet ministers, like John Profumo, liaised with good-time girls like Christine Keeler and Mandy Rice Davies. The hostesses were allowed to give their phone numbers and they were often asked to 'parties' afterwards. The girls weren't obliged to fuck the clients, that was not a condition of employment, but some did – including Kathy herself, so Hanna gathered, when the deal was right. Hanna didn't – which must have been damn disappointing for the guys who'd spent the evening buying her bottles of champagne at who knows how much a pop.

Hanna was, in a way, naïve, an innocent in clubland. I remember one night when I picked her up, she was in tears because all evening she'd listened to a Danish executive visiting London telling her about the emptiness of his life, and enquiring about hers. She'd told him about me and our child and the richness of the life we'd found but, when closing time came, ignoring all this, he demanded she come back to his hotel, and became very nasty when she refused. 'He seemed so nice,' she kept saying, 'but it was all so as to get me back to his hotel so he could fuck me . . .' I tried to comfort her. Poor pilgrim soul; poor Hanna. She was very drunk. It was an occupational hazard; every night she was tiddly, at least. The girls were expected to help empty the bottles, so the punters would buy more. Experienced girls had a deal going with the waiters to water down their glasses somehow. But Hanna's club work brought in good money. Often, she'd charm a client into giving a big tip. At home, she'd squeal with delight as she pulled the roll of banknotes from her bra and we'd count it together on the bed. She was very brave: we were a team; we'd risk anything. We were working to buy time to make a new life, to free ourselves of the subjective desires and sorrows. Material goods meant nothing to us. If somebody had given us, say, a fancy watch for a present, we'd have flogged it to get money for Formentera. We feared that if we were in the city too long, we might be infected or trapped and lose the state of grace, lose the dream.

We saved hard and when we headed south in April 1964, we had the old Zephyr half-full of Mike Darby's purloined provisions. We also had a gun – a six-chamber pistol, a scaled-down, chrome-plated replica of a Colt 45 that shot .22 bullets. Hanna had inherited it: her father had been an air raid warden in a London borough during the war and it had been presented to him afterwards, along with a medal. When I saw it in a cabinet, gathering dust, I said that maybe we could sell it to a gun shop somewhere; it looked good. Once, I'd brought it to Ireland to show it to my father, who enjoyed shooting. I fired it carelessly in the direction of some rabbits in a field and was amazed and contrite when an unfortunate rabbit keeled over, dead.

As we travelled, the gun was buried deep amongst the exotic foodstuffs under Aoife and, although on our trip south we crossed the Belgian, French and Spanish borders, we were never searched and so brought it all the way to Formentera.

The provisions and the money we'd saved kept us going just fine until July or so, when Mel, with his Maxatone-mad mind, limped back into our lives, sick and suppurating from a hundred Tangier nights and a hundred dirty needles, and we were obliged to save his life by lending him most of the money we had left, for his scams. Had he mailed back what he owed us, we'd probably have eked out a few months more before returning to London again, but now that he'd said the scams had worked for him, I figured they'd work for me, so I was into doubling my money at least and giving us a new lease of life on Formentera. The idea of launching a raid on London and high-tailing it back to the islands appealed to me. Me, Carlo and Rick – we'd be a sort of a holy Hole in the Wall Gang, raiding the banks and making a get-away, like Butch Cassidy and the Sundance Kid. We'd rip off only enough to keep us going for a while; we had no interest in riches or property. Possessions tied you down; you didn't own them, they owned you. If you owned nothing, you were free.

The same went for love and relationships. As Kahlil Gibran said in *The Prophet*: 'Love one another, but make not a bond of love, let it rather be a moving sea between the shores of your souls . . .' Bruno had given us the book and we read it together, Hanna and I, in C'an Pujolet, our house on the Cap de Berbería.

'Sing and dance together,' Gibran said, 'and be joyous, but let each one of you be alone, even as the strings of the lute are alone though they quiver with the same music. Give your hearts, but not into each other's keeping. For only the hand of Life can contain your hearts . . .' And so on. There were tears in Hanna's eyes as I read. I didn't ask her why; I was hip to the fact that I hadn't given my heart into another's keeping, at least not, so far, into hers. For me, Gibran was a tad too simplistic and too flowery but a lot of people hung on his every word. He expressed the new unpossessive lives we aspired to lead.

Now, the one-time killing fields of northern France slipped by on either side and I was driving the graveyard watch as we approached Calais. Rick, riding shotgun, had long since fallen asleep. I clicked the dim switch on the floor as the occasional early morning truck approached and passed, then turned the lights off altogether and drove in the grey dawn, the mist like a wet, army blanket on the landscape. Behind us, the sun was rising, slivers of dawn shining in the wing-mirrors every now and then.

At Calais docks, a few trucks were parked, with drivers standing around, shaking themselves against the cold, cigarettes cupped in their hands, their breath like steam. Without waking the others, I slipped out and went to the shipping office and found I'd been right – there was a boat to Dover at seven; we were in plenty of time. A white-painted kiosk opened its window and a Frenchman with a Gauloise in his gob proceeded to brew up coffee and take croissants from a cardboard box and put them in a glass case. I ordered a milk coffee and a croissant, while lighting yet another fag.

When the ferry office opened, I went and bought tickets, then decided I'd go back to the car and maybe catch some kip before it was time to drive on board. The others were still asleep, Carlo, with his moustache, earring, and blanket looked like an Albanian shepherd without the sheep. Rick, with his hat, his grey jowls, sunken eyes, zipper jacket done up to the throat and hands deep in his pockets, looked like street-wolf in a city, some guy standing in a doorway whom you'd avoid. He woke as I climbed in, and he woke Carlo, and they went to score coffees while I crashed out for a while.

On the boat, we headed for the washrooms; there was a free shower, which we took turns using. It was the first shower I'd had in months – except for Hanna pouring buckets of water over me. The boat was only half-full, mainly with truckers; there were few holiday-makers so late in the year. It was as well to be spruced up before we hit Dover, and UK Immigration. I was OK, but Carlo and Rick, being Americans, could be asked how much bread they had before they'd be let in. They carried all the money we had, split between them, but it would hardly have been enough to satisfy Immigration that they weren't bums. We certainly looked out of place in the north, what with the worn and faded clothes and the dark suntans. I told Rick it'd be better to take off the hat and had half a mind to advise Carlo to take out the earring. He wouldn't have minded; he'd have to do it anyway for the scams.

In London, we stood out amongst the city-dressed people, all pale and formal. Not many of the Brits took Mediterranean holidays then, and a suntan on a Caucasian made him somewhat exotic; only movie stars and millionaires had suntans in wintertime. This worked perfectly for the scam. My plan was that Carlo and Rick should present themselves as well-off American holiday-makers who found themselves in embarrassing straits. For my scam, I'd pretend to be a freelance journalist on an overseas assignment. It wasn't glamour; it was just the best story I could think of to explain what a twenty-four year old Irish guy was doing carrying travellers cheques.

Rick and Carlo got through Dover with no hassle, and it was great, a few hours later, to be steaming into London town in the old jalopy, bums as we were. My friends being strangers to the city made me feel sort of international and proprietorial at the same time. It was a bright autumn day, one of those days when London is at its most beautiful and I was already giving them the tourist spiel. '*Earth hath not anything to show more fair . . .*' I told them, quoting my school Wordsworth as we drove over Westminster Bridge. They thought London bobbies looked quaint, and I told them how best to deal with English cops.

We drove through St James Park and passed Buckingham Palace and on through Hyde Park, with the trees in their autumn beauty, and then headed for Notting Hill. In run-down St Stephen's Gardens, Sikh kids in turbans were playing cricket in the street, and Jamaicans in pegged pants and slope hats were standing outside pubs in Ladbroke Grove.

First stop was Henekey's pub on the corner of Westbourne Park Road and Portobello, where, if we got lucky, we'd meet Mel and I'd get the money that was so essential to our plans. It being a Saturday and the Portobello street market in full swing, Henekey's was heaving. However, no Mel – but, lo and behold, my old pal Mike Darby of the carpet-bagger suit, twirly goatee and twinkling eyes was there at the bar. With a big grin he said: 'Eh, squire, you were expected. I've something for you from your old mucker, Mel.' Mel had apparently taken off for Paris two days before to hear Bud Powell playing in the Blue Note and he was heading for Tangier from there. Mike discreetly slipped my money across to me – and told me he'd been to the south of Turkey and had scored some dope. I felt him drop something in my jacket pocket, and when I put my hand in, found a sizeable lump of hash, maybe half an ounce. Wow, things had certainly changed in the six months since I'd left London! The last time I'd talked to Mike about dope, he was still a member of the dope-rots-your-brain-but-drinking-ten-pints-of-booze-a-night-is-cool school. Now, suddenly, he was a convert. Suddenly, London was turning on, or at least beginning to.

I introduced Rick and Carlo but they weren't much at home in pubs and soon moved off. Mike was his usual self, friendly but abrasive. When I said we were in town to do some scams, he corrected me, 'Confidence tricks. Speak the Queen's English, old boy!' The pukka fucker was having me on, of course, 'winding me up' as the English say. When I said my friends and I were going to make some 'bread', he insisted that that was American jive-talk too. I asked him hadn't he ever heard of 'bread and 'oney', Cockney rhyming slang for money. That shut him up.

He told me he'd recently met a rich divorcee and had hopes of a windfall. No, he wouldn't come to Formentera, not if my would-be-partners-in-crime were an example of the people he'd meet there. But he'd like to see Hanna again.

Rick and Carlo came over and said they were going to slope down Portobello for an hour and would be back. A little later, a long-legged English bird in a short skirt came over to Mike and asked him if he'd seen Mel. When he told her Mel had gone, she looked at me curiously.

'Are you Mel's friend from Formentera?' she asked.

'That's me,' I replied.

'He mentioned you,' she said. Then she walked off and joined a girl sitting on the long bench under the window; the light was pouring through the smoky panes above them, so I couldn't see her well.

Mike saw me looking. 'How's Hanna ?' he asked pointedly.

I said she was happy and sent her love.

Cutting out the bullshit for a minute, he looked me in the eye and asked 'You looking after her, then, are you?'

It was this fatherly thing with Mike, a bit like with Rick. Neither of them had the balls for a long-term relationship and I found it rich that they were worried about mine. 'Who's the chick?' I asked him, ignoring his question.

'Fran.'

'Nice-lookin' bird.' I said, to bug him, but it was true.

He pulled a face, finished his pint and said he had to go and back a horse at the bookies. He'd see me if I was in the pub that night.

Now I was alone and the only guy I knew in the pub was a Scottish metal sculptor but he was already pissed and swearing, even though it was only two o'clock. I turned to look at the girls and found they were looking at me. The small one beside the tall one waved cheekily. I went over. It turned out they'd met Mel a couple of times and he'd told them about his travels and said he wanted to go to Paris but was hanging on in London waiting for a Formentera friend. Mel had turned them on, but smoking a joint or two together was as far as it went. They were all questions, like 'What's that ring you're wearing?'; it was a ring I'd got from Hanna, I told them – a worn-down Italian cameo. 'What star sign are you?' they asked – that kind of stuff. I didn't come on strong; I didn't really come on at all. The small one, who was called Nicole, seemed to be setting up me and Fran, acting like a go-between. I liked her. She was *gamin* and mischievous, with an elfin face, but the tall one seemed to have staked her claim on me already. I wondered if they were after me because they thought I might have some dope or because they thought my Formentera friends and I were exotic: three *bandidos* riding into town. I agreed to meet them later. Maybe it was the old story of the beat guys attract the best-looking chicks. Fran, with her long body and pretty, doll-like face, was putting me on an ego-trip I knew, but I couldn't resist her.

By the time Rick and Carlo came back, the pub was closing anyway, so we moved on. I had the feeling Rick wasn't too happy to see me with the chicks. Maybe he was on a Mike-trip about Hanna, or thought I might forget about him and Carlo or get distracted from the scams. He needn't have worried; nothing was going to distract me from making some dosh.

Next stop: Bernard's. However, when we hopped in the car, it wouldn't start. The two chicks, emerging from the pub after us, found this pretty funny, the three *bandidos* broken down. However, Rick and Carlo gave me a push and I jump-started it. To reassert our dignity, I roared away. This wasn't hard, given that the exhaust pipe was shot and it raised a racket anyway.

Bernard agreed to put us up for the night and asked if we'd brought any dope from Spain. To Rick's consternation, I produced a last small piece of my Moroccan, enough for two joints. Somewhere as we drove through France, smoking what he thought was our last bit of kief, he'd got sort of paranoid and demanded to know if either Carlo and I were carrying any dope into England, because we were going to London to rob banks, not to get busted for smuggling. He was right, but I'd buried the little piece of Moroccan so deep in the back seat of the car that nobody would ever have found it. There were no sniffer dogs back then, although I do recall a friend of mine called Zee telling me about a red-haired Customs woman in Tashkent who regularly sniffed out backpackers heading for Europe via Russia with dope from India or Nepal. He'd seen her do it.

When I produced the serious lump of Turkish hash Mike had given me, smiles broke out all around. It was great dope. I told them what Mike had said about how the Turks harvested it, running between lines of dope plants in the fields, making the heads swish against the leather aprons they wore, and then scraping the pollen off the aprons at the end of each row. It was sticky hash, rich in oily resin. We smoked and talked about Formentera and mystic things and philosophies, the books we wanted to buy, and where to get them. I let Bernard tell the visitors where to find the bookshops.

Kathy arrived and she and Rick and Carlo got to talking about methadrine, which was injectable speed, and various other such shit I knew nothing about. Americans tended to know about injectables; there'd been a junkie culture there for a long time. Neither Rick nor Carlo had ever been strung out and I thought their interest was a bit weird, given they had taken acid. What were they doing looking to score *that* shit? But maybe they were holidaying. Kathy said she was going to the clubs that night and would try to score some.

I was into going back to Henekey's, but neither Rick, Carlo nor Bernard had eyes for that: they just wanted to sit and smoke some more of the Turkish. I must say I found that strange, what with my *compañeros* being in London for the first time and there was so much to see out there on the town. I headed off, found the car wouldn't start again and walked down the Grove where I had sausage-egg-and-chips in a 'caff' and then hit Henekey's. Fran was there, and she was alone. We walked down Portobello Road and I played the fool, watching my shadow skipping under the street lights, walking with attitude, making her laugh. We went back to her pad over a shop in Westbourne Grove, where she had a bottle of Chianti waiting. That night I slept in her bed and never did make it back to Bernard's and the Hole-in-the-Wall Gang sleeping in their blankets and ponchos on the floor.

Fran was dreamy, long and lissom, affectionate but passive, almost prissy in a way. In the morning, she made breakfast, and went down and bought the Sunday papers. We parted in the late afternoon and I went to Bernard's, where I got the old banger started by cleaning up the battery leads. I had Fran's phone number, and she said I could give her a ring if I was free.

Sunday evening, about six o'clock on one of those lovely, slow London evenings, Kathy came back from wherever she'd been the night before, bearing drugs in ampoules. Rick and Carlo set about fixing themselves up. I'd never seen this before and watched in fascination. There was the ritual of tying a belt around the arm, of cracking the top off the ampoule, of sucking up the clear liquid, of easing the needle into the pumped vein, of drawing back the plunger so that red blood was sucked like smoke into the clear liquid in the syringe, of easing the plunger down and seeing it empty, of drawing it out, of leaning back against the cushions, eyes closed, of letting the syringe fall. Carlo offered to fix me up, and I agreed. He did it in a careful, almost loving fashion, touching my inner arm with his fingertips, massaging up a vein. I looked down at my arm and watched the needle enter. I felt the rush, the wave of warmth that spread through every atom in my body like a tide, the warm, womb-like comfort and I smiled and said, in a distant voice, 'Wow, where can I get more of this shit?' I heard my friends laughing, and after the first headlong rush, I opened my eyes and we were all sitting there on the floor in the evening light pouring through Bernard's top-floor London windows, and love and peace was amongst us, like we were touched by the Holy Ghost.

It wasn't the same a few hours later when we began to come down. Speed is always edgy, tense. However, we had Mike's dope to ease the descent and we'd hit up early in the evening so that by eleven o'clock it was all over and we were able to sleep. We crashed on the floor at Bernard's. He and Kathy had the bed. I didn't ring Fran; I had things to do in the morning, taking care of business TCB. It was my role to get things together, to keep us focused. Besides, it was in my own best interest and, in truth, that came first. I had the tribe to think of: Hanna, Aoife, Con and Kilian. I was in London to make bread, and neither sex nor drugs would distract me. The methadrine was a one-off: I'd seen what Maxatone had done to Mel.

My confidence was, in part, down to experience. I had once been taken on a very successful kiting expedition to posh London shops. 'Kiting' was an upper-class word for bouncing dodgy cheques in posh department stores. London banks would be similar; if you presented yourself in the right way, nobody would dream of asking you for ID before cashing your travellers cheques.

When I'd first dropped out of medical school and come to London – before Scotland, before Nancy – I'd met a guy in a London jazz cellar called Cy Laurie's that used to stay open until dawn at weekends. I'd seen him before once or twice. He would come in, an arrogant-looking kid of my own age, a junior city gent, with bowler hat, rolled umbrella, neat suit with waistcoat, blue striped shirt, white collar and club tie. He'd leave the paraphernalia in the cloakroom, and in collarless shirt and pants proceed to dance. He danced like a demon; he'd spin and catch and spin and catch, and have the girl flying around like a carousel on two legs, and he'd sweat like a horse, mopping his brow with a large white handkerchief. He and I took to one another some-how, and became good friends; we ended up sharing a small flat. I was doing casual work – a few weeks as a block hand in the Quality Inn restaurant in Leicester Square, then a few weeks in the Hudson's Bay Company in the cold rooms three floors below the street, hand-carting up stacks of beaver pelts, Arctic fox, whatever, for the perusal of buyers. James Whittaker, later to become chief 'royal watcher' for the *Daily Mirror*, introduced me to his set, and I went to parties and met Hooray Henrys, also known as Debs' Delights, and the debutantes themselves, mostly not so much aristos as landed gentry. Some were the Hon. this or that; they and their girls would be lords and ladies as soon as their parents died.

I already knew somebody in that set; a louche and interesting erstwhile Polish count. We'd been friends at my boarding school in Ireland. In London, he took me to The Ognisko Polski in Princes Gate where the aristo émigrés hung out bemoaning the vast estates they'd left behind in Poland after the war, knowing that if they'd stayed Stalin would have buried them in a forest or send them to a gulag. The English were worse snobs than the Poles but they all let you know who they were and that they were listed in Burke's Peerage or the Almanach de Gotha. But some of the British ex-Rodean and Cheltenham Ladies College 'gals' were wild, and one day, when I was sitting at home with no work, three of them descended on James's flat to offload the spoils of a kiting expedition. They'd kited so many items they could no longer carry all the shopping bags around and had taken a taxi to drop them off before going on to hit some more shops in Bond Street and St James's.

As they sat around smoking fags and drinking kited bubbly, they instructed me in the art and urged me to don one of James's suits and a cravat and join in the fun. I wasn't hard to persuade. Half an hour later, arm in arm with one of the girls, I strolled into Simpsons in Piccadilly where, under her critical gaze and attended by an obsequious young shop assistant, I tried on selected Daks sports jackets and expensive trousers. When it came time to pay, I whipped out the chequebook she had given me and, with suitable disdain, told the unfortunate minion that I'd be paying by cheque. He went to a floor walker in an impeccably tailored suit and florid tie who discreetly looked us over and then gave him the nod. We walked out with a bag of booty and laughed our heads off as we swaggered down Piccadilly, past the Ritz, to buy me a shirt in Savile Row. The best thing I scored that day was the pair of Cuban-heeled suede boots from Annello and Davide which I later wore while teaching in London and was still wearing now, even as I drove to London with Carlo and Rick.

It was no big deal, kiting. At the time, the account-holder's name wasn't printed on personal cheques. With the right accent, the right image (hacking jacket, Tattersall shirt, cavalry twills) and the right air of confident disdain, one could shop with a chequebook borrowed from a friend, it having been agreed that, in return for getting him a few selected items, he wouldn't inform the banks of the mysterious 'disappearance' of the chequebook until the following day. So kiting cheques was an occasional diversion for the more outrageous idle rich, particularly the Sloanie girls, who revelled in it. Running up debts was, in any case, still the prerogative of the gentry, and the young men thought ripping off the bowing-and-scraping merchants was quite a wheeze, almost a divine right in fact.

Telling Carlo and Rick about the success of the kiting expedition boosted their confidence. The scams would be simple: each of us in turn would buy three hundred bucks' worth of cheques, 'lose them' and then claim a refund. All three of the American travellers cheque companies guaranteed to refund up to three hundred dollars – one hundred pounds – of lost or stolen cheques on the spot. Meanwhile, one of the others would cash the 'lost' cheques at local banks. A counter-signature would be required, so whoever cashed them would have to make a fair stab at reproducing the signature of whomever had bought them. However, cashiers paid little attention, according to Mel. We'd start out with my hundred quid capital and by doubling this three times, we'd each make three hundred bucks. All we had to do was dress convincingly and have convincing stories ready if the travellers cheque companies asked for details of how the cheques had been lost.

I was good at stories. I suggested that Carlo could say he had met an English girl in France and had crossed the Channel to visit her in London. However, she'd told him she'd found another lover and was off to Greece. He'd got drunk, gone to a club in Soho, gone to a room somewhere with a hooker, woke up back at his hotel next morning and found his cheques and wallet were gone. He'd be suitably ashamed and contrite, but hung-over and not to be messed with when he asked for his refund. If it came to it, he'd cite their guarantee, advertised in *Time* magazine: the instant replacement of lost cheques up to the value of three hundred dollars.

After Carlo's scam, we'd have two hundred quid total and, next day, Rick and I would take half each and do two more numbers, doubling up again. Rick could play the part of an amateur American artist sketching his way around Europe. He'd buy his cheques at Bank of America and, when he returned to report them missing, would say that when he'd been sketching in Hyde Park, people had gathered around to watch and an hour later, he'd found his bag had been rifled and his cheques gone. He would be carrying a folio and might even show sketches; we'd buy a couple from a guy who sold them on Bayswater Road.

As for me, the phoney freelance journalist, I'd buy my cheques at First National City Bank and, if asked my business when I went to claim the refund, would say I'd bought them because I was about to travel to Sweden to follow up a story about a GI deserter from Vietnam. All this preparation was, in a sense, academic – it was unlikely we'd be questioned at all: the scam was for a small amount, and refunds were automatic.

Rick and Carlo joked that I was contriving all these backgrounds simply because I enjoyed it – and I was. But, like I said, I wasn't into getting busted and I'd protect them as I'd protect myself. Also, I was already working out a scheme to make a bit more money before I went home.

And so, on Monday morning, we were wide awake and spruced-up bright and early – embryonic rip-off artists, ready to go.

Chapter 8

FIRST STOP WAS AN OXFAM Charity shop where we got Carlo fitted out with the kind of gear straight Americans would wear. I scored myself a dark suit and white shirt and, for a few bob, we got Rick a pair of desert boots that looked like new. He was still wearing the tyre-soled sandals he'd bought in the tienda in San Francisco Xavier when his Detroit footwear had worn out.

After that, we zoomed down to the Haymarket, where I parked alongside the pavement fifty yards below the American Express office. In the car, I handed over our entire hundred and twenty quid to Carlo, and we ran through the procedure once more.

First thing he should do was buy the cheques in dollars, denominations of ten, twenty, and fifty. Later, he'd cash ten dollars in a change office on Shaftesbury Avenue within spitting distance of the Soho strip-joints where he'd later say he got ripped off. Getting fifty- and twenty-dollar denominations would make life easier for me when I came to cash the 'stolen' cheques.

Also, when he was in the AmEx office, Carlo should ask a few dumb-ass questions so that they'd remember him when he came in to report the missing cheques the next day. He could ask had they any holiday packages for two to Amsterdam and Copenhagen, and would he need visas for there 'cos, you see, he was going to take his girlfriend on a holiday, etcetera. He should also take away a bunch of brochures, American-looking things; I'd use these as props in the banks where, cashing his lost cheques, I'd be playing the earnest Yank on tour. Finally, he should make his signature easy to forge.

When Carlo emerged from AmEx, business done, we drove down to Soho where he cashed a ten buck cheque as per the story he would tell. In Greek Street, we cruised past the strip-clubs where he would say he'd met the thieving hooker.

That night, we went to Fran's. Her friend Nicole was there too. She was pale-faced and medium-pretty, sort of serious. She wore no makeup and with her black stockings and shoulder-length hair, looked like a French high school pupil. She sat on an armchair by the gas fire, upright, maybe slightly uptight, her knees primly together, hands clasped in lap, like she was waiting outside an office for an interview. She laughed easily. I thought she was a bit like the woman in Modigliani's paintings; his mistress who had died of consumption. I was romantic about consumptives; when I was about ten, I'd fallen in love with a girl called Geraldine Brennan who had tuberculosis and duly died the next year.

At Fran's, we smoked some of the dope Mike had given me. Carlo strummed Fran's guitar, and I saw Nicole looking at him a little wistfully. Come half past eleven, she dashed out to catch a night bus home to the boon-docks. Fran seemed to think I was staying and I wasn't averse to that. I offered to drive Carlo and Rick back to Bernard's but they said they'd prefer to walk. I drew them a map.

At half past nine next morning, I collected them at Bernard's, catching the keys Kathy threw down to me. Carlo appeared, all dressed in his scam-ming outfit, although he still had his earring. We had breakfast at Mick's Café at Blenheim Crescent, a Greek-Cypriot greasy-spoon of high quality, and headed for the West End.

I pulled the car in at Ken High Street and hit a Barclays Bank and then a Midland Bank, chop-fuckin-chop. I got a special kick out of scamming the Midland, the bank that had refused me the one pound loan when I wanted to take Nancy and the twins to London from Slough.

I hit four more banks and had no trouble at all. By noon, I'd off'ed the whole wallet and had our outlay back in my pocket. Now, it was down to Carlo to get the replacements and we'd double our money. As we drove to American Express, I said, half-joking, that he should do it like a method

113

actor, feel the fuckin' hangover and live the part. He was all for that. He started moaning right away and we had to tell him not to overdo it.

I'd read a couple of years before that some guy had convinced AmEx that he had the entire world's soy supplies stored in three huge tanks in New Jersey and that if they invested a million dollars, they could make a killing. However, he fixed it so that they inspected just one tank on each of three consecutive days. Overnight, he pumped the oil from that tank to the next. Instead of having just one tank full, it appeared he had three. And AmExCo lost a million dollars for their shareholders. So what did it matter that we were ripping them off for a few hundred bucks? Never mind the moon shots and the satellites, we were spending Uncle Sam's dollars supporting the arts and Inner Space exploration.

Carlo took out his earring before leaving the car. The way he walked away, all slumped and dejected, was positively Stanislavskian. He emerged with his replacement cheques and turned them back into cash in a bank in Park Lane. We now had six hundred dollars, two hundred pounds. I took Rick straight to the Bank of America – AmEx might have got suspicious if two Americans arrived on consecutive days claiming to have lost newly bought cheques overnight. I went in after him, just to see what the bank was like. Rick stood at one of those shelf-desks that run along the walls and conspicuously sorted through some drawings before putting the lot back in his folio and approaching the cashier. He was wearing his straw hat, a Bermuda shirt, his new second-hand desert boots and he had a line of pens and paintbrushes in his pocket. He bought three hundred dollars' worth of cheques, signed them in a simple scrawl and left the bank.

Next day, he was back in there, telling them his sorry I-got-ripped-off-in-Hyde-Park tale. By then, I'd already taken Carlo to leafy Wimbledon in the old Zephyr, and he'd offloaded the 'ripped-off' cheques in a few banks there. Rick got his replacements and we'd made a profit of six hundred bucks so far. Split three ways, it would keep Rick and Carlo for four months in Formentera and me, with my two families, for at least half that time.

I bought cheques at First National and City Bank's one and only branch in London. I cashed twenty as a token and gave Rick the rest: I'd offloaded for Carlo, and Carlo for Rick, and now it was Rick's turn to offload for me.

All went well and, a few hours later, I returned to the bank and reported I'd lost my cheques. I was a man in a hurry, briefcase and airline ticket to Sweden in hand, just in case (I later cancelled the ticket and was refunded in full). I lit a Gitane with a bit of flair and a polite effort to conceal my impatience, and a minute later they came through with the bread.

So we had almost nine hundred dollars profit; we divvied up and that was supposed to be the end of scamming. However, I had a new idea. I ran the scheme past Rick and Carlo, explaining how they could do the same, but they both declined. Enough excitement they said; they didn't need the money. I did – but it would be unwise to do any more numbers in London. I'd hit mainland Europe: but there one had to present proper ID to cash cheques. My plan was to approach Bernard and ask him to 'lose' his passport and not report it missing until I'd used it for a day. I'd offer him a hundred quid and the price of a replacement. It was a good deal, no danger to him, and he agreed.

I'd travel to Holland on my own passport, take his with me, replace his mugshot picture with mine and then do a whistle-stop tour of three or four cities. In each, posing as Bernard, I'd buy three hundred bucks' worth of cheques. Using the same freelance-journalist-chasing-a-story line, I'd report them missing in the next city, get replacements and buy more. I'd offload both originals and replacements as I went, then destroy Bernard's passport and fly home a whole lot the richer on my own passport.

By extraordinary coincidence, next evening on the train to the Harwich-Hook of Holland ferry, I ran into Mike Darby. He was going to visit a Dutch girl in The Hague. Her parents would be away, so he invited me to stay. She turned out to be a young and pretty ballerina – what she saw in Darby was a mystery to me. She met us with a taxi and took us to her home, a lovely house in the suburbs. She gave us wine and showed me to a bedroom. It was now midnight, and I had a marathon day ahead. I hadn't yet altered Bernard's passport which I was carrying in the briefcase I'd borrowed from him. If it had been found by Dutch Customs, I'd've said he had lent me his briefcase and must have inadvertently forgotten to take out the passport. Bernard would verify the passport story if they phoned him.

But now, at one in the morning, I still had to change the mugshots. I refused the proffered joint, had a large coffee and headed to my room. On an antique table, under an antique light, I laid out the tools I'd brought – a scalpel, an eraser, an italic-nibbed pen. Carefully, I set about replacing Bernard's picture with mine, embossing my photo to match the surrounding embossing. Meanwhile, I could hear Mike and the girl screwing like happy rabbits in the room next door.

I was about finished the passport when I heard Mike shouting, 'Hey, old chap! Get in here smartish, Evie wants you!' He called me again and again. I put down the pen, and walked across the landing. The door was part open; I pushed it and walked in. The girl was lying with her bare breasts above the coverlets, florid Mike beside her, a twinkle in his eye, a glass of wine in one hand and a smoking joint in the other. 'Plenty of room in here, old man,' he said, winking. Beside him, Evie smiled. 'C'mon, Irishman,' she said, holding out her hand, 'Time to come to bed . . .' It was very difficult to get out of the situation but I had business to take care of first thing and, anyway, the last thing I fancied was being in the same bed as the naked Darby.

I've sometimes thought of that girl since – but then, we probably all regret sexual opportunities missed or under-explored in our youth. I apologised and said I was having trouble replacing the passport photo. Mike shook his head, despairing of me. The irony was that while he didn't think it right that I should have eyes for chicks in London, it was OK for me to help him screw young nymphos in Holland.

In the morning, as mist was rising in the suburbs, I left the house without waking Darby and his doxy, and hit the street. Europe lay before me. The pre-arranged taxi took me to AmExCo, where I bought three hundred bucks' worth of cheques, presenting myself as Mr Bernard Price. I used one of the window counters to conspicuously repack my briefcase. Arriving by train in Amsterdam, I took a taxi to the AmEx office there and told the clerk I'd just discovered that the cheques I'd bought fifty minutes before had gone missing: I'd probably left them on the counter where I'd unpacked my briefcase to organise notes for the story I was writing. I was given a new book of cheques to replace the loss.

Using Bernard's passport, I cashed the lot at various banks and bought new cheques from Bank of America and from First National City, each time doing the packing-unpacking-my-notes routine. All done, I jumped on a train to Düsseldorf. Upon arrival, I phoned the Amsterdam banks from the station to ask if my cheques might have been found on the counter where I'd unpacked my briefcase. No, they were nowhere to be seen but I should report the loss to their branches in Düsseldorf where replacements would be arranged. It was all sweetness and light, poetry in motion. In Düsseldorf, I converted the replacements into D-marks and scored new cheques from American Express.

A couple of hours later, I crossed the border into Belgium on a train. I had four wallets of cheques down my trousers with the plastic covers sticking to my belly. Now, all I had to do was convert them all into cash so that I could dump Bernard's passport. But time was running very short before my plane.

It was a roasting hot evening, and as I dashed along the big street of Antwerp, a problem became evident: the fuckin' banks were beginning to close! I couldn't risk hitting any single one with too big an amount. I had four options: risk taking the cheques back to England, with Bernard's passport; stay overnight in Belgium and risk cashing them next day; dump the remaining cheques and Bernard's passport; or run like fuck and change them all before catching the plane.

There were change offices along the street, grubby little joints, with sleazy-looking dudes behind the counters. They took commissions but who cared? Just gimme the money, I'm in a hurry! I raced from office to office, tie pulled down, lathered in sweat. And then, with one half-book left, and my pockets bulging with cash, the last change office closed in my face.

There might be an exchange at Antwerp's little airport, I thought, but I hadn't wanted to use it. I'd be flying from there and didn't fancy leaving a Bernard Price trail. But here I was, still Bernard Price, jumping in a taxi, hoping for an airport change-office – my last-chance saloon!

Vite!, I told the taximan. He was a gypsy cab and he got my drift. When we screeched to a halt outside the breeze-block airport, it was only twenty-five minutes to take-off. It was a tiny strip and there would be no more planes that day.

I whizzed inside, braking on my Cuban heels, and scored a ticket to Southend, near London, the only destination out of Antwerp-Deurne. I spotted a change office nearby. There, as I shakily signed the last ten cheques, sweat running down my forehead, hair falling into my eyes, I noticed a guy standing behind me. I could feel that he was taking an interest. He looked like a cop in plain clothes. He moved closer and would certainly have heard the clerk address me as 'Monsieur Price' and seen that my passport was dark blue. Crossing the small departure hall, I quickly dropped Bernard's passport into my pocket and took out my own. Now, as I went through Immigration, there he was again, right behind me, and the passport I was presenting was green. I felt his eyes on me, and thought I'll feel a hand on my shoulder at any second. However, it never happened. It was simple paranoia. I never saw the man again.

Suddenly, I was through into the departure area and about to board the flight but I still had Bernard's passport to dispose of. I couldn't just dump it in a bin. The local cops would have reports of a Bernard·Price doing scams; my progress might be traced, tickets and names put together. My flight was being called. Then my name was being called for the flight! I scuttled down antiseptic corridors towards the plane. There was nowhere to stash the passport – nowhere. I had to, at least, get my picture out of it. I whipped into a men's toilet. My name was called again on the Tannoy. 'Last call . . .'

I bang into a cubicle, shoulder first. I slam the door. I take Bernard's passport and rip out the name pages. It's like trying to tear a fuckin' telephone directory! I start on the others – each has an ID number, perforated on the page. With superhuman strength, I rip them out and go to stuff them down the john, around the U-bend, but I can't get my shirt sleeve open – I'm wearing cuff-links, part of my scamming get-up. In desperation, I take my cigarette lighter and try to set fire to the pages; at the time, smoke alarms were rare or non-existent. Smoke billows up, and the flame dies. Now, with more superhuman strength, I rip the shirt-cuff open and plunge handfuls of ripped passport down the bowl and around the bend. My hair is in my eyes, I'm sweating like a bath attendant, smoke is still rising from burnt fragments on the floor. 'Final call for—' and it's me! I crash wild-eyed, wild-haired out of the cubicle, wet shirt-sleeve hanging, smoke rising around me. The loo outside is half-full of dark Oriental men who've suddenly entered: maybe there was no loo on the small plane from Southend. They look at me in terror and draw back as I plunge past them and race for the plane.

I make it. A nice man is in the seat beside me. I am euphoric and let him tell me his life story. He says why don't I come back to his place when we reach England. I firmly, but nicely, say no.

When I landed in England, the money was stuffed in my boots and every pocket as I went through Customs at the little airport on the Essex marshes. As I'd figured, Southend was much more relaxed than Heathrow. My only luggage was Bernard's briefcase which now contained my necktie and a newspaper.

I took the airport bus into Victoria, where I changed to a double-decker for Notting Hill. I could have taken a taxi but the ride would cost the equivalent of a week's rent in Formentera. I was high out of my head on the thrill of having pulled the whole thing off. When I closed my eyes with fatigue, I dreamt of arriving in the farmhouse and Hanna coming towards me and me telling her 'Honey, I've brought us a year!' 'My hero!', she would say, and kiss me and be so happy she would cry. I just wished I could have phoned her but there were no phones on the Barbary Cape, of course.

Meanwhile, I had Rick and Carlo's reaction to look forward to. I'd pretend things hadn't gone so well and then: surprise, surprise! I didn't even know how much I had; there hadn't been a free minute to count it. I'd paid out fares and taxis and change-office commissions but, after straightening out Bernard, I'd still have the guts of five hundred pounds. I'd never had so much money in my life!

Aboard the bus, sitting with wads of banknotes in every pocket was uncomfortable; I felt like a stuffed duck. Under cover of the seat back, I put it all in the briefcase. From Notting Hill, I walked the last five minutes to Fran's place. I pressed her bell, and she looked out, but instead of throwing down the key, she came down and opened the door. 'You OK?' she asked. I smiled and said, 'Sure, baby . . .' 'I'm so glad,' she said. She was making me feel like a husband coming home.

I went up the stairs ahead of her and pushed open the door. Rick, Carlo and Nicole were sitting on the floor, with an incense stick and some candles burning. They looked up expectantly, smiles mixed with apprehension.

'How'd you do, man?' Rick asked.

I shrugged and said 'OK.' I turned and took off my business jacket. I let the silence linger. Then I lifted up the briefcase and undid the zipper. I held it above the space between them and turned it over, and banknotes in four different currencies fell to the floor.

Just before I arrived, they had all taken the Romilar Rick and Carlo had bought in Ibiza, twenty pills each, and they were just getting into tripping. Carlo held out a tube of pills to me, and Fran gave me a glass of water. I upended the tube and swigged them down in one go. Rick passed me the joint and I sat down and joined the circle, Fran beside me. It was good to be back amongst friends after my wild day in the world of commerce. We all smiled in the slow glow of the Romilar. Carlo quietly strummed the guitar. Romilar isn't a break-neck, head-buzzing trip like acid: insights, maybe, but no revelation, just brilliant colours, detachment, human warmth, love. We said almost nothing. Every now and then we passed the joint and exchanged smiles.

Later, I volunteered to go out to score milk from a machine for coffee, and Nicole came with me. As we walked, she asked me about Carlo: what kind of guy he was; if I thought he liked her. He'd asked me something similar about her. She was living with her mother in south London and he was sleeping at Bernard's. They had nowhere they could be together, even if they wanted to.

When she mentioned that she had no work next day, I said why didn't she come around to Fran's in the morning and we'd pick up Carlo and Rick and go shopping; I had to buy Dieter's Coltrane and Chris Longley's oil paints and there were things I wanted to buy to bring home. Kathy had told me about a new shop called Biba's in Abingdon Road where I could get something nice for Hanna. Talking about Hanna was sort of deliberate. I'd told Fran about her and Aoife from the start. Now, maybe Nicole would reinforce the message: I'd be going home.

That night, I stayed at Fran's again. She went off to work in the morning, and I woke up in the flat alone. She'd left a note, 'See you this evening . . .'

I'd said I'd take her and Nicole out for an Indian meal. She'd fed me twice and I owed her. Sleeping with her was great, and a whole better than sleeping on Bernard's floor. If Hanna made love to someone while I was away – although, in truth, I didn't think she would – it would be none of my business. As long as it was still us when I got back, what happened when we were apart didn't matter.

Nicole came by a few minutes after I woke, letting herself in with her own key. I was still in bed, and she made me tea and toast. She was wearing a dark coat and dress and black stockings. I lay there, enjoying the breakfast-in-bed, and we had a cigarette afterwards, and talked; it was a bit early to go around to Bernard's anyway. I liked Nicole a lot. I felt easy with her and she seemed to think of me as a sort of father-figure, although I was only four years older than her. When she was a kid, her father, a Czech who'd come to England during the war, had left home one day to go and buy cigarettes; a month later her mother got a postcard from Australia saying he wouldn't be back. Her childhood had been tough, her mother struggling to feed her and her sister, to send them to school, then secretarial college. She was a typist-secretary now, doing temp-work, but she was smarter than that; she'd spent a year in France and spoke good French. She was funny with it and loved to clown. If she hadn't helped set me up for Fran, I'd have been happy to spend my time in London with her. As it turned out, it might have been a good thing. Carlo would not have become Nicole's lover and she would have been steered away from a fate that, two years later, took her life.

Some time before noon, we drove around to Bernard's, honked the horn and Carlo and Rick came down. Nicole went to sit in the back so that one of them could use the front seat, the better to see London. Rick took it, of course.

It was a beautiful day and as I rhapsodised about the joys of London and the style of the secretaries in their short skirts eating lunchtime sandwiches in St James Park, Carlo lit and handed around a pre-rolled joint, and he and Nicole joked about the roadside attractions. Near St Martin's Lane, I parked the car and we decanted into Watkins bookshop, where we spent an hour perusing the thousands of esoteric titles on offer. We left with copies of the *I Ching*, *The Tibetan Book of the Dead*, *The Tao*, *The Psychedelic Experience* and Hesse's *Journey to the East* and *Steppenwolf*, and a book of haiku poetry which

I later grew to love. We spent more money on books than on anything else; we were earnest, if naive, scholars.

As we left the shop, Nicole suddenly said to Carlo, 'OK, will we go to Charing Cross Road and get your guitar strings then? We can walk from here.' Carlo grinned and said 'Sure.' I think he was a bit taken aback. 'Alright,' said Nicole breezily, turning to me and Rick, 'Meet you back at Fran's place . . .' And with a wink and a jerk of her head to Carlo, she said, 'C'mon.'

Rick and I went back to the car and headed for Pall Mall. I wanted to get a new International Driving Licence at the Royal Automobile Club, and I thought Rick might like one too. We scored passport photos from a machine in Boots Chemist in Piccadilly Circus, and then drove up to the RAC. They were 'good chaps' at the Driving Licence counter – it was a Gentleman's Club, after all – and they accepted my story, delivered in an underplayed Hooray Henry voice, that I'd left my British licence down at the cottage in Berkshire, having quite forgotten it in the rush to collect my American friend at Heathrow. That evening we were both catching a flight to Rome and driving up to Florence; I'd need a licence to be able to share the driving, of course.

I was good at accents. I easily slipped into the language and gestures of the milieu in which I moved. During my childhood, my father's job had meant that the family moved to towns in the four provinces of Ireland, and it became second nature for me to slip into the accents and vocabulary of the local kids. Childhood moving made me a nomad too, unafraid of new places, knowing the knack of fitting in. Like Roma gypsies, the children of peripatetic Irish civil servants learned to speak in divers tongues.

Rick decided he'd like another joint. We crossed the Mall and sat on a bench and watched the ducks and the girls, at least I did. Rick rolled the jay, shoved the dope back in his pocket and lit up. The sun was almost as warm as in Spain.

After half an hour or so, we hauled back to the car and missed a beat when she wouldn't start. I got my feet on the street, one hand on the steering wheel and my shoulder against the door frame and Rick shoved from the back. We pushed out into the traffic and gained momentum. I hopped in, slammed her into second, and she fired.

All was going well up Piccadilly but just as we came on to Hyde Park Corner, I saw a cop on the central reservation and I knew immediately that he was pulling in bangers to check them out for valid insurance and tax. Meantime, the chances were that while he was persecuting banger-drivers, Rollers and Jags full of the Kray Bros and heavies with guns were passing right by. I tried to stay on the outside lane, to keep trucks and buses between me and him but his hand went up, pointing at me, calling me in. I'd have pretended not to see him but he had a motorcycle cop beside him, ready to give chase, and I didn't want to make things worse than they might already be. I bounced us up over the kerb of the big central reservation under the arch at Hyde Park Corner, right opposite the St. George's clap clinic where Hanna and I had had our first date. 'You holdin'?' Rick hissed, slipping his dope out, leaning forward to push it into his shoe. 'Shit!' he said, as it fell on the floor.

The cop came to the window. He was a London bobby, helmet and all – the full Gilbert and Sullivan regalia. 'Is this your car?' he enquired, to which I answered in the affirmative. I'd been through this before.

The fact that I had no road tax was a problem, but it worked out fine. I told him my friend and I were English language teachers working in Spain, and I couldn't tax the car from there. In fact, apart from seeing family, renewing the road tax was the reason I'd come home; once it was taxed, I could legally keep it on in Spain. I liked right-hand-drive (none of that Continental nonsense!) and it was a good old car, despite its looks, and, well, wages weren't high in Barcelona. When he asked for my driving licence, I promptly passed him the International Licence and said I'd bought it that morning. When he asked to see my current British licence, I told him I'd gone home in between, and left it, along with my passport and other papers, in the pocket of a jacket which I'd been wearing when I went to the RAC. Rick sat shtum and listened to all this, his hat held in his lap, and wearing a sort of sickly smile. As far as my certificate of motor insurance was concerned, I told the copper I had Spanish insurance and a 'Green Card', which allowed me to drive in most European countries, including the UK. I'd left that in the jacket too.

The cop took all this in, and then asked me to turn on the lights, then the indicators, then to honk the horn. All of them worked; I could hardly believe it. This done, he turned to have a word with his colleague, the motor-cycle cop. I saw what was coming. The cop asked me to step out of the vehicle and, as I did so, I reached down and palmed Rick's nub of dope off the floor. I held it in my palm as I watched the motorcycle man kneel down, lean in, check to see that the pedals had rubber on them and then depress the brake pedal with his gloved hand to establish that I had working brakes. It was a lucky fucking thing his dope wasn't still on the deck, I knew Rick was think-ing. He sat there, trying to show a discommoded interest. He looked like someone dying to go to the jacks.

Inspection completed, the bobby took out his notebook and assiduously copied my name from my new licence, along with my fictitious address, a house in Kangaroo Valley full of transitory people, the house where I'd had my kisser altered by the bookie's heavies, in fact. He handed me a slip requir-ing me to present my UK driving licence and motor insurance documents within five days at the Earls Court Road cop shop. I assured him I'd do so before my imminent return to Spain. I started up the banger, hoping he wouldn't, as an afterthought, decide to do me for a faulty exhaust. As we got moving again, I handed Rick his dope. He was highly apologetic. No sweat, I said, the cop mightn't have seen it anyway.

Rick asked me how come the Law couldn't trace me through the car own-ership papers. I'd never registered the banger in my name, of course: it remained in the name of the guy who'd sold it as scrap to my friend, the bi-focalled New Zealand dope-smoker, old furniture dealer and banger-mechanic extraordinary, Jim Lowery, who had patched it up somewhat and sold it on to me. So, should the cops try to find me, they'd come upon a bloke who'd be able to demonstrate he hadn't owned or even seen the car for some time. 'You're outrageous, man!' Rick told me, as we limped past Marble Arch, the engine still on stop-go.

We got to the Biba shop at about five; we were killing time so as to give Carlo and Nicole some space when they got back to Fran's. The minute I went in, I saw an itty-bitty dress that I thought would look great on Hanna, so I scored it in a size 8 and left. Shopping like that suited me; in-and-out, short and sweet like an ass's gallop. It cost two quid; she wouldn't have wanted me to spend more. She'd live in flour sacks if it would buy us more time in Formentera.

When we arrived at Fran's, Carlo and Nicole were sitting together on the floor, Carlo's fat, new hardback copy of the *I Ching or Book of Changes* open in front of them. A classical Chinese text of divination, it had a foreword by Carl Jung, the psychoanalyst and inner space explorer, and was held in high esteem by followers of Taoism and Buddhism, providing day-to-day guidance on how to proceed to greater harmony with the world. Three coins were thrown six times. How they fell, face up or down, signified a hexagram, the meaning of which could be looked up in the book. We all had a go. Carlo put some store by it, Rick was respectful, I was simply curious and the girls thought it was witchdoctor stuff. But then Rick, who'd talked about travelling to the East, threw the hexagram entitled The Wanderer, and Nicole threw The Marrying Maiden. Blushing, she said, 'Not bleedin' likely!' Carlo grinned widely and we all laughed.

Chapter 9

ON SATURDAY MORNING, THE CAR began to seriously fuck up as I drove over to Bernard's and there was no starting it again. Getting new wheels was now the most important business of the day. I went through the interior to make sure I'd left nothing behind, and then pushed her alongside the pavement and said goodbye. She'd been a good old car.

I found a phone box but I didn't have coins to pay for the call, so I tapped out Jim Lowery's number on the cradle of the handpiece, like Morse Code. He told me come over. I walked to St Stephen's Gardens off Westbourne Park, where he lived. Jim wasn't your typical Kangaroo Valley Antipodean: he was of a different stamp.

We stood on the wide steps of one of the fine houses around the square, then in terminal decay, where Jim rented a couple of rooms. A three-piece suite of furniture sat in the 'gardens' in the middle, where somebody has left it out to rot. Black kids and Sikh kids with their hair done up in top-knots were playing around it. For all the ravages of neglect, the sun through the London plane trees and the kids running in and out of the shade made it a beautiful, almost tropical, scene. The smoke from our cigarettes curled upward in the clear air.

It turned out old James knew of a car. 'Wait'll you see her. She's a beaut'!' he said in his wide-awake New Zealand accent, 'She belongs to a sheep-shagger I know.' Fifteen minutes later, we're looking at the car, around in All

Saints Road. It's a long, low-slung, cream-colour Triumph Roadster Convertible 2000, circa 1949, body falling apart but soul perfect, so Jim says. She'd probably once belonged to some RAF type who drove her with the hood down, scarves and mustachios flying, and lank blond hair; it was maybe the kind of car in which Isadora Duncan got her scarf caught in the back wheel. It had the age and it had once had the class, but at this stage it was no longer a vintage sports car; it was a wreck. Jim said the guy wanted twenty-five quid. This was twice as much as I'd ever paid for a car before, but if she went well it'd be worth it.

In front was a bench seat of scuffed tan leather, wide enough for three. The front was the 'convertible' part, covered by a fold-back hood a bit like the hood on the second-hand Pedigree pram we'd bought when Aoife was born. Behind it, the boot had a lid that opened in two halves. The lower half hinged back over the rear bumper and contained two comfortable, leather-upholstered buggy seats, while the upper half opened upward to make a split-pane windscreen for the passengers that sat in them. I asked what would happen to the people in the back if it rained. 'They'd probably drown,' the sheep-shagger told me, chewing a match as he spoke.

I pointed out that the big headlights that stood proud of the front wings were wonky – she looked cross-eyed from the front. Jim said he could fix those, no bother, so I said let's start her up and drive her round the block. She'd been standing some time, so the battery was down; however, she fired after a few swings of the starting handle and off we went. I had to admit she drove beautifully but, nevertheless, I told Jim's Antipodean buddy that he was asking five quid more than I was going to pay. We split the difference, and I got her for twenty two pounds ten. The guy slipped Jim a quid, and we left.

I dropped Jim off after giving him a bit of dope, and I made a beeline for Bernard's. When Kathy opened the window to throw me the key, I pointed at the car and yelled for them all to come down. With myself, Rick and Kathy – in froufrou bedroom slippers and a kimono – in front, and Bernard and Carlo in the buggy seats, I took them for a drive down Ladbroke Grove. Outside a Gospel Hall in Basing Street it was like Antigua or Barbados on a summer's day, pale, bleached cops in shirt-sleeves directing all God's 'chillun' as they walked in procession, singing and shining in the sun.

That afternoon, we went to Portobello market and toured the antique and bric-à-brac stalls and the barrows selling everything from kumquats to plantains. Rick came across a pair of enamelled opium pipes some ancient sailor must have brought back from China, and scored them for a few bob each.

Rick and Carlo asked Kathy if she could get them some more heavy drugs. Carlo wanted to try heroin; he thought maybe the governments were all lying about smack like they lied about grass. In America they put out all that 'reefer madness' shit, saying that smoking dope would turn you into a violent thug and rapist. We knew that wasn't true. If they lied about that, how could they be trusted to tell the truth about any other drug? Like acid, maybe other drugs, if used right, would take you to the sort of peace money couldn't buy. Maybe, said Carlo, the bankers and merchants who controlled the world didn't want us messing with our heads for fear we'd see the light, and love and fair distribution would prevail. They'd no longer have consumers hooked on their tacky products, or slaves or soldiers to go to war for them. Alcohol wasn't banned. Alcohol was OK: when you got over the hangover, you'd go back to work and be a compliant citizen. You could drink all you wanted and go home and beat your wife but you couldn't smoke a peaceful joint without going to jail. Meanwhile, Harry Anslinger, J. Edgar Fuckin' Hoover and the US Army were experimenting with LSD for brain-washing and mind control. If they had their way, any day now it'd be 1984.

But I couldn't help Rick and Carlo score smack. They knew that Bernard was acquainted with Alex Trocchi, the guy who wrote *Cain's Book* about New York junkie life, and they asked him if he would hit on Trocchi on their behalf. I drove them all down to Vicarage Gardens where the Trocchis lived and, while the others waited in the car, I went upstairs with Bernard; I'd read the book and wanted to catch a glimpse of the master. Poor Trocchi looked like death warmed up, with sores and grey skin; he was the physical refutation of any romantic view Carlo might be entertaining about heroin. Furthermore, he wouldn't come across with any drugs. I wasn't unhappy about that. If they'd got it, I'd have tried it. I'd try anything but, in the case of smack, I wasn't in any hurry.

When we met Fran and Nicole in Henekey's, Fran was breathless with the news that she had a friend in the box office at the Albert Hall who could slip us tickets to hear Ravi Shankar, the world-famous sitar player.

So, it was fish-and-chips for supper and off to the concert. We drove through Hyde Park with the hood down and Fran jammed between me and Rick in front. It was lucky the gear stick was on the steering column, otherwise I don't know where she'd have put her legs. Carlo and Nico sat like postillions in the jump seat; I thought maybe we should have rented them top hats. The sun was shining red through the trees, low in the sky, like it was already deep autumn. Rick, the collar of his jacket up, his hat in his lap, passed a joint around. Off to our right, across the gilded lawns, Prince Albert sat in his stone temple, watching the evenin' sun go down.

Outside the Albert Hall there were crowds of straight-looking people – bespectacled music-students, Indian women in glorious saris with husbands in Nehru jackets – with a sprinkling of bums like ourselves. Fran scored the tickets. The seats were behind the circular dais where the musicians would sit; it was an ace of a place to hear from. It was amazing to be there, anyway, crossing the great space of light, outcasts from the islands, Rick, his hat held to his chest, slight baldness at the temples showing, smiling nervously, bobbing his head to audience and ushers as we passed. 'Far out!' Nico whispered, wide-eyed. Right on, thought I, far fuckin out, Nicole! I'd never seen anything like this before.

Soon a silence fell, punctuated by small coughs. A whisper rippled across the hall. Three small dark men, in white kurtas and cotton trousers, walked onto the stage. One, scrawny and hawk-like, carried a long-necked stringed instrument which caught the light. Ravi Shankar, himself, maestro of the sitar.

They bowed low and then sat themselves down, cross-legged, on the floor. Now, I tell myself, I am in the presence of genius. Soon, I had lost all thought in music and images born of music. Brown hands on the tabla whirring, brown fingers the sitar caressing: they swept me away so fast I almost giggled, and the tamboura's hypnotic drone filled my mind. The tabla slowed and tapped like droplets on leaves, and the sitar slid over the notes like flowing water. Fran took my hand in hers. I released my hand. She simpered. Fran, I wanted to tell her, I do not want you to simper; simpering at me makes me feel unfree. I reclosed my eyes. The drone of the tamboura reclaimed my mind, the tablas rattled like rain on a tin roof and the sitar sang like a woman. In the silences between the notes one could almost women's their voices in the languid heat. I wanted to tell Hanna about this. We would go to India. I would take us to India, if it was the last place we ever went.

On the way back to Fran's, I stopped the car in Hyde Park for a minute. I was still in outer space. A long glow-worm of cars moved down Park Lane, beyond the trees, under the sodium-yellow sky. Lights of a plane winked, flying to God knows where. Jesus, it is so good to be alive! I had five hundred quid, for me and Hanna ! It was beyond my wildest imaginings.

Homeward, then, up the Bayswater Road, the tyres singing, songs of the nomad nation in my mind. I felt as if I could drive on and on, onward to India, where Nancy and I once set out to go but never reached. At traffic lights, I heard Carlo, in the back telling how, at Benares on the Ganges, he had seen the pundits cracking the skulls of the bodies burnt on the Ghats. Pop, they would release the soul; pop, pop, pop-pop, at the sunset hour of the evening. Flats and sharps, different each one.

On Sunday morning, Fran again made breakfast, and went down and bought the Sunday papers. It was all getting too cosy with Fran. It was time to be leaving London anyway. Take the money and run was the way I'd always thought of London, much as I loved it. In those years, I used it only to get together the bread to go elsewhere, or to have my kids; the hospitals were brilliant, and they were free.

When I met Rick and Carlo at Bernard's, we talked about plans. They didn't have any. Rick thought he'd maybe head for India, via Amsterdam. He asked me to take his opium pipes back to Formentera and keep them for him until he got back. Carlo thought he might stay on in London a while; Jim Lowery had said he had a back room in his pad and they could share the rent.

The next Sunday afternoon, we went over to the Cromwell Road to meet a friend of Nick Phillips who'd said he and his wife would be glad of a lift down to Barcelona and they'd share the gas. We made a deal. That night, Rick, Carlo, myself and Fran and Nicole went to an Indian restaurant in

Westbourne Grove. Bernard arrived with Kathy but she came and went, all dolled up, paint, powder and high-heels. She said she had business to take care of. Who knew, except Bernard, what she meant by that? She didn't seem to find it any problem, whatever she was doing; in fact, she may have left because she found us bums a bit dull. Afterwards, I drove us back to Bernard's, with Nicole sitting on Carlo's lap. Soon, Fran said she'd have to go; she had work in the morning. I wasn't sure I wanted to go back with her but I could hardly let her walk when I had the car. At her place, she asked me wasn't I coming in, and I came in, and next thing she was lifting her dress over her head and walking over to me and, of course, with the dope and all, it was good but really I was thinking of Hanna.

Afterwards, Fran rose to take her alarm clock, wind it and set it. I was lost in another world. Had I thought any more about coming to Greece? she asked me; she'd had the idea that I might go to Greece with her before returning to Spain. No, I hadn't. Well, to book tickets, I'd have to make up my mind soon . . .

Poor Fran. She was truly lovely. Most guys would have given their right ball to be in bed with her but I knew my heart was with Hanna, second-best Hanna who'd become part of me, always there in my mind.

The most sensible thing for me to do now, I figured, was to leave. Fran was half-asleep anyway. I murmured that I was going back to Bernard's to smoke another joint. She told me take the spare key and said she'd see me the following evening. I didn't take the key and she was too out of it to notice. I wouldn't be there in the morning but the key would be. I figured she'd get the message; I was sorry but it had to be done.

As I drove away, I felt a sense of liberation. My own version of a Dylan song was playing in my head, '*When the rooster crows at the break of dawn, Look out your window, baby, I'll be gone, Don't call on me 'cos I'm travellin' on, But don't think twice, it's all right . . .*' I hadn't started things with Fran, and I'd never pretended it would last.

Rick was going to Amsterdam. With a handshake, a pat on my shoulder and a laconic smile, he said he'd see me in Formentera sooner or later, whether he made it to India or not. He'd get himself some acid if I could give him a Dutch connection. I couldn't. I knew Simon Vinkenoog but he was a psychedelic scholar, not a dealer. However, Rick would meet someone for sure. Carlo had moved into Jim Lowery's room.

I was heading south again, in the old Roadster with Nick's friends, Geoffrey and Jennifer Ford-Holme, my passengers. They were bubbling with excitement; it was to be their first time in Spain, the first time on such an adventure, and I liked them a lot. Sometimes, they enjoyed sitting in the buggy seat in the back, and I watched them in the rear-view mirror and talked to them over my shoulder. They'd enjoy themselves back there so long as it didn't rain.

We stopped in Paris and I looked up Zelda Bloom, an American actress with the Living Theatre whose address Mel had given me when we'd last met. She lived in an atelier in rue Grégoire de Tours. She wanted to go south too. She was warm and she was fun and she sat beside me on the bench seat in the front while Geoff and Jenni sat in the back. Before we left Paris, Zelda took me all over the Left Bank and to the Café Deux Magots and Le Dôme where Sartre and Simone de Beauvoir hung out – but they weren't there that day. At her local café in rue du Seine, an old white-haired guy said good morning to Zelda in a most courteous way. She told me he was Marc Chagall and that they often said good morning to one another when they breakfasted there.

On our first night out of Paris, we stayed at a Routier place in a French town. Next morning, Zelda hauled me into a lingerie shop, insisting I should buy a sexy present for Hanna. Small fripperies would have cost as much as a month's rent in Formentera but, laughing, she held them against herself, to show how they would look when they were worn. I honestly hadn't thought of such sexual sophistication before.

Next day, as we drove, I dreamt up the idea that we should all go to Africa sometime and take acid and syringe out each others' ears as the sun rose and the dawn chorus began on the Serengeti Plain. We all agreed we'd do it one day. Zelda told me about the ranch her father had left her in the redwood forests in northern California and said why didn't I come and spend a while there with her. I said I'd love to some time. 'Don't make promises you can't keep . . .' she laughed. We could have made sweet music together, Zelda and me, but I was heading home to Hanna and Aoife. And that's how it was with me.

We got into Barcelona during the siesta and killed time at a café on the Ramblas. Then I went and found the guy who'd fixed the wheels of the Zephyr and asked him if he knew anywhere cheap and safe where I could leave the car. Thing was, with the English reg., if I left it in the street the canvas roof was likely to be slashed by somebody wanting to thieve from it. The guy said I could park it in his yard for eight *duros* a month – forty pesetas. So now it was going to cost me to keep it, even when I wasn't using it: it was an object lesson in the problems property can bring. But the price wasn't bad – about the same as I'd pay for a packet of fags in England at the time.

After we'd dropped off the car, Zelda and I headed for the port to catch the night boat to Ibiza. Geoff and Jenni wanted to stay in Barcelona for a few days. I said that if they made it to Formentera, to come out to the Cap de Berbería and I'd find them a house if I could.

When Zelda and I landed in Ibiza, she was into catching the boat to Formentera right away; she planned to stay at the Fonda Pepe in San Fernando. I said I'd take the evening boat and see her when I'd see her – Formentera was a small island and we couldn't fail to meet. Meanwhile, I had things to do in Ibiza, I wanted to see the kids, give Nancy a lump of money, Dieter his Coltrane disc and Chris Longley his oil paints.

Nancy was at the Montesol with the kids, and they were overjoyed to see me, not only the boys but her too. I gave her a wad of bread as promised, enough to make up what I owed her, plus a few months in advance. I had reading books and pens for the kids, a dice game with letters instead of numbers and a couple of Superman outfits; I was going to get Batman and Robin but I thought there'd be fights over who was which. I'd bought them Indian spinning tops in Portobello Road. They found some string somewhere, and I made them whips and in no time at all they were lofting the tops six feet off the ground in the middle of the Vara de Rey.

I was looking for Chris and when he didn't show by lunchtime, I asked Brunswick if I could borrow his motorbike to go out to the *finca*. He said to keep it until I caught the Formentera boat in the evening and to drop it off at the Domino before I left. I piled the kids aboard, gunned the engine and headed for the hills with two miniature Supermen behind me. Chris's place was a lovely old *finca* he was house-sitting for a couple of German guys. He gave me the bread for the paints and made tea from fresh chamomile and we looked at some dope plants he was growing behind a sheltered wall. Afterwards, the boys climbed back aboard and we headed down to the sea. I let each of them help steer the bike, taking turns to sit on the petrol tank in front of me. Time passed so fast, we had to hightail it back to Ibiza before I missed the boat. I left the bike at the Domino and the boys ran beside me down to the pier to see me off.

When I'd left Formentera, I hadn't told Hanna when I'd be back and by the time business was taken care of in London, there was no time to reach her by mail. It would be a great surprise when I suddenly turned up out of the night. The sun was setting as we made the twenty-kilometre voyage between the islands. The only other foreigner on the boat was the French-Egyptian guy I used to see when I'd cross to Formentera to get away from Nancy. With his dark-jowled face and big nose, he looked, more than ever, like a French movie star playing a gangster. No doubt – although nobody knew it then – he'd be typing up phoney provenances for Elmyr's paintings in the dead of the night, as he'd done when I was penning my doleful lyrics in the room beside him at Fonda Pepe.

Arriving at La Sabina, we both took the island bus. I got out at the junction for San Francisco, hefted my bag onto my shoulder and set off to walk the five kilometres to the house. It was a lovely night, with the moon rising, which was just as well because the bedrock of the *camino* was often pocked by ancient lava flows or the runnels of old rivers, and walking it in the pitch dark wasn't easy. But the moon rose over the sea and shone out over the land, silvering the fields, whitening the dust, brightening the one or two whitewashed farmhouses I passed, in which could be seen glimmers of light. I met not a soul but heard an owl calling. I walked steadily, looking forward to seeing Hanna, looking forward to arriving, triumphantly, home.

The dog barked as I came to the gate and, as I crossed in front of the house, half the big door opened and there she was, standing against the candlelight of the kitchen, crying out and running to me and throwing herself into my arms. Next thing, Aoife was beside us, grabbing our legs, all wet because she'd jumped out of her plastic bath and come running – as I lifted her, I saw that the bath must have tipped because a river was running out of the kitchen door, shining in the light as we picked her up and hugged her all wet and naked between us, with the dog jumping up and down, standing on my bag and wanting to get in on the act too. With Aoife's arms around my neck, and toting my bag with the other hand, I walked into the house, and dropped the bag on the floor. I put Aoife down and reached inside one boot top and then the other and produced, like a magician, two wads of banknotes. 'I've brought us a year!' I said. Hanna's eyes were bright with tears.

We had supper. I unwrapped Aoife's presents for her – reading books, wooden animals for a farm, a wooden cart which clicked when it was pulled around the concrete floor. After I'd put Aoife to bed, I gave Hanna the dress. She tried it on and looked even prettier than she had before. I produced the carbon light I'd bought so that she could paint at night, a two-litre iron cylinder like a camping gas bottle that had an aperture with a screw top where one dropped in the pieces of carbon and then added the water, and a spout where the gas emerged which, when lit, produced a brilliant, white naked flame, turning night to day, like a kleig light, lighting corners and niches of the high walls and roof beams we'd never seen before. We marvelled at it, and then doused it. We sat by the fire and smoked a joint. I took a glass of water from the bucket by the door and there was a red mosquito larva in it, a small worm with feathery gills, like a miniature seahorse. There weren't supposed to be mosquitoes hatching in the well but, in the clear glass, in the clear water, it looked very beautiful, blood-red, swimming up to the surface, drifting down and then, with a beat of its tail, rising again. We looked at it and looked at one another, and in the space between us there was nothing to be said.

I touched her and found I was in love again with all the contours of her body. I had learned love from her; women (but not Nancy) had taught me what women enjoy, each different, and I had been an attentive student. We made love. I wanted to satisfy her more than to satisfy myself, to hear her murmurs and to see her body responding, taking her away. From the time I met Hanna, I'd sworn I would always remember her, that I would wait for her and I would love her more than I'd love myself.

I'd brought tea from England and we had some afterwards. We smoked another joint and in the big, vaulted bedroom, in the silence of the Formentera night, I fell into a deep and dreamless sleep.

A Love Supreme

Chapter 10

DAYS PASSED ALL BUT TIMELESSLY during the weeks afterwards. We seemed to be suspended in time. Certainly that was the way Blind George appeared when we saw him one afternoon as we walked back from Mitjorn beach, me with Aoife on my shoulders, he with two Swedish girls of arresting beauty accompanying him almost like handmaidens, I thought. They led him where the ground was broken and later, at our house, they rolled his joints like sisters in service, wrote down addresses for him and attended to his every need. When he said he felt like going home to bed, they rose and walked out beside him, for he could certainly still see the door with the light blasting through it into the big, cool room with its single window, but maybe not the bucket of water beside it or the low step outside. He looked like Jesus Christ, with his shoulder-length hair, gaunt, ascetic figure, wispy beard and blue but almost sightless eyes.

Rick didn't return but wrote to me saying he was heading overland from Amsterdam for India; he'd heard it could be done on the cheap by taking local buses from town to town, city to city. He'd be back, of course, but it might not be for a while. If he had to, he'd go home to the States after India, earn some bread and see us all again in Formentera, in a year or so at the most.

Bart Hughes came to the house one day to show me the hole he'd bored in his head. He too was accompanied by women, not quite the slim beauties that escorted George but two earnest American acolytes following him as he roamed like a wandering sadhu around the island from house to house, selling a scroll, beautifully printed, describing the ancient and esoteric history of the Third Eye. The girls wrote in their 'journals', as was the wont of Americans, I don't know why. 'Here and Now' was where we all wanted to be and, anyway, the mind retains the important memories and forgets the rest. Besides, for obvious reasons I never kept a diary of my felonious career; the stamps in my passport were record enough but they could be incriminating too.

Bart was a self-effacing guy, and he kept the hole hidden under a lock of hair. But for those who wanted to see it, it was there, bored with a dentist's drill in his flat in Amsterdam to the horror of poor Barbara – who'd given us our first acid trip – who really didn't like the idea at all. But Bart had drilled away courageously, determined, like the rest of us, to follow knowledge whatever the cost.

He told us he'd read a report that the CIA was doing controlled tests with LSD to see if they could use it for brainwashing spies or for telepathy in war-zones. We'd already heard that psychiatrists were experimenting on schizophrenics to see if mega-doses would have the effect of a reversible pre-frontal lobotomy, which would, of course, have been a whole lot better than turning the poor bastards into irreversible vegetables.

While Bart was the sole pioneer of the ancient Third Eye, none of us shirked the dangers involved in seeking enlightenment. Carlo and other Americans had gone to Mexico and tried peyote, although you were guaranteed to be as sick as a dog for hours and to vomit your guts out before you came within even twinkling distance of Nirvana. When he wanted to try smack in London, he knew it was playing with fire but thought that maybe all needs would be reduced to only one. Material needs, sexual desire, false concepts of duty would all fade; illusion would fade, and all would dissolve into a dream of pleasure domes and damsels with dulcimers. In a sense, he was right. When you're there, you're there, amongst the palaces. In an opium den in Calcutta, I have experienced the ultimate detachment. You lie on a pallet in the soft glow of the candle and let the man light your pipe for you and be your ministering angel. Your troubles and the world float away.

Bart was an old friend. I'd met him when he was a medical student on a few weeks' holiday in Ibiza in 1961, wearing a sports jacket with leather elbow patches. We'd hit it off in the Domino Bar and got on our bikes that very night and, with a small flashlight, gone out to the olive groves to look for tree frogs. For all his fame – or notoriety – he was as unassuming as ever and we half-thought of going to look for tree frogs again the night he and his entourage stayed at our house. He told me that the hole in the head induced a mild, marijuana-like high – no more than that – but it had provenance amongst the magicians and shamans of various cultures and, eager to learn, he'd tried it out. He and Barbara were no longer living together. Barbara was with crazy Brunswick now.

One day, Ramón, the local *carpintero* and our nearest neighbour, asked Hanna and me if we'd come to his house that evening to see his wife's new outfit. I didn't quite get it, but Hanna said he might mean that Maria would be wearing modern clothes. We feared what we'd see but, for her sake, we had to go. We liked Maria more than Ramón; in fact, I was a bit wary since he'd called me into his workshop one day to show me dirty pictures, black-and-white postcards of 1920s' women in hats and stockings and nothing else. I pretended interest; I didn't want to put him down. He talked about modern women in their short skirts and wanted to show me pictures he'd cut from magazines. I laughed it off and made a polite escape. However, I could hardly blame him for his fascination. While the Formentera women, including girls from sixteen or seventeen upward, wore dresses to the ground and never went swimming or appeared in bathing suits, some foreign women wore scanty skirts and sometimes lay on the beaches half-nude. They were cautious about this; Formentera had no Guardia Civil but maybe some scandalised local might denounce them to the authorities in Ibiza and they'd be deported from Spain.

Maria was twenty-three or twenty-four years old, and had one child. We'd always admired her tall, straight figure, the way she moved so gracefully over the rough paths in her long black dress, hitched up when she was hoeing the fields and showing all sorts of coloured petticoats. On her head, she wore the traditional straw sombrero and a headscarf, and a pigtail of jet black hair descended to the small of her back. I guess the headscarf was to protect her face against the sun – maybe it was an Arab influence. Over the millennia, these islands had been colonised by various North African peoples.

We walked to the house after dinner, Hanna carrying Aoife on her hip, and got there about sunset. Ramón gave us a glass of wine from a barrel in the shed; we sometimes bought wine from him, bringing our own bottle. Maria was nowhere to be seen. At last, he went into the other room and a few minutes later emerged, Maria behind him, eyes shyly downcast, looking mortified. She wore a short-sleeved, knee-length, flower-print dress from which her legs and arms protruded, white as tubers. Her face was half-tanned, half-pale, with her pigtail shorn and replaced by a pudding-basin haircut in the 'modern' style. She tried to smile. Our hearts went out to her but what could we say but that she looked lovely. She turned at Ramón's command, to show us how she looked from the back. She was the first woman on the island to go 'modern'. Afterwards, I tried my best to avoid Ramón. I think he figured out why, but I didn't care.

One night, at Cala Sohona, a baby was born to Jacey and Lorna, Californians living in a small house on the edge of the pine *bosque* and the sea, and they called her Maria-Juana, which I thought, personally, was not a good idea. I argued with her father as we walked along the beach afterwards, while simultaneously congratulating him on the child. I said that as soon as Immigration read the name in her passport, she'd get shook down at every border she passed through. So what?, he said, she'd be able to deal with it. It didn't make sense to me.

Bruno had come to our house at about one in the morning to tell us Lorna was in labour; he thought that maybe she'd like Hanna, being a mother herself – the only foreign mother on the island – to be there. We woke Aoife and carried her along the paths through the umbrella pines, under a big moon, to their house on the beach. A few other people had already turned up to congratulate them and to see the child. It had been born in the house, by the light of candles and firelight and to the sound of the sea, with Jacey boiling water on the hearth for the local midwife, who came in her black robes and headscarf when he walked along the beach to fetch her. She brought her daughter, and they carried fresh sheets and enamel basins, and they ordered him about and demanded water for washing, first for their own hands and then for Lorna, lying on the mattress on the floor, and, later, the baby. It was delivered as Jacey stood there in the silence: there was only Lorna's breathing and the waves breaking, and then the baby's cry. After the birth, the midwife and her daughter fussed about outside in the moonlight, wringing and hanging out clothes, noisily turning the handle that lowered the bucket into the well.

Hanna made yerba maté tea, and we drank from bowls and jam-jars: there weren't enough cups to go around. Afterwards people went home. It seemed to me a singular miracle that, only three hours before, there had been two people in the solitary house at Cala Sohona and now, as we left them, there were three.

When we arrived home at C'an Pujolet, a guy called Marvin was sitting outside, rolling a joint. Longini had told me about him; he was from New Jersey; he had a rented motorbike from Ibiza and he went around calling at every foreign house, without invitation. Longini had found him sitting on his front porch, which was surrounded by fly screens; he'd just opened the door and let himself in. He then proceeded to ask Longini why he had such a thing about flies. Who the fuck did this asshole dope-tourist think he was anyway? Jack demanded. (In fact, this Marvin had a point; Longini spent half his home-life wandering around with a fly-squatter ambushing flying insects – but that was his business, and Marvin seemed by all accounts to be a prick.) It was strange to find him at our house; the door hung open, he'd gone inside. All the same, we offered him coffee. He told us he thought Maria-Juana was a great name and that he'd half-suggested it to Jacey in the first place. It was a lovely morning and we decided to take Aoife to the beach. Marvin suggested giving Hanna a ride, with Aoife, on his motorbike but she said no, she'd walk. We were glad when he took off and left us.

Lorna's baby thrived, although there was no doctor or health care on Formentera until years later. The only medical help available was the *practicante* who lived in San Fernando, not a *médico* but a drug dispenser and injection-giver. As far as giving injections were concerned, one or two of the

Americans had had plenty of experience, so foreigners had no call on the *practicante*'s services. He provided pills or medicines in any quantity requested, but stayed off the drugs himself.

Before him, there had been a glum young woman who came across on the boat from Ibiza once a week, stayed overnight and opened the island pharmacy in a room off the *tienda* in San Francisco Xavier. Longini's list of pills had probably excited her curiosity and, one way or the other, it looked as though she was trying everything the *estranjeros* asked for: uppers and downers, semi-psychedelics and trippers, Centramina, Romilar and the rest, with the result that she was mostly either half-asleep or frantic and was shortly replaced by the new *practicante*. Later, we heard that she'd taken up residence with an American speed-freak in Morocco and was supporting them both by belly-dancing for the king. This was an Ibiza myth that spread to Formentera. Expatriate communities on small islands thrive on myths. The more fantastic they are, the more they are retailed.

Even in the idyllic world of Formentera, Hanna and I didn't always agree on everything and one day we had a serious run-in when she made Jacey a present of my book of haiku poetry. When I found it missing, she explained that he'd dropped in for a glass of water and had admired it. She'd said he should take it; it was obviously meant for him. I asked her what the fuck she was doing – it wasn't as if Jacey was a poetry reader and the book was something I treasured. That was all the more reason to give it, she said, and she accused me of being hung up on possessions and not able to give. It wasn't that, I said, reminding her that I'd laid money on half-a-dozen people since I'd got back. We ended up yelling at one another. Of course, we got over it. My rancour died quickly. Maybe Hanna was right: giving money was easy – I had no love for it. To get free of material desire, we had to give away the things we really loved.

Sometimes, I was afraid of what would happen to her if I walked out because I couldn't stand being trapped any more. She would be so down; would she be able to pick herself up? What would happen to Aoife? She needed parents – but not parents who regularly fought. I'd been there, a child split sometimes between two parents. I didn't want that for her. The boys hadn't suffered that. It had been a clean break. Nancy had made sure of that. She had been right, in a way.

Hanna and I decided that we'd take acid again: our second trip. Bruno and Desiree had four trips of pure Sandoz, on sugar cubes. They offered us two, and we gave them two hundred pesetas – the same as they they'd paid for them. Nobody was making money out of acid; love was the motivation. I said I hoped they wouldn't mind if Hanna and I took it alone, as we'd done with the first trip. 'Put a note on your gate to say you are tripping,' Bruno said. 'So nobody will bozzair you . . .'

However, despite the note, Suzy, a big Australian girl, along with Black William from London and a pair of unknown Americans, all of them also tripping, arrived out of the night and skipped into our kitchen where a single candle was burning and Hanna and I were sitting by the fire in the music of silence, the roar of the psychedelic tides in our minds and the soughing of the seas. In the midst of this, with their games and their bullshit, they arrived.

We turned our heads to watch them. We didn't say anything; we didn't move. They found our stash of candles in a recess in the wall and began to light them. They lit up the big room like a church or temple, and they began to chant and dance in a circle, the high, beamed ceiling a dark void above them. They came forward, hands outstretched and reached for us to join the circle, the whirl of bodies passing in front of the candles. I didn't yield to the pull of the woman's hand but peeled her fingers off mine, but her other hand was on Hanna's, drawing her forward. As she rose uncertainly, I feared for her and wanted to protect her but they spun her away. When she looked at me as she passed, I held out my hand but she didn't take it. They danced on the wide floor, wild and chanting. I sat hunched over the fire, the Australian girl dancing around me like a gauche Salomé. The eyes of the others, as they danced past, watched me as if I was some sort of pitiable creature, unenlightened, unevolved, unfree. I met Hanna's eyes. She looked away as if she denied knowing me.

When I looked again, she was sitting on the floor near the door. She was weeping. I got up to go to her, but the woman held up a hand to ward me off. I reached out to Hanna but she shook her head and buried her face in her hands. I stood looking down at her but no words came to me – words were too far away – and I returned to the fire, dismayed.

Later, sitting helplessly, I watched the woman wash Hanna's face at the well, as if to cleanse her of some sin, and then dress her, red-eyed and runny-nosed, in a white shift they'd found somewhere, and lead her off to a place in the field where they sat around her as dawn broke. I could do nothing. I circled them like an outcast and, disgusted with what I was seeing but having no words, the words too tremulous to form, I walked down to the sea.

As I stood on the shore, my anger rose in waves over the acid. Who the fuck were they to arrive with their phoney rituals of purification, their beatific smiles and their holy-Moses dancing? Who were they to lay their holier-than-thou trip on my poor innocent Hanna, high on acid and so vulnerable? Who were they to assume that she needed cleansing, who the fuck were they to use her as a toy in their childish games? I wanted to go back, to beat them like philistines out of the temple, but I couldn't do that. Hanna was out in the stratosphere, in a dangerous place. She was under their spell and who knew how she would view me if I intervened? I would sit by the sea, and wait for them to go.

With acid, the passage of time is unreal, if there is time at all. When I returned an aeon later, I skirted the house and saw Hanna sitting on the step of the wide open doors with Aoife. The others were gone. When she saw me, she looked away and held Aoife closer as if to protect her, and I wasn't sure if I should approach her yet. I stood in view, about thirty feet away, looking out at the sea. The acid was still there but now it was only a ghost of itself, there one minute and gone the next, fading. I knew it'd be the same for her. I went closer, and then stood beside her. She looked up at me, biting her lip, her eyes full of tears. 'I'm sorry,' she said, but there was nothing to forgive. She'd fallen under the spell of game-players and charlatans; in acid, we are infinitely suggestible. Later, when we talked about it, she said she had seen me as a dark force, imprisoned in my mind, unable to let go.

For me, there was a whole difference between letting go and joining the rituals of a self-appointed priestess, a would-be wizard from south London and a couple of acid tourists seeking Enlightenment-on-Five-Bucks-a-Day. My view was: avoid false gods if you want to find the real one. Brought up a Catholic, I'd seen the smoke and candles before. I didn't say this to Hanna, though – she felt bad enough already. We were fine again before long. Our unwanted visitors had divided us only because we were very different anyway. We didn't hold it against them and, indeed, often met them again.

I record the happenings of that night only because they relate to Hanna's insecurity, for which I was partly to blame. The game-playing and mock-magic was symptomatic of the time. Behind drugs, the sincere were easily led: they thought Nirvana was to be found via the right guru and the journey to the East where you could buy enlightenment, like dope, off the shelf.

Hanna and I had in common the desire to live in an awareness of nature, and to love and care for the world and for one another. It was a simple enough dream. Together we watched dawns and sunsets, the pinewoods of the Barbary Cape churning in the wind, the waves lapping on its shores, birds in flight, the mosquito larva in the bowl. We swam in the sea, and I read her poetry. Sometimes, we smoked grass before we made love. We lost ourselves amongst the stars at night, lying on the roof, Aoife indoors, sleeping. We could ride with the moon and understand why our ancestors worshipped the sun. The contours of a stone, the colour of earth – we were intrigued by these things. Some people drank and deadened their senses, made gross their instincts, fuelled aggression and ugliness, lost control of their minds. We sought only peace, beauty, love for one another and for everything. Yes, we were romantics; we were all romantics. But love is a sustaining creed.

Came the Italians to Formentera, Paulo and Gianluca, the Renaissance men, speaking four languages or more, conversant with all European literature and thought. I was deeply impressed. Gianluca looked like a Velázquez Jesus Christ, thin as a rake, with intense eyes, dark skin and curly, shoulder-length, black hair. Paulo was the opposite, a slightly pink Italian, with bottle-end glasses, thinning hair and a modest moustache. Gianluca knew a lot about everything and was somewhat arrogant in his knowledge; he'd sit down, start talking and expect the company to gather like disciples around him. I listened for a while but preferred to hang out with Paulo. We had been friends in Ibiza; in contrast with his companion, he was a quiet, unassuming man. I loved talking to Paulo: he, like me, was trying to write poetry and he could tell me about Dante and d'Annunzio, the Provençal troubadours and the German poets Schiller and Rilke. One day, at the Casas Baratas, we sat on rocks and he took a slim book from his jacket pocket and read some of d'Annunzio's poems and translated them for me.

Paulo drowned in a bath tub in Ladbroke Grove in London the following year because he was half-stoned and fell asleep. The flame on the Ascot water heater somehow blew out and the gas leaked and he succumbed slowly and peacefully, I guess, sliding beneath the warm water and back, perhaps, to the womb.

We sat outside on a couple of logs at C'an Pujolet the evening they first came to Formentera, I remember, and there was a small fire. We had a smidgen of grass but no skins and would have had to walk three miles to the Fonda Pepe to buy some. On the spot, I invented a potato pipe by boring a slim spud down the middle with a broken scissors blade and putting a bit of foil from a fag packet, perforated with a pin, on top. It was a cool smoke, like a chillum. However, afterwards, you couldn't eat the spud.

Aoife was wandering around, and sitting under the fig tree. To give Hanna a break, I took her indoors when the time came, bathed her in the plastic bowl and put her to bed. I made up a story to tell her and she went to sleep quickly, and I rejoined the company outside.

Bruno and Desiree arrived with a bottle of farmhouse wine and passed it around. Bruno, waving the bottle, said something like, 'My friends, my ambition is to attain Nirvana and then snuff out like a mosquito in a *pissoir*. There he is and – zap! – there he isn't, floating on piss to the enormous sea . . .' His eyes widened, and he laughed at us. Desiree's arms and legs were so long and her clothes so tight, she looked like a stick-insect towering over Bruno.

At dusk, lamps began to glimmer in distant farmhouses and the velvet night came down. Bill Hesse was there that evening, quiet and unassuming in the rap and the laughter, a gentle American who'd been on Formentera for a year, living alone, parsimoniously, making his money stretch. He had legal residency in Copenhagen, where he worked in the Blue Note jazz club. We talked a lot together. His mission in life was to achieve enlightenment but he felt he was failing in it. He was missing his Danish girlfriend, the Blue Note and the cutting edge of music, but it was a trial to be endured. He didn't smoke dope but had taken acid. As he put it, he had seen The Man, he had seen the light. I believed him; in his eyes, whether they shone bright with eagerness or were dimmed in humility, the light was always there.

Bill lived below us in a house towards Punta de l'Aguila, a single-room house surrounded by stone walls and rocky fields. He had a fire and a primus stove, and cooked regular meals, although he didn't eat much. He was very thin, usually wore black and had a dark, trimmed beard. On some mornings, he would stand balls-naked outside his house and blow his saxophone to the sea. If the wind was blowing from that direction, we'd hear snatches of riffs and numbers, surreal sounds in the silence of Formentera.

Bill lived for music. When I came back from London and told him I'd bought Coltrane's *A Love Supreme* for Dieter, he got up next day at dawn and crossed on the boat to Ibiza to hear it at the Domino Bar. He passed by our house that evening, to tell me about it. There were almost tears in his eyes as he hummed Coltrane's words like a mantra, '*A love supreme, a love supreme . . .*' It got into my head and I found myself humming it too.

'Love' was a word much used amongst the free spirits on Formentera. While I had no problem expressing my love for those whom I held dear, I found it impossible to tell people I hardly knew that I loved them. But others had no such problem. It was an ideal they aspired to, and who was I to criticise?

The night the Italians came to C'an Pujolet, a Swedish guy, whom nobody knew, showed up with a lean dog. He sat against the house wall in the shadows, with the dog across his lap, stroking its ears and saying nothing. Later, when everybody was leaving, he asked if he could stay and we said yes and gave him a sleeping bag. Some hours later, I woke up to find him, fully dressed and with his boots on, climbing in between me and Hanna. This was 'love' gone a little too far. I told him to go and sleep elsewhere. There were no hard feelings. In the morning, we found him crashed out on the floor in the front room with the dog on top of him.

Col and Kilian came over from Ibiza, and we spent a whole day on the windswept, sun-scorched Mola looking down off the cliffs and watching an Elanora's falcon we'd spotted stooping on small birds migrating to Africa. Next morning, after taking them to the boat, I was walking home when I heard the screams of a pig from a farmhouse I was passing, and then other pigs starting to scream too, farther and farther away, in every direction. Five minutes later, the screams abruptly stopped.

In San Francisco Xavier, I met Longini hefting a sack of *pimento* into his jeep with the help of a boy. He was driving my way, and I took a lift from him. The *pimento*, made from local peppers, was for his neighbours. They'd killed a pig and would be making *sobrasada* sausage; it was the traditional *sobrasada*-making day, a fiesta for everybody but the pig. I went with him to the house where a dozen locals were assembled, the men dressed up, wearing their best berets, the women in their long dresses and sombreros.

One of the little black pigs they raised on the island lay dead on a white sheet in the yard. It had been de-haired with a blow-torch and the butcher was carving the carcass into cuts. A machine like the old hand-turned man-gold-choppers I'd seen in Irish farmyards stood nearby: it turned out to be a meat-mincing machine. Longini and I talked with the locals, drank wine and watched pieces of meat being fed into the maw while the boy turned the handle. Ground meat fell into a wooden trough. Women cast scoops of pimentón and herbs on top and, arms red to the elbows, mixed the lot with their hands. The mix was then spooned into the pig's intestines and the ends tied with string. When his job was done, the butcher packed his knives into a scabbard and secured them on the back of his little *moto* before taking off to kill another pig; he was over from Ibiza for the day. I wondered if the pigs, upon hearing the first one scream, knew it would soon be their turn. Maybe it was pig-telepathy. I loved homemade *sobrasada* yet couldn't but feel sorry for the pigs.

At about that time 'The Sheila', as she called herself – Suzy, the Australian love-priestess – mentioned that she had a brother who'd left a VW camper van parked up in Barcelona. Maybe that was where my troubles began; however, in truth, I was getting restless as the days passed uneventfully and my boot heels were '*ready to go wandering*', as Bob Dylan's song put it the following year.

When I heard of the van, I thought what a fine thing it would be for me and Hanna to go wandering together, maybe to the green Rif mountains of Morocco and sojourn there a while, or even to cross Europe as we had conceived to do back in our the Earls Court bed-sit, albeit in a gypsy caravan. So when the guy came across from Ibiza, I asked him what he was doing with the wagon and he said he didn't have a lot more use for it because he was shortly going to London. I told him all about my Triumph Roadster and how it had English plates and would be a fine, stylish car for him in Kangaroo Valley, where VW vans for sale stood in lines in the street – clapped-out wagons that the Antipodeans had used to tour Europe before spending their year in the Old Country being temp secretaries or pulling teeth before going home to a middle-class life Down Under. He liked the idea of the Roadster and we exchanged a set of keys and papers, the latter being dodgy in both cases; my car wasn't registered in my name, or the VW van in his. I gave him a letter for the guy who was minding my car, telling him to release it. If he didn't like it when he saw it, he could put the keys and papers in an envelope and leave them for me at *Lista de Correos*, Barcelona. If he liked it, he could leave the papers of his wagon there instead.

I got a postcard from him a week later saying we had a deal. Just a few days after that, Jacey came over to the house, with Carlo, who had now returned to Formentera, bringing Nicole. Hanna and Nicole, both Londoners, got on well; Nicole assuming a sort of 'daughter' role to Hanna's 'mother' role in the hierarchy. Maybe Hanna would hear about Fran but I didn't think so; she wouldn't have wanted to know.

Jacey said that he'd come up with a bright idea. Carlo had told him about my friend, Mike Darby's, dope trip to Turkey, how cheap and good the dope was there. Dope was regularly in short supply in Formentera so, now that I had a VW camper, why didn't he, Carlo and I drive to Turkey and score a few kilos? Everybody would chip in, either before we went or when we came back. We'd cover the dope cost and the expenses, no more than that; there'd be no selling and no profit. The three of us would have an adventure and we'd come back with hash enough for everyone in Formentera and stories to tell. We'd sit around the fires and talk of the nomad nation and how we'd bring up our children like the natives in *Coming of Age in Samoa*, wandering free, away from materialism and illusion, in places where conch shells would be the currency and we would be another race.

Carlo would leave Nicole on the island, I would leave Hanna, and Jacey would leave Lorna. Then, at the last minute, Jacey said his money from America hadn't come through and that he couldn't leave but that he'd send Carlo money care of AmEx, Istanbul, to cover our trip home. So, one morning Carlo and I crossed to Barcelona, just the two of us, picked up the van, and with no thought that we were heading into a bitter Turkish winter, set off.

Turkey in Winter

Chapter 11

THE VAN HAD A BULLET-HOLE in the windscreen, down low. The wind whistled through it, until Carlo blocked it with chewing gum.

A home-made camper, the interior was plywood-lined inside and the small windows were covered with fussy little gingham curtains. There was a fold-down table and a bench seat that converted into a bed going back to the rear window, which opened up, but no sink, no amenities except a gas stove. The single light on the roof was dim and made the inside look dingy at night, but candles would light it and warm it up. It had begun life as a commercial vehicle so there was a bulkhead behind the front seat, and the only way to get from the cab into the back was to either climb over it or haul yourself outside and enter via the side doors. It was 1952 vintage, with a split windscreen, double cargo doors in the side – a sliding door came with later models – and, as we were soon to discover, an underpowered 1100cc engine that made passing long trucks a nail-biting experience. At night, the six-volt battery added to the excitement; the headlights were little better than bicycle lamps, so there was a lot of guesswork on roads where there weren't white lines, or where trucks came at one lit up like Chinese festivals. It turned out that we met a lot of these. Otherwise, the old wagon seemed sound.

Carlo got in, turned the key and she started. We threw in our bedrolls and were on our way. We had a map, but had no idea of the journey ahead. Before leaving, I'd paid up-front rent for C'an Pujolet and left every *centimo* I had –

except for travelling expenses and money to buy dope – with Hanna. Carlo had left almost all he had, which wasn't a whole lot, with Nicole. He planned to do a scam on the way, using an old passport. In the used-furniture business, Jim Lowery regularly came across out-of-date passports in houses he was clearing, and had given Carlo a couple. We also had the pretty pistol, which we figured we could trade. We'd buy whatever dope we could afford, and Jacey's money would cover our trip home.

We came out of Spain through La Junquera with what cash we had in our pockets, the scamming passport and the gun stashed in the panels; we had no ammunition for it and wouldn't have carried it if we had. We turned right at Narbonne, crossed the south of France along the famous coast road above the Riviera, and passed through Monaco, just north of Monte Carlo. It was night and, but for lights glittering in the villages below the viaducts that soared from hill to hill and some lights on the sea, we saw little.

Then we were in Italy, changing a few bucks for Italian lira and being given banknotes half the size of newspapers, stopping at a pizza stall on the roadside near Milan and then driving into town to see La Scala but – bad timing – the opera was over and the place was shutting up. It was raining; it rained all the way across Norhtern Italy until we reached Venice, where we were mind-blown by the immensity of blue sky above the Piazza San Marco and how the square somehow contained it, like a roof. Then, the church itself, the porticos and entrance all painted by Michelangelo, and only four continents shown on the ceiling because only four were then known. I fell in love with Venice. I thought of living there, with Hanna, in that eternal city subsiding into the lagoons; there were no conservation agendas in 1964.

The pigeons in Saint Mark's flew over us with a rush of air and we smoked a joint sitting on a bench, jaw-dropped in wonder. Here was man-made beauty, of a style we had never before seen.

We pushed onward to Trieste to do a scam and get Carlo some bread. Trieste was an austere and secular city of grey rococo and Gothic buildings without much fun in it, we thought. The old Lowery passport was British as it happened. I got to work with my pens and erasers in the back of the van and, an hour later, acting as pro tem British Honorary Consul in Mr. Joyce's Trieste, I issued Carlo with a passport, lately renewed. He went and bought three hundred bucks' worth of AmEx travellers cheques.

We drove through Ljubljana in Yugoslavia as darkness fell and, in the dark, through Zagreb and, two hundred miles farther on, Belgrade, where women in headscarves and rubber boots were sweeping snow off the broad boulevards under the street lights. Belgrade felt like a Soviet city, grey, closed and cold.

At dawn, we came out of the night-long tunnel of potholed roads with unlighted horse-drawn carts the size of trucks, into the bright sun of Serbia where, at Niš, in the south, we hit a Sunday market with men in baggy Turkish pants and women with bright bandanas and rings in their ears. They were either Muslims or gypsies; we were in Asia Minor and Sunday was a business day. Another race roamed among the stalls of live chickens and geese, rabbits in cages, fruit and haberdashery, a grey race, quite different, presumably Serbians, who are Slavs. We were intrigued by the jewellery of the market women: the bracelets and headdresses, the brilliant colours of their clothes. I could almost smell the exotic East and, indeed, as southward we went across Kosovo and into Macedonia, more and more did we see of these gypsy-like Eastern people, the women walking with bundles on their heads on wide plains under a blue sky. We stopped at the extraordinary town of Titov Veles – where, again, I wanted to live some day in one of the houses perched over a deep gorge with the river running blue and white far below, houses built into the cliffside, like apartment blocks, with bay windows and wooden decks hanging out over the abyss. Here, the people were even darker, more Eastern-looking. And then we were at the border with Greece.

We came into Greece at night; the Customs post was bleak and bare and in the cold office where we presented out passports was sitting a black American who had been there for three days, he told us, because they thought the papers for his shiny Merc, parked outside, were not legitimate, and they'd taken the keys. If his colleagues in Germany for whom he was driving the car didn't come up with better papers, he was going to jail. The Customs guards hadn't bothered to manacle him or lock him up because there was no way out of there. He was sleeping in the car. We gave him some smokes and ten bucks in dinar, and said we hoped he wouldn't still be there on our way back.

Saloniki was a bustling bazaar of a city. Down by the port, in a narrow street of cafés, cheap shops and money-exchanges, we found the dingy office of the travel agent who acted as the local rep. for American Express. Carlo presented him with the receipt for the cheques he'd bought in Trieste and had, somehow, 'lost'. The agent barely glanced at the British passport into which I had so painstakingly inscribed fair copies of the border stamps we had acquired on the journey, and paid up without demur. Since he had the passport, Carlo would have no problem offloading both the replacement cheques and the originals – but we knew we should then leave Greece without delay. When he came to cash the first cheque, the guy asked us where we were going and we said to Turkey and he said he could give us a good rate in Turkish lira if we cared. Greece was at war with Turkey over Cyprus, and Greek banks wouldn't exchange Turkish lira for drachma or any other currency. We did, indeed, get a good rate, twelve lira to the dollar in the street in Saloniki, rather than ten in the street in Istanbul. An old guy told us that Saloniki had been all Jewish and full of business before World War II, but the Nazis had cleared out the Jews, and only he and a few others had survived to return.

As soon as we had our money, we left town, burning the British passport in a pine grove. We had wanted to visit the island of Mykonos, where we'd heard there was a small foreign scene. We were up for meeting new people; for myself, I hoped that sometime I'd meet a woman and fall in love as I had with Nancy. When I thought of Hanna, I felt a sense of caring, of concern for her, but of frustration too. I was not free. We had been together for three years; she was in love with me as I had been in love with Nancy, and there was nothing I could do to change that. I sometimes wished she'd meet someone who would make her happy, which I couldn't. She would go of her own volition, and I would support Aoife and remain close to them both.

In the event, Carlo and I gave Mykonos a miss. We were out of sync with the seasons. The Aegean Sea would have been stormy and the Aegean islands as cold, or maybe colder, than Ibiza and Formentera at that time of the year. There would be no sun-browned, sun-blest girls cavorting on the beaches in bikinis, no sitting around beach fires and smoking dope – if there was a dope scene there at all.

And so we passed by on the high road to Turkey, through Kavala and Komotoní, sleeping in the van which we'd drive into fields or forests when tiredness overcame us. We had a small pouch of kief hidden away, and Centramina pills, if we wanted to stay awake. We talked as we went, and lived in a world of our own, counting down the miles. About three hundred miles after Saloniki, we passed through Alexandropolous and crossed the border into Turkey at Edirne. I still have the passport, and the border stamp, with date and place. Carlo could no doubt find the same stamp in his if he still has it; he wasn't one to keep souvenirs. His passport was so crowded with visas from Morocco and his road trip to India that the US Embassy had to add extra pages. It opened like a concertina, full of exotic stamps. It was the best passport I'd ever seen.

In Istanbul, we found a one-star hotel in Underground Cistern Street, the Gulhane Palace, near the Blue Mosque. Istanbul was a dreary city in November. Men stood bundled in overcoats and flat caps, dangling their fishing rods over the Galatea Bridge; every café was full of steaming refugees from the cold outside. They sipped their tiny coffees and ate their honey-dripping baklavas, and the huge, overloaded ferries crossed and recrossed the Golden Horn, the Bosporus, the Sea of Marmara, constantly.

The city swarmed with steaming humanity, wrapped against the chill. Huge taxis, packed to bursting with passengers, plied the streets, honking and swerving between the foot-porters who spent their medieval lives bent double as they carried towers of huge cauldrons, bed frames and woolpacks as big as wardrobes on their backs, or pulled carts with rubber tyres loaded with scrap-iron, or sold tea and water from tanks carried on their shoulders. The Grand Bazaar and the Jewellery Bazaar were noisy with cries of vendors and the hammering of coppersmiths, and smoky with the fires of smiths and welders, and the Spice Bazaar was aromatic with the multicoloured mountains of cardamom and turmeric and chilli on the vendors' stalls. There were dried bats and snakes and live leeches in jars of water at the medicine shops, and it was all mind-blowing, especially after a joint.

Hustlers and money-changers got to know us quickly and didn't bother us, and it was only the youngest and most naive of shoe-shine boys who offered to shine our unshinable shoes, for the older men knew we weren't like the guided, gilded tourists who came in summer. We were another kind of foreigner, more like them.

We went to the Blue Mosque and the Aya Sofia; we gazed in open-mouthed wonder at the tiled interiors, the great vaulting domes, the huge spaces where the faithful, in ranks, prostrated themselves to pray. We saw them take off their shoes and do their ablutions in the freezing water at the small fountains and taps before entering. Afterwards, we watched them emerge from the mosques in their hundreds, men hand in hand. We sat in the warmth of the Blue Mosque Café and steamed alongside them, and there we met the first foreigner we had encountered since the lone Afro-American on the Greek border, a Chilean called Tola, a slim young man with lank black hair who wore a black, tailored overcoat and who had been in the city for some months. He had dreams of Kos and Mykonos, as we had, but he was embroiled with Turkey, and a Turkish girl. He bought some dope for us, and we smoked together.

Then one night, out of the blue, two uniformed cops with greatcoats and bristling moustaches suddenly came through the door of the café and Tola jumped up and ran for the yard at the back with them charging after him through the tables, one of them pulling a gun. We heard shouting outside and then a muffled gunshot. We sat frozen, like everybody else. A minute later, they dragged him back through the café. There was no visible wound but he was as pale as death. His eyes met ours as he passed; his glance told us not to get involved. The cops threw him into a police van and sped off. We asked the owner did he know where Tola lived; we thought we might find an address and inform his family in Valparaiso. But the owner was uncommunicative. We never saw Tola again.

He had told us we could maybe sell the gun to a taxi driver at the Hilton Hotel, or exchange it for hash. He said they could deal in kilos but that the hashish might not be as good as we could get farther south, near the hemp fields; this was what Mike Darby, back in London, had told me too. Mike had said Gaziantep was the place he'd scored, but we thought we might as well try the taxi drivers first; it might save the long journey south. In Istanbul, the pavements were white, and snow fell every day.

We went to the Hilton. Carlo carried the gun. What with his dark shades, dark moustache, unshaven jowls and earring, he looked like a bandit or a Turk. I did the talking, as always. I approached a driver and said the magic words 'hash-hash' and 'gun', in English; he understood both. He nodded to his car, a big, broad American job. As we walked towards it, he nodded to other drivers who were watching us, their elbows sticking out of the windows of their cabs; in Turkey, there were always eyes. We climbed in the back seat, as he indicated; he and two mates got into the front.

'Gun?' he said, turning to us.

'Yep,' I said. 'Gun.'

His friends turned to view us, and we viewed them back. Carlo and I exchanged a glance; they seemed friendly enough men – one had gold teeth, another with a small scar – and I said to Carlo, 'OK, show them the gun.'

Carlo hauled it out and held it, shining, in his lap. I took it and broke the breech. I was demonstrating the spinning cylinder, with its six chambers, when our host said, 'Stop!' I stopped.

'Gun . . .' he said and reached for his inside pocket – and his friends, as if in a Damon Runyon chorus line, both did the same, pulling out pistols one third the length of my arm. 'Gun!' he said again, holding his piece in my direction, 'Your gun, no good.'

'It's good,' I told him. 'Look, it will take bullets – bang-bang-bang, it shoots you dead!'

'No,' he said, shaking his head ruefully, and then he told me, in fatherly English and German, that my gun was a danger to myself, that I should throw it in the Bosporus. In a gun battle, you must first knock your opponent down, he said; when he is down, you can kill him at leisure; he is no longer a danger to you. With the pretty pistol, except I hit him between the eyes (he used his thumb to mark my forehead) or in the heart (he patted my breast), he would keep coming and, if he had a gun like his and hit me anywhere whatsoever, I would be knocked on my ass and before I could get up he would deliver the *coup de grâce*. Dangerous gun, he said, and I shrugged and told Carlo to put it away.

Then, we turned to other business. How much was hash-hash a kilo? I asked him. He told me the price. It was twice what we wanted to pay, so we took it no further, shook hands with all three and left the car. He reminded me of what he'd told me about the gun. In the real world, our point 22 was no better than a decorative peashooter. Actually, I was sort of glad of that.

We determined to go south in search of dope, to seek the source, to buy at the price Mike had told me about in London. In Gaziantep, he'd scored half a kilo for thirty-two bucks – eleven quid. We set off that night – clock time didn't mean much to us – driving across the Ataturk Bridge on the Golden Horn and, with a moon like a peach hanging low over the Bosporus, proceeded to another bridge where we crossed to Üsküdar and entered Asia. I had never been in Asia before.

Chapter 12

FROM ÜSKÜDAR, WE DROVE DUE south across the Anatolian plateau, with snowfields and mountains in the distance, heading for 'Antep. We hoped we'd get lucky there. Mike had given us no contacts. He had bought his dope and gone, making no liaisons. The journey was twelve hundred kilometres; it would take us from the Black Sea coast to the shores of the Mediterranean and beyond. When Carlo was driving, I studied a little Turkish phrase book. I learned to count and to say 'Yes', 'No', 'I want', 'How much?' and 'Too much!' We thought we should start asking about buying dope as we went. The towns we passed were bleak places. In spring or summer maybe these high plains, these vast distances, were beautiful, but in November, coming on December, they were drab.

We stopped in towns. We sat in cafés, smoking cigarettes and drinking tea, playing 'spot the dealer' or at least 'spot the smoker' – only it wasn't a game. It took balls to approach someone in that alien world where we knew little of the language and nothing of the customs – or whether they'd cut our throats or rob us or take us to the police. But balls we had in plenty, even if we didn't have a lot of sense.

We were driven out of more than one village with angry shouts. As we backed towards the van, we tried to pretend we hadn't really said '*Istiyorum hash-hash*' but '*Istiyorum ekmek*', and that we were only trying to buy bread. But the villagers were so freaked out, they didn't listen. The men shouted and the head-scarved women shooed us away. The Turks are hospitable people and in a couple of other villages they acted as if they hadn't heard us right and, indeed, brought us slabs of bread and bowls of honey. Maybe they wanted to assuage us, or maybe they thought we were crazy – as indeed we were – and needed humouring. '*Youk, youk!*' they said, when we mentioned hash-hash, tossing back their heads and clicking their tongues against their palates, making tssk-tssk, admonitory sounds.

Everywhere we went, our enquiries met with the same *youk, youk*, like a Turkish joke, while we were convinced there was hashish all around us. It was no joke, however. The men in those piss-poor, mud-house villages on the Anatolian plain were seized with consternation and held their wrists together signifying handcuffs and cried '*Besh yil, besh yil!*' meaning five years in jail, warning us, with near panic in their faces, before sending us away. Five years. We didn't even think about it; we weren't going to get busted, Carlo and me. We didn't think about Turkish prisons – the movie, *Midnight Express*, which showed the horrors and brutality of the prisons, wasn't made until years later. Meanwhile, the Turks we approached treated us as miscreants or idiots, and wanted shut of us, ASAP.

When we drove out of the villages, sometimes gangs of men and youths half-blocked the road. Tola had told us that villagers would fill a bag with sheep's blood and throw it at the front of your wagon and then phone the cops in the next town and tell them you'd killed one of their sheep. The cops would stop you and escort you back to the village where the farmers would produce a dead sheep and the cops would make you pay the owner compensation – plus slip them plenty baksheesh. It was a fuckin' lynch mob, and the cops would protect you only if they got paid.

The hole in the windscreen let in a pinpoint draught when the chewing gum Carlo had sealed it with fell out. The hole seemed ominous. The Sheila's brother had said it had happened in Yugoslavia as he drove; a gunshot, almost certainly. He hadn't seen anyone fire at him; it might just have been a missed shot or a ricochet from hunters. We wondered if, in the wild country we were passing through, there might be loons who'd take a pot-shot at us just for the hell.

Four hundred kilometres south of Istanbul, we passed through the town of Afyon. 'Afyon' means opium, and the best opium was produced in that province. But we weren't into scoring opium. Opium was heavy karma, next worst thing to smack. We decided we'd give up trying the villages and wait until Gaziantep, where Mike had scored, eight hundred kilometres farther south.

Sometimes we slept in the wagon but it was cold – and colder than a warlock's bollocks in the middle of the night if you had to go outside to take a leak in the snow. So we paid for hotel rooms; they cost pennies.

We'd eat at roadside truck stops; the only other vehicles on the road were trucks and long-distance buses. The counters displayed open trays of mouthwatering roasted peppers, tomatoes, aubergines, mutton and goat stews, glistening sheep's hearts, and cauldrons of yogurt and thick vegetable soups. And there was always chai or thick, sweet Turkish coffee, with fine grounds filling half the little glass. We often pulled up outside these places in the deep of night and walked in and the men – never a woman – looked up at us from their beat-up car seats ranged around the braziers made of tar barrels with the tops cut off and welded back in a foot or two lower down, the space above them filled with earth and pebbles, with the stove pipe chimneys poking through them and through the roof above. You could take a handful of warm pebbles in your pocket when you left. Sometimes, we'd sleep in the van parked outside. We'd eat early breakfasts and head on at dawn, through the frozen fog.

We drove through Konya, a big city, and through Adana, near the Mediterranean coast, without stopping. The road east to 'Antep passed within twenty kilometres of the sea; why we didn't go there and warm our asses on the beaches in the winter sun, I do not know. Later, we passed the underground cities of Cappadocia and never stopped to regard them – dumb, hell-driven dopesters as we were! Letting neither beauty, nor blizzards nor long-gone history deflect us, we plugged on. There was no radio in the truck and while one of us sometimes whistled a tune as he drove or thumped the steering wheel to a rhythm in his head, we did not go in for Boy Scout sing-alongs but sang stuff like '*I don't care if it rains or freezes, I'm OK with my plastic Jesus, Ridin' on the dashboard of my car . . .*'

We had no camera and never thought of buying one. The journey was a moving picture, a constant stream of impressions and images, too vivid and fast to capture. To stop and take photos would have atrophied the flow, like trying to photograph poetry in motion. Capturing the moment was not our thing.

We recited poetry in motion, though, Carlo and me. One balls-freezing dusk we stopped for a leak in a copse of snow-bedecked pines and Carlo suddenly said, out of nowhere, '*Whose woods these are I think I know . . .*' I saw him grinning to himself, and said '*His house is in the village though . . .*' which is the next line of the poem, and we both laughed and recited the whole four verses of 'Stopping by Woods on a Snowy Evening' as we watched our piss stain the snow in that lonely Turkish wood where the only sound was '*the sweep Of easy wind and downy flake*'.

Carlo told me that 'Stopping by Woods . . .' was the only poem he's ever learnt, apart from 'The Song of Hiawatha', and when we climbed back into the wagon and started moving off we repeated '*The woods are lovely, dark and deep, But I have promises to keep, And miles to go before I sleep, And miles to go before I sleep . . .*' and then got into a rap about how Robert Frost moved on with his little horse because he – as a human, a Master-of-the Universe – figured he had promises to keep to himself and to the world. The horse and the woods and the snow had no such hang-ups. They were serene and part of nature. The human being, alone, had ego and aspirations and was out of sync with the natural world.

I said to Carlo that he, being a Buddhist, might agree more with the horse or, indeed, with a poet called W. H. Davies, who spent years living the hobo life, riding freight cars across North America and didn't, it seemed, give a flying fuck about promises. He wrote: '*What is this life if, full of care We have no time to stand and stare? No time to stand beneath the boughs And stare as long as sheep and cows.*'

Carlo liked that poem. Yeah, I agreed, it expressed a whole lot better attitude than the character in T. S. Eliot's 'The Love Song of J. Alfred Prufrock' who said '*I have measured out my life with coffee spoons*'.

'What turned you on to poetry?' Carlo asked. I thought it was probably my father's songs, *Moore's Melodies*, and so on, which he'd sing as he drove us home from the seaside on summer Sundays. My father could recite too –

'Dangerous Dan McGrew' and 'The Green Eye of the Little Yellow God'. Poems were music; they stayed in your head like a song and sometimes expressed your thoughts better than you could express them yourself. For instance, a poem I'd learned in school about Ulysses, the Greek hero and wanderer – his trip was '*to follow knowledge like a sinking star, Beyond the utmost bound of human thought . . .*' That's what we were doing in Formentera, I thought, with the acid and all. Carlo agreed with me. He said he liked poetry too.

I told him what stories I knew about the poets, about Dylan Thomas, his heavy drinking and, yet, his perfect recollections of childhood in 'Fern Hill' – and about Wilfred Owen who wrote about the First World War – '*What passing-bells for these who die as cattle? Only the monstrous anger of the guns. Only the stuttering rifles' rapid rattle.*' He'd died himself, just before Armistice Day. 'It was carnage,' I said, 'Forget Vietnam, forget Stalingrad, imagine Flanders . . .!'

Poetry was one of the few things I'd liked when I was at school. Wordsworth had turned me on back then, and I'd since realised that some lines he'd written expressed exactly what I felt after the acid trip Hanna and I had taken in Ibiza – '*The earth, and every common sight To me did seem Apparell'd in celestial light, The glory and the freshness of a dream.*' He and his mates all did laudanum, and Coleridge was heavy into opium. It had also occurred to me that old Wordsworth, when lying on his couch in '*vacant or in pensive mood*' and seeing a host of golden daffodils, was probably stoned out of his head at the time. In school, we learned Irish poetry, too, I told Carlo, and there was nothing like Irish to echo the onomatopoeic clanging bells, as it did in a poem about the end of the Irish woods, cut down to build English warships, and the ruined churches, where the bells no longer tolled.

Carlo was highly impressed by my half-assed rendition of bowdlerised lines and misquoted verses, recalled from when I was teaching school-exam literature to kids in classy London drawing-rooms. Given the boredom of the whited-out landscape and snow hitting the windscreen hour after hour, he'd probably have listened to a sewing machine or a train shunting to relieve the tedium.

As I drove and rapped, he climbed into the back and started making coffee. We stopped and, as we sat side by side drinking coffee by candlelight, I demanded he gave me *Hiawatha* and, next thing, I had him chanting '*By the shores of Gitche Gumee, By the shining Big-Sea-Water*' and both of us stamped to the rhythm until we made the van shake. Poetry was music, and the man that hath not music in his soul is fit for treasons, stratagems and spoils! Never mind the meaning – poetry is like opera. You may not understand a fuckin' word of what the fat lady is singing, only that your heart is swelling like her chest!

We reached Gaziantep, and sat all day in steamy cafés where men with big moustaches, baggy trousers and flat caps ate cakes with small spoons and drank sweet coffee from tiny cups. I talked to a young guy, following him into the john, because we figured he looked stoned on something.

He apologised politely, '*Youk* hash-hash.'

'A smoke?' I asked him, holding up one finger.

'*Youk . . .*', he said. No smoke.

'Where hash-hash?' I asked, smiling like I was a pothead simply looking for some light relief.

He looked serious, put his finger to his lips, then waved it at me as a warning and left.

The second or third day in Gaziantep, we saw a couple of clean-cut Americans – they couldn't have been anything else, with their crew-cuts, half-mast pants and big shoes. They walked through the crowd like they knew the place and when we saw them stop at a stall, we caught up and said hello. They were with the Peace Corps, they said, working with the Turks on an Aid programme. We told them we were adventuring, driving east to India, stopping here and there on the road. To see how they'd react, I said that a strange thing had happened that morning – a guy had tried to sell us hashish. Don't take it, they said; it's five years in jail for possession of five grams, a year per gram. They were not longer smiling now, so I shrugged and said fuck drugs anyway and we'd better be on our way. 'Fuckin' CIA!', Carlo said, as soon as we left them. We decided it was better to get out of Gaziantep. We'd go farther east. The east was full of promise, as they say.

Beyond 'Antep, we descended from the mountains and followed a road that ran parallel to the Syrian border, and wondered if we might be able to score in Halep, a.k.a Aleppo. We turned south on a side road and reached the Syrian border after half an hour. Two soldiers emerged from a concrete hut with guns at the ready and told us to go back. We would have to use the main Gaziantep-Aleppo road to cross the frontier.

We decided to forget about Syria and continue east. That day we saw, off to our left, a string of Kuchi nomads moving across a stony desert between the flat road and the dry hills capped with snow. They drove herds of sheep and goats, and their belongings travelled on the backs of donkeys and camels, bundles as big as beds with tent poles sticking out at angles, like knitting needles in balls of wool. A few rode asses but mostly they walked; their flocks and dogs following at a distance. Many of the women wore black robes but the children were immensely colourful. There was a small group walking by the roadside, amongst them a young girl with a half-hobbled sheep in tow. She smiled up at us as we puttered past. She was wearing a woven jacket and bright ribbons in her hair; she shone in the morning sunlight. Although I saw her for only a second, her image as she turned, wild and beautiful, her black hair swinging in a pigtail behind her, is imprinted on my mind's eye still.

The sight of her got us to talking about Hanna and Nicole. 'But if you wanted to split, you shouldn't have had children,' Carlo said; he meant Aoife and the child we'd lost. He was right but, well, you live with a woman and it's good at times, and you make love – and contraception doesn't always work.

I was missing Hanna and he was missing Nicole, but Turkey in winter wasn't a place where you'd think much about sex. Tola had told us that in the caves at Matala, in Crete, there was a small scene of people like ourselves. We joked about going there and finding a couple of gorgeous hippy chicks waiting for us on the beach. However, we both knew that as soon as we'd done our business, we'd head for home. I wanted to see my kids for Christmas, to bring them presents from the East – frankincense and myrrh – and to lie in Hanna's warm embrace. I remembered the night I came home from London, the mosquito larva. It could be so right with her.

Carlo and I saw many accidents on the way. At one, a bus was overturned and bodies lay covered in white sheets on the slopes down which it had rolled.

169

We saw trucks broken down in the snow, with men sitting beside them around small fires. The old wagon kept going, plugging on through blizzards where the snow chased ahead of us on the road like sand devils on a beach and the wind howled and rocked us. Sometimes, I made the coffee as Carlo drove.

Once, in a snowstorm, we came upon a small car, a Deux Chevaux, broken down and half-buried in snow, with a figure in a long black overcoat standing beside it, waving us to stop. It was a young Frenchman and his Vietnamese wife, driving back to France from Lebanon. They climbed into the van and, with the wind buffeting us, we made coffee. They told us their headlights had cut out and they couldn't proceed in the dark. If they waited until dawn, they would certainly freeze to death. We set off again in convoy with us driving ahead, carving a path of light for them through the darkness and the flying snow, until we reached a truck stop, where we left them. And went on . . .

Chapter 13

WE GOT AS FAR EAST as Djarbakir, the wildest town we hit in the entire journey, near the borders of Iraq and Iran. Here, we learned, the people were Kurds. The men wore chequered cloths on their heads and some toted shotguns on their shoulders. One morning, a car passed through town with guys shooting guns out of the window. We wondered if it was a Kurdish drive-by or a marriage celebration. We saw no dope; we smelled no dope. We decided to head back the way we had come.

There was more ice than before on the mountain roads between Djarbakir and Gaziantep and it got hairy at times. Huge trucks would loom up on the hairpin bends and blind us with full heads and blast their klaxons so loud the sound waves would almost sweep us off the edge of the road and into oblivion. 'Fucking tourists!' – we could almost hear the shaggers laughing as they passed.

It was cold too. The heater didn't work too well and we drove wearing gloves and jackets. Once we saw, in the middle of nowhere, a shepherd standing with his back to the blizzard in a huge coat of stiff leather down to the ground, like a grey wall or a standing stone, making a windbreak for his twenty or thirty sheep that trailed away from him in the winding shelter of his wind-shadow.

So here we were, three weeks out of Formentera, and where the fuck was the dope? If we didn't score soon, we'd have no option but to head back to

Istanbul and score from the taxi drivers with the guns. We could've done that three thousand kilometres before but – what the hell! – we'd seen a whole lot of Turkey. We'd try for a bit longer. We were in a land of dope and sooner or later we'd score.

The next town was Adana, a big town. We had passed through there on the way to Gaziantep but hadn't stopped. We barrelled in there one morning about eleven o'clock. The town was a mess, with pools of melt-water in the street – at junctions it was deep enough for pigs to wallow in. The poor bastards between the shafts of the big flat carts loaded with bales of wire or tyres, or whatever, were up to their balls in sludge, with the kids who pushed from behind straining to get a run on before they hit the next wallow.

We parked up and decide to take a stroll. It was a cold, bright morning and the town was bustling; it might have been a Saturday, and the people were out shopping after the Muslim day of rest. Around the bazaar, the streets were packed with Turks, the guys all wearing overcoats and Battleship Potemkin caps. We were the only foreigners. We moved through the crowd, through a market with birds and chickens and ferrets in cages and even an unfortunate bear. We came to a café with chairs running along the outside wall, facing the sun. We bought *chais*, green teas, inside the café and went outside to find seats.

The clientele were all men; you only ever saw women in cafés in the business district in Istanbul. Some guys grunted dozily as we stood looking at them and they moved along to make room for us to sit down. The sun was so strong, we had to squint when we faced it. The guys around us sat with their little tea glasses in their hands, the saucers on the pavement between their feet. A kid came with biscuits. They looked dry and hard but were good, and we needed some sort of breakfast. After eating them, we lit cigarettes and sat, digging the scene. Across the street, a couple of heavy characters were sitting inside the window of a café with their caps on, watching us as they spooned baklavas under their moustaches, big hands and tiny spoons. They stared shamelessly at us two *gringos* in their midst and, every now and then exchanged a remark. Could they be fuzz? Who gave a fuck; we weren't carrying anyway.

And then, as I lean forward to put my cup down, I notice that a guy a couple of chairs down is shooting me a wide smile. I smile back; he looks more than just friendly. Carlo takes a gander to check him out. As we look, he takes a cigarette from an inside pocket. He's about forty, and wearing Western clothes, cheap and kind-of flashy. He lights the cigarette, a roll-up, inhales and blows the smoke in our direction. He smiles a big smile, like he's a clever fucker indeed. It's hashish, alright. He holds the joint out to me. Now, what am I to do? I dig the two cats in the window across the street; they're still watching us. They're either wound-up toys or they're spellbound because they're still doing the same thing, spoon to baklava, spoon to mouth, spoon to baklava. Are they the Secret Police?

It's the moment of truth; either I accept the jay or we blow the opportunity. What the fuck – if we ain't ready to take chances, we shouldn't be here. I glance at Carlo and he's not saying no, so I take it, and take a toke. I pass it to Carlo, who takes a hit, and I hand it back to the guy. So, we've confirmed our credentials. Now what? Half the street is suddenly watching. As if with bated breath.

The guy talks out of the side of his mouth; it's all like a B-movie. 'Hash-hash?' he whispers. 'OK,' I say, shrugging, playing it cool. He grins broadly, like he knew we were heads the minute he saw us, and makes some sort of gesture meaning swallow your tea and follow me.

And, so, we are off, into the bowels of the bazaar. He pauses only once: hash-hash, do we want? I tell him, yes – kilos. Cheap, cheap – but good, good. He nods and smiles.

For some reason, we're taken to a tailor's shop, where the tailor and his assistant, labouring under some misapprehension, attempt to measure me for a suit. I let him go ahead, looking at our new-found friend with curiosity, knowing that he knows, and I know, that I don't want a suit. The tailor has a mouthful of shiny, metallic teeth, which is mildly disconcerting when he looms up out of the shadows of his shop, smiling broadly. A baddy in some James Bond movie had steel teeth. The whole thing is like a movie from now on.

When he discovers we aren't there to be fitted for suits, the tailor doesn't seem too happy with our reprobate companion, who looks like an ageing *bon vivant* seriously under the weather. In fact, after the reprobate whispers in his ear, the tailor flips out and starts to shoo us all out of the shop. But he is pre-vailed upon and calms down, and we are invited to sit on the carpet in the tiny premises full of hanging suits and bolts of suit-cloth, and take tea, which is brought by a boy, as is the custom in outlets of suits or carpets or home-made artillery all the way from Istanbul to the Khyber Pass. We sit in the silence, smiling and nodding at each other, language-less. And then, another guy arrives, a kid of eighteen or nineteen, and says follow me; meanwhile, the reprobate has disappeared. The kid leads us through the alleyways; people stand aside as he leads us into places foreigners do not go.

We arrive at a hotel. It's a dump; we see women in the corridor in bras and slips. They smile at us as we follow the kid upstairs and we realise that the place probably doubles as a knocking shop. He opens the door of a room, indicates with a sweep of his hand that it's all ours, and leaves us.

The room is a flophouse classic. Paint is peeling off the walls and the only window is small and high up at the back. The light is a flyblown bulb hanging from the ceiling. The beds are narrow, with thin mattresses and stained cov-erlets and the bedside locker is scorched by cigarettes. The toilet down the hall is Turkish and malodorous, with a shower basin without a curtain and a small hand basin, cracked.

We lie on the beds, backs against the wall. We smoke cigarettes and wait. We talk for a minute about how brother Rick is probably baking his ass off in India, maybe in Pondicherry meeting Krishnamurti. Carlo says Pondicherry was nice – sea, sand and meditation – but he didn't meet the great philosopher. He mightn't have been enlightened enough, he thinks. He laughs. We're both sort of nervous, waiting.

(Recently, I met an English friend of mine, an upper-class old lag who'd served time for botched cannabis deals in many countries and had just come out of an open prison in the UK at age seventy two. I asked him why the hell he hadn't given up the business long ago. 'Because when it's happening, it's so exciting – it's like being in a movie,' he said.)

And so there we are, Carlo and me, lying on the beds in that dingy hotel room. There wasn't a lot to discuss: it was a case of sit back and await developments. We smoked fags. Carlo half-nodded off. And then we heard a light knock on the door, and there was the kid again, with another guy, about our age, whom he introduced as Cesar.

We all shook hands courteously. They sat on one bed, we sat on the other. Conversation drifted for a minute. Sign language – Turkey, thumbs up! Right-on! Good people. Yeah, cold! Shiver, shiver. You want hash-hash? Yeah. You got hash-hash? Yeah. How much, the hash-hash, how much the kilo? That much? That's too much, too fuckin' much! Hey, that's laughable. We can get it for less in Istanbul!

I'm doing the talking; Carlo is sitting there, behind his darkened-out glasses staying sthum. He looks like my back-up; the heavy who might pull a gun and blow everybody away. He smiles quietly, not unfriendly, just not too forthcoming. It's a movie, like I say.

We reach an impasse. The kid, with a nod from the boss, rolls a joint. It's as big as a beer bottle, and he puts half an ounce in. The dope looks good, and it sure smokes good. '*Güzel!*', they say. Yeah, '*chok güzel*' – real nice, but wrong price. No business. Oh, well. Time passes, the joint passes. Impasses.

My wallet is lying on the small table between the beds. I open it. There's a picture of Hanna and Aoife. My wife, I say, passing it to Cesar. Oh, yeah? He's taken aback but he politely pretends interest. You married? You got kids? I ask.

He shrugs and is silent. The boy grins. C'mon, he tells him, own up! Cesar sort of squirms so I pursue it, c'mon, how many kids you got? *Bir? Iki? Ewch? Durt?* The boy is grinning ever wider! *Besh, alti, y—?* Stop there and go back. Cesar confesses, 'OK, I've got five kids.' Wow! Carlo and I grin. Five kids, how many years have you? 'Twenty-five,' he says. 'Me too, now,' I say. 'One kid'?, he says. No, more. *Bir? Iki? Ewch? Durt?* Carlo now starts grinning. Stop there. Three; sorry, I got two less than you. We smile. Small women, good women, many children. The two mothers is too complicated to explain, Nancy in Ibiza, Hanna in Formentera. It doesn't matter anyhow. Some ice has been broken. We're both young dudes with families to support. He passes the joint to me without smoking himself; I pass it straight on to the boy. Do you have money? he asks, rubbing his thumb and finger together, the universal gesture. Yep: I flash the stash, or part of it. OK. He stands, he nods, let's go.

On the way out, I stop at the desk. Book us a room, I tell the clerk – I want our new-found friends to know that our presence in this town has been registered. All right, the clerk nods. But when I put my passport down on the desk, he pushes it back to me. '*Youk,*' he says. So if we disappear in Adana, no one will ever know we've ever been there.

Cesar and the kid led us to the van. They knew where it was parked. So much for being strangers in a Turkish town in the early 1960s. The minute we arrived, those with business interests were on our case.

They jumped in the van with us and we drove through a labyrinth of dark streets and alleyways, led by them. I had the wad of lira – five hundred bucks' worth – inside my shirt, under my sweater, inside my donkey-jacket coat. We parked and crossed the empty street to a small door, and ascended a narrow stairs. We emerged into a barn-like room on the first floor with a low ceiling, and some light coming from an L-shape at the near end. We turned into the L-shape and found a surreal candle-lit scene: an old man and a boy squatting beside a brazier made from a perforated oil drum. Behind them was a giant Technicolor cinema poster: Charlton Heston, driving a chariot across the wall, with a larger-than-life Kirk Douglas, as Spartacus, on the wall opposite.

They rose to greet us. The man wore baggy pants big enough for two. He had a broken nose and a gnarled face, one that had seen life in plenty. The kid was open-faced, too shy to meet our gaze, probably blushing if there'd been light enough to see it. Cesar bids us sit; there's a line of wooden chairs along the wall. We sit. He goes to a guy we haven't noticed. He's young, a soldier, dressed in military uniform that doesn't fit too well. Cesar says something to him and he takes out cigarette papers.

A guy arrives who looks like Cesar's older brother. He shakes our hands. Give him your car keys, Cesar signals. Huh? It's cool, he signals, relax. I give him the keys. We're in Cesar's hands; we gotta trust him. He and his brother leave.

I make some conversation with the old man in sign language. The weather, shiver-shiver, cold. Today, warm and clear – hand gestures towards the sky. He tries me in funny German; I learnt some German when Nancy was in hospital: I get the drift. You come from Amerika? *Nein, Irland. Irisch?*

Long way. He has a son in Australia. He shows me an envelope with an Australian stamp. The soldier passes the joint. Once again, it's as big as a Havana cigar. He's a conscript, I reckon, probably doing his national service, a clownish kind of character, laid-back and humorous, not a committed military man. It's wonderful the way one can crack jokes, with no language; I guess it confirms that there's a Family of Man. The Family of Man isn't always jokey or welcoming, of course – but here the vibe was good. We sat, getting more and more stoned – we had to continue to confirm our credentials – with the brazier going and Spartacus waving his sword and Ben Hur riding his chariot in this shrine to Hollywood in a barn in a back street in Turkey.

The *Tao Te Ching* says 'The Way is that there is no Way', and the only way for Carlo and me now was to have faith, have trust in our instincts, because these seemed like good people. Our fate, whatever it was to be, was already decided. We'd steer it as well as we could, but if things got heavy, there wouldn't be a thing we could do.

Now, as we sit sharing a joint with the soldier and the old man, other guys start to arrive. They're all young and they're either shy or shifty, arriving in twos and threes, and watching us out of the corners of their eyes. We nod to them, they nod back, an at-arms-length greeting. Great cinema posters! I say. Yeah, they agree. Cesar's brother makes like he has a movie camera in his hand. He pretends to film us and put our poster on the wall. They're proud of the posters, we can see; they think they're real cool – and, indeed, they are.

Carlo is maybe smiling a little too hard, as Americans often do with 'natives', but that's OK; there's nobody I'd prefer to have with me here, except maybe Rick; in fact, given Rick's propensity for paranoia, I'd prefer Carlo. I'm keeping my wits sharp about me, concentrating on winning hearts and minds. I fall into a rap with the old man. I'm telling him that in Gaziantep when we asked for hash they were terrified; I mime the handcuffs bit. Some of the kids laugh. The old guy shakes his head in disgust, like, Yeah, in 'Antep, they got no balls, not like here in Adana. Me and the old guy are getting on like a brazier on fire and maybe this is having the right effect on the onlookers. Carlo and me are big-time dope dealers, after all, nice guys but not to be fucked with!

By now, there's maybe ten or more newcomers standing around, listening, watching – enjoying the show. Cesar comes back, checks to see that we're cool and then sets off to the other end of the barn and up an open-tread staircase that disappears via a trapdoor into a room overhead. He's followed by every-one except us, the old man, the soldier and the boy. The trapdoor closes and we hear footsteps above us. Then we hear raised voices. The boy is saying something to the soldier but the old man tells him to shut up. They all listen intently. There's some sort of discussion going on. There's tension in the air.

For me, it's the feeling of being in a movie again: the eyes looking down at the brazier, then up at the ceiling, the glances exchanged, Spartacus in arrested animation. Then, whatever it is the old guy hears, he suddenly smiles to us and nods. It's cool, no worries; it's all been sorted. Next thing, the trap-door lifts and Cesar's brother is beckoning us upstairs.

Upstairs is a big room, with no ceiling, the rafters in shadow overhead. There are candles and a brazier going, and mattresses on either side of the bra-zier, some guys sitting on them, some standing around. We're beckoned to sit, and space is made for us. More tea. More guys show up. They look us over and hear the news about us, whatever it is. Ahmed, the guy we met outside the café, suddenly appears now, obviously out for the night, shaven, pink and powdered. He's an old queen. He carries a long cigarette holder and wears his coat draped theatrically over his shoulders. We greet each other like old friends. This bit of drama over, we sit again, taking the joint when it's passed, playing it cool as the Turks gossip all around us. Carlo and I hardly speak to each other at all; rapping in English may change the vibe, make them uneasy. All this is like walking on eggs. There's nothing to say anyway. We're both hip to the situation. Then, suddenly, the vibe changes.

We have our backs to the trapdoor and the stairs. The guys sitting on the mattress on the other side of the brazier look up; it's clear that somebody spe-cial has arrived. We turn to look. A guy is walking towards us out of the shad-ows: a well-dressed guy, about thirty, with a spivvy suit, a bootlace tie, a thin moustache and heavy-lidded eyes. He is flanked by a cohort of companions. He doesn't look friendly. He walks around us to the other side of the brazier. He takes a handkerchief from his pocket and spreads it on the mattress in the place that has been vacated for him. He steps forward and sits his ass down. It's a dramatic entrance.

A henchman whispers in his ear. He turns his head towards us, regards us and lowers his eyelids – that's the extent of his greeting. I think what the fuck is this asshole about? He comes to the point quickly, and I sort of like him for that. He does the rubbing finger-and-thumb gesture, have you money? I nod. He extends an open palm. Caesar is standing behind him. Our eyes meet. He nods to me. I lay the money in the guy's palm. He looks at it. He's like a fucking actor. For a beat, he's silent; then, he explodes. 'Turkish lira, Turkish lira, Turkish lira!', he bawls, holding it up to the assembly. He leans forward and waves it in my face. He's gone from nought to sixty in twenty seconds. '*Dolaresi, dolaresi, dolaresi?!*' he screams, followed by a jabber of Turkish, a declamation to the assembly. We get the drift, the fucker wants dollars. We ain't got dollars – but Turkish lira is bread!

Hey, I tell him, 'Lira *güzel*, lira good, for fuck's sake, this is Turkey, man!' He holds the wad of six thousand Turkish lira up and spits on it. He throws it on the brazier. Shit! What the fuck . . .! I look at Carlo. Carlo looks at me. The money sits on the brazier. The coals are dark, with red bits in between. The bottom note begins to singe, to go brown along the edges. It's all the bread we've got, but it's a poker game. If I pick up the money, I'll be putting it back in my pocket and, at best, we'll be on our way, dopeless in Adana, scoring at a rip-off rate in Istanbul. If I leave it where it is . . . well, it hasn't actually caught fire yet, and I don't think anyone is actually going to let five hundred dollars' worth of lira go up in smoke.

We sit: he sits. He stares at me. I look at him and shake my head like: What a dumb thing this is to do, but if you want to send my six thousand lira up in smoke, that's your prerogative. He sneers back. Then, at the last second, it all happens. Just as the edges of the bottom notes begin to flame, Cesar suddenly reaches in, across the flash cat's shoulder, and lifts out the wad. He blows on it, and hands it across to me. Take it, he says, keep it! I take it. It's hot and still smoking slightly.

Now, Cesar addresses the assembly. His voice is forceful. 'Lira' is a word he mentions often, 'lira' and 'dolaresi'; it isn't hard to figure out what he's saying. There are grunts of assent from the listeners. The spiv interjects, but nobody's listening. Dollars is wishful thinking; we have no dollars. Six thousand lira is six thousand lira. The spiv and his sidekicks are overruled.

He rises, in umbrage, and he and his cohort sweep off into the shadows, without even the grace to say goodbye. The Turks are a mannerly and hospitable people, but these are exceptions. Maybe they've been infected with the dollar fever, the American dream.

After they'd split, things settled down again. Half the people left. A joint was passed around. We were in no hurry. I was enjoying it. Carlo, beside me, seemed totally at peace and as bemused as I was. Now a couple of nervous-looking kids appear – they look like small-time street-hustlers – and start some *sotto voce* rap with Cesar's brother. He turns and says something to the old man, who gets up and leaves. A few minutes later, a loud rhythmic banging starts up in a room beyond the stairs, beyond the shadows. Cesar's brother sets off towards it with the kids, and then beckons for us to follow.

Through a low door, we advance into a room with banging and shouting coming from a lighted area at the far end. There's smoke everywhere and such a smell of dope you could get high just by breathing. The floor is trembling and we find ourselves in the middle of a hashish production line. We're bid to sit down, and we do so, on a carpet on the floor. Cesar's brother is there, and the spiv, again, and others. The old guy is hunched over a brazier, his baggy pants around him, using tongs to turn and lift wet, steaming paper packets off the coals; in the smoke, he looks like Mephistopheles. Nearby is the boy, spooning golden-green pollen from a half-hundred-weight sack into narrow cellophane envelopes as fast as he can. He folds the openings and slides them across the floor to the soldier, who's tearing brown paper into strips, dipping the strips in a basin of water and wrapping them around the cellophane packs. Then he tosses them onto the fire, which is red and glowing but without flames. Fat, wet packets of pollen steam and smoke on the embers, the old man's tongs expertly flipping them over before they burn. When the packets scorch and the edges catch fire, he tosses them onto the floor where Cesar's brother and a beefy companion begin to stamp on them, pounding them flat, then kicking them off to one side. They're both glistening with sweat, rocking on their feet, shouting comments as they stamp. Smoke and steam swirls under the low ceiling, half-hiding them. The voices seem to be chanting and calling to one another – or maybe I'm just super-stoned. The floor is jumping, and the ceiling appears to move in the rhythm of the stamping. A joint is handed to me. No, I gotta say no. I pass it on to Carlo. Crazy Carlo takes it, and grins.

Suddenly, everything slows down and stops. The old man cooks the last package; it's flattened, unwrapped and stacked. The smoke clears. The young hustlers crouch down beside Cesar who has stacked the bars in neat piles and is busy tallying them. His brother comes over, wiping sweat off his face with a towel. The kids start counting out money on the floor. Everyone seems happy. Cesar comes over and asks us if we're OK. Yep, I nod, we're fine . . . acting like we spend every second day in the middle of a hash factory.

A thought suddenly strikes him and he holds up a finger for attention. With a grin, he walks to a wide, whitewashed cupboard standing against one wall. With the gesture of an impresario, he swings open the door. The whole inside is divided into small compartments, each containing one or two white doves. They stir, blink and coo in the sudden light; pairs strut minuets around each other. Then, one flies out in a flap of wings, circles twice and comes gracefully to rest on our man's outstretched arm. He strokes it, smiling proudly. We're rapt: it's some movie, this one. Meanwhile, the street kids stuff bars of hashish into their pockets. Off to work. With a wish-you-well grin to us, they turn and split.

My head isn't as together as it might be when Cesar leans across a couple of minutes later and asks me for the bread. I give it to him, sure. He counts it, nods to the others and hands it back to me. Now, he crouches down to talk. Carlo moves closer. Cesar is grave, now, as he addresses us both. He's explaining something to me but I don't get it. He explains it again. I still don't understand. I can see that this is embarrassing for him; the spiv snorts contemptuously. Carlo thinks that he's saying something about tomorrow. I listen intently, trying to get the drift. The communication between me and Cesar – the basis of this deal – is suddenly falling to pieces. The spiv laughs out loud to the assholes around him. What the fuck's Cesar saying? Then, suddenly, he holds up one of the bars of hash and calls to the kid to bring the gunny sack of pollen. He holds one beside the other. Suddenly, I'm hip to his meaning: it'll take hours to bake the amount of dope we want to score! '*Yarin* . . .', he says – *tomorrow*. I tell Carlo. We look at each other and have the same thought: *mañana* may stretch to *mañana-mañana*, as in Spain – and who knows what could go down if we wait around? If we take it tonight, it'll be in pollen and much bulkier to stash – but we've got the van, we've got space and – hey! – we'll bake it up ourselves back in Formentera! Carlo shrugs; we're agreed. '*Youk*,' I say, '*Boogewn* . . .', which means today. Cesar gestures, why not sleep, eat, relax – go tomorrow? '*Youk*,' I shake my head and say again, '*Boogewn* . . .' He shrugs, OK, and he nods to his brother. They indicate that they'll go out and come back; meantime, have more tea.

Ten minutes later, the kid returns with a kettle and two glasses. He pours us steaming green tea. The good soldier has another joint going; we all smoke and drink, exchanging pleasantries, killing time. Then there's noise on the stairs again, and it's the brothers with a sack. They put it down beside the brazier, untie the neck and take out a clear, litre-size plastic bag of pollen; there are more bags inside. They open it and hold out a spoonful of greenish brown pollen for us to see. We look at it, smell it, rub it between our fingers. It's sticky – as good pollen should be. So, OK. They drop the bag back in the sack and invite me to lift it. It's heavy.

'*Cach para kilos?*' I ask.

'*Besh kilos*,' Cesar tells me.

I invite Carlo to try it. Five kilos, I tell him. He lifts the sack and asks me, 'You know what five kilos feels like? I don't . . .'

'You got the scales,' I tell him, 'Do we weigh it or don't we?' Without words, we agree no. Carlo does everything right; he's the perfect partner. 'Pay the man,' he says, 'and let's get out of here . . .' I nod. Boss hash for a hundred bucks a kilo, thirty-six quid – we've done better than Mike.

I count the notes into Cesar's hand; he watches carefully. His brother picks up the sack, says something to him, shakes hands with us, and splits. Cesar signals that we'll all leave together. OK.

He leads us to the wagon and hands me the keys. What's goin' on? we wonder, exchanging a glance. There's gotta be a reason they're doing it this way; they know the ground. We pile into the van, the three of us on the bench seat, me at the wheel, Carlo in the middle, Cesar by the off-side window. 'Go!' Cesar tells me in Turkish. I start the engine and we go.

'Whaddafuck, whaddafuck – it's happenin', we're on the move, baby!',

I'm thinking as we gather speed, following Cesar's hand signals, right, left, down dark lanes and unlit alleys.

'Slow now . . .' he signals as we turn into a dim-lit street and I slow. Suddenly, there's a guy on the pavement and another coming out from behind a truck, and Cesar has the window open as his brother, running, throws in the sack, and peels off into the darkness. Cesar drops the sack to the floor. 'Go!' he says again, and there is urgency in his voice and concentration in his face as he guides me out of the labyrinth onto a wide, well-lit street. 'Istanbul!' he says and points straight ahead. I pull over. The handshakes are brief, but with feeling. Opening the door, he pauses a moment and smiles at us. 'Good luck, compadres!', he says – or whatever it is in Turkish. His brown eyes are warm and reflect his soul. In a moment, he has slammed the door shut and is gone forever.

A minute later, I'm pushing the old bus through the gears and we're headed once again for the deep, dark hinterland of Turkey, the empty roads beyond the edge of town.

Chapter 14

AS I DRIVE, CARLO CLIMBS over the seat and into the back, and shoves the sack of dope into a locker. He lights the gas stove and makes instant coffee. I drink it as I drive. We're high as kites; we've fuckin' done it, we've scored, and at what a price! Now all we gotta do is get it safely home! Already, we're talking about the scene we'll have in Formentera, baking it. Never mind a clambake like they have in New England, this'll be the hash-bake, man! We're dying to weigh it, bustin' to weigh it. Five kilos, he said, is that true? There's no traffic and, about ten kilometres out of town, I pull onto a by-road and stop. I haul myself over into the back too, and we light a candle because the interior light is so shaggin' dim we won't be able to read the scale. Carlo holds it, and we suspend the sack from the hook, and we look, and it reads 5kg, spot on! Spot fuckin' on, it reads five kilos, not a gram less. Hey, but Cesar and those people, they're good people. We paid our money, and they came up with the weight. If they'd said at any point, never mind the fuckin' bargaining, just give us your bread and get out of here before we kill you, we'd have handed it over like lambs. But they didn't do that; there was honour amongst dope dealers then; dope dealers weren't thieves. We sat, and celebrated in the candlelight, with drifting snow slowly covering the windows. Then we drove on.

Most of our money was gone now, but the money Jacey had said he'd send Carlo should be waiting for him care of American Express, Istanbul.

Istanbul was a thousand kilometres north from Adana. We decided to go back a different way, not through Afyon, the town called Opium, but through Ankara, the capital. We thought the roads might be better, and that we could maybe make fifty kilometres an hour if we got lucky so it would take us just twenty hours if we stopped only for gas and grub. First thing, we stashed the dope a bit securer. Inside the sack, it was in plastic bags, ten of them, each five hundred grams, about a pound. We put a few bags here, a few bags there, in corners, under cushions. In Istanbul, we'd undo the plywood panels and stash it properly. Meanwhile, we had a long drive ahead.

The first shift was mine. After we'd hopped out and, standing side by side, had a quick and steaming piss in the snow, Carlo said he'd like to crash out for a while. When we got back in, he pulled out the bed and covered himself with blankets. I blew out the candle and climbed back into the front and started out again, the tyres skidding on the snow as I reversed onto the road. I was so elated up there in the cockpit, with the snow hitting the windscreen and the old wipers arching back and forth, back and forth, barely coping, but coping, that I felt I could drive on and on for ever, back to Formentera right there and then. I tapped and I sang, tapped and sang any old song for an hour afterwards, making them up as I went – '*They're gonna put me in the movies, They're gonna make a big star outta me, The greatest fool that ever hit the Big Time, Just for actin' natcherly!*' I was full of the glow.

Back in Istanbul, the first thing to do was to check American Express to see if the money from Jacey had arrived. It hadn't, but Carlo was sure it would. There was a letter from Hanna, a letter telling me that she and Aoife were OK but that she wished I was at home *right now* – why *right now* I didn't know. Nicole was living with her while I was away and was looking forward to seeing Carlo. The guy called Marvin had called around. Rick had written from Teheran to say he'd be back soon. It was great to get her letter and I read it more than once over the following days.

Between the pages were some sketches of Winter moths she'd drawn. They came into the house at night and flew to the candles and she and Aoife shooed them away before they'd burn. She closed the shutters to keep them out, although then she and Aoife couldn't watch for falling stars – so many fell! I realised that, more than anything, I loved the pilgrim soul in Hanna. From our first acid trip – from first meeting her – that was what I'd loved; her fierce belief in truth and love.

Now again, like that morning at the Montesol, the day I left for London with Carlo and Rick, I saw Nancy as she really was. Dazzling, vivacious, garrulous Nancy, always a laugh-a-minute – but how boring and oppressive that could be. How much more real was Hanna – quiet, unaffected Hanna, faithful and sincere. She had put up with so much from me! I had seen her as second-best. As long as I lived, I never would again.

Istanbul was as bleak as before. Once more, Carlo and I took a room at the old Gulhane Palace in Underground Cistern Street. The waiting was costing money; we could give it a week, no more; we could sell blood in Greece to pay for gas if we had to; Carlo had done it before, on his way back from India. In the meantime, we ran into a couple of jokers I knew from Ibiza. Bobby G and his friend, M. Zee, were two middle-class New York Jewish kids who'd come to Europe to jump a marijuana rap against them in the States – they became serious dope-dealers later. They had money and were staying at the Istanbul Hilton, no less. When they heard our story and where we'd been, Bobby said, 'You're in Turkey with five kilos of hashish and a gun? You're outta your fuckin' heads, man!'

They invited us up to their room overlooking the Golden Horn, a river of lights, lit-up bridges and fairy-lit ferries, with the city like a dark cloth with gold spangles spread out on either side. We were overawed. Zee came over and stuck a small pipe in my mouth; it contained crystals of something called DMT, Dimethyltryptamine. He said, 'I'll light it and you suck . . .' I did that and I was blown away in a second, my head swirling and all the colours brightening and a rush sweeping over me, like a trip. It didn't last long but it sure was potent, with no revelation much, except the sense of some moments frozen in time.

We'd brought a bit of pollen with us and we told them how they baked it in Adana. Bobby phoned down for an electric iron and we proceeded to bake some up, right there in the room. They smoked it, and said it was boss dope, as good as they'd ever smoked anywhere. Then they suggested we go out and dig the town.

We got into a taxi outside. 'Girls!', our hustler friends told the driver, 'Find us some girls!' Carlo and I, to tell the truth, weren't up for this at all. We tried to excuse ourselves by saying we couldn't afford it but both M. Zee and Bobby were extravagant in their generosity. They said they'd pay for everything; we should just relax and have a good time.

The cab driver took us out into the suburbs, and stopped outside a house in what looked like a poor neighbourhood. He went and banged on the door; a woman came out and, after some exchange, she waved to us to come in. She stood back to let us pass and we walked down a corridor and into a room lit by a ceiling light where there were rugs on the floor and stuffed chairs arranged along the walls. The woman wore traditional clothes, a full-length *djellaba* and a headscarf. She bid us sit, then left. An older woman appeared, then another, and they sat too. What the fuck's going on? our hustler friends were asking the cab driver, who just kept saying they should wait, everything was OK.

Minutes later, the first woman reappears, now with two young girls in tow; the youngest can't have been more than nine years old. They're all dressed up in traditional clothes but with mascara on their eyes, and garish lipstick. I didn't know what to think might happen next but I figured the cab driver had misunderstood my friends' intentions, and the little girls would do a traditional dance after which G and Zee would be hustled to pay and that would be it. The thought that they might be offered for sex didn't cross my mind – it was a more innocent world then – and I don't think that was the intention, anyway. In any case, M. Zee immediately got up and said, 'Let's go!' As we filed out, the woman stood in the way, asking for money and the cab driver told Zee to give her some, and he did, maybe five bucks. We split into the night, glad to get out of there. In the cab, Zee and G read the riot act at the driver, calling him a fuckin' idiot and a yo-yo. 'Girls, women!' they said, 'Fuckee-fuckee!'

The more they got into this, the less happy I was, and Carlo too. I was all for sex and women but I knew that if I had to pay for it, I couldn't do it. I don't think this was because I thought of the exploitation of women but more because I needed to feel I was desirable for myself, not for my money – otherwise I didn't think I could raise a hard-on.

Zee and G were getting madder and madder with the cabbie as he gave them the run-around. There had to be whore shops in Istanbul, they said. The taxi-driver was getting pissed off with them too and I think he decided he'd give them their come-uppance. Next thing, he stopped on a flyover, told us to get out of the car and pointed to a street below us. There, a long queue of men stood outside a pair of doorways that opened now and then and let one out, one in, working men, in overcoats and caps. Through a line of dirty windows, we could clearly see women inside – not glamorous young women but tired, dishevelled women in stained slips – coming into the hallways and taking man after man with them, like dehumanised fuck-machines, into nearby rooms.

It was horrible, filthy and degrading, and I think we all felt it. Zee and Bobby went quiet, and told the driver to take us back to the hotel. He sniffed, like, 'So, my big-mouth friends, now how do you like the reality?' And back we went to the Hilton to smoke another pipe and a couple of joints.

Zee told us about what had happened to an Australian chick he'd been travelling with in India. On an acid trip, she reverted to babyhood and stayed there. She couldn't speak except in goo-goo language. He had to spoon-feed and wash her; she couldn't walk or even use the john. Her parents came to take her home. She was still fucked-up, he thought, or he'd have heard from her. It was good acid too – but not good for her.

Zee and Bobby were flying to Amsterdam next morning. Years later they got into dealing heavy drugs until they got banged up which, much as I loved them, I had to say wasn't a bad thing, given the powdered death they were purveying.

Our money was very short now but we kept our faith in Jacey. Meantime, we still had the gun and we figured we must be able to sell it somewhere. Zee and Bobby had advised us to throw it away. If we were caught with it, we'd go down forever. This was probably true but we didn't much reflect on this possibility. We'd hidden the hash, stuffing the bags behind the plywood panels that lined the inside of the wagon, which was parked in the street; we had even put bags in the roof lining. We had dumped the scales.

One freezing winter evening, Carlo and I went to The Grand Bazaar, where hustlers and money-changers hung out. The corridors and alleyways were all lit up, the tinsmiths and coppersmiths banging, the tailors' sewing machines humming, the spice merchants sitting behind their pyramids of many-coloured spices, the apothecaries smiling from behind their jars of bears' balls in aspic and dried tigers' dicks. In the gold bazaar, the windows and display cases glistened with chains and trinkets, and nobody bugged us to buy. We didn't look like we had a bob to spend.

Then, a kid of seventeen or eighteen with a baby beard stepped up and offered to sell us hashish. No hashish, I said, but would he be in the market for a gun? 'Gun?' he said, show it to me, and we followed him into a shop. His eyes lit up when Carlo pulled the nickel-plated Colt 45 real-shootin'-replica from under his jacket. The kid held it up to the light and spun the cylinder like a cowboy. Had we bullets? No. 'OK,' he said, 'I'll have to try it out before buying . . .' He'd need an hour, he said. The Turks we'd so far dealt with hadn't burnt us, so we decided to take the chance.

When he got back, he wanted to trade for the gun alright, but he had no money. All he could offer us was a half-kilo of hash. We wanted cash, not hash; we had enough hash already. However, we had no money for presents to bring home, so we offered to trade. We ended up with a couple of beautifully embroidered jackets for Hanna and Nicole, a small carpet, a furry jacket and slippers for Aoife, a necklace for Hanna, some amazing wooden animals for the boys, a string of beads for Nancy and a pair of fur-lined boots each for Carlo and me. Now we had gifts to bring home – but still no money to get there.

Next morning, we were back at AmExCo again. Again, there was a letter for Carlo from Nicole, but none from Jacey. I was beginning to think this Jacey was a little California-flaky. I'd wondered from early on if he was maybe taking Carlo for a ride. That was Carlo's business but, for me, it was getting personal. I realised we should have asked Bobby and Zee to stake us, but it was too late now.

Days passed. The hotel bill was mounting. We'd seen the sights and there was nothing much to do except sit in the steam of the thawing Turks in the

Blue Mosque Café and nurse our coffees. The café was the best place to meet travellers if there were any in town. One day, an English couple came in. The man was a huge, bearded, bear-like guy and the woman was tall and skinny with long hair in a plait and a red nose. They both wore Afghan sheepskin coats which smelled of their original owners: Father Christmas and his red-nosed bride. When we told them we were heading west and could take them as far as the south of France if they'd pay the petrol, they went for it. Naturally, we didn't tell them they'd be practically sitting on a cargo of dope. No point in making them nervous and, in the event of our getting busted, it would be better for them if they didn't know.

They paid us the gas money in advance so we decided to abandon hope of Jacey's money and head for home. We plotted a new course. Instead of going through Greece, we'd cross Bulgaria on the road through Plovdiv and Sofia, then go north through Yugoslavia and across the north of Italy into France. We set out with the Christmases one day in mid-December. Old Santa Claus was a mean bluesman on his harmonica and he played us on our way. My battered old passport says that we left Turkey at Edirne on 11 December. We had a lot of hard travellin' to do, two and a half thousand kilometres to make it back to Formentera for Christmas. It could be done provided we didn't delay. But a delay happened to us in Bulgaria; and it almost plucked our festive goose.

Chapter 15

ONE MORNING, AT THE BREAK of dawn, I was driving, alone up front, with the others all asleep in the back. I came up a hill surfaced with cobblestones outside some Bulgarian town. Freezing fog was blanketing the road and lying on the snowfields below me on one side. It was a sort of cutting into the hill-side. As I topped the rise, I hit black ice and the wagon took on a mind of its own and started to pirouette, light and graceful as a ballerina. I watched as the world spun by in a full circle, as if I was on a fairground carousel. Somewhere on this magic roundabout, I caught a glimpse of two uniformed cops standing by the rock face of the cutting and, as the wagon momentarily pointed towards them, I thought that one jumped into the other's arms, like something out of the Keystone Cops.

Coming out of the spin, we were heading down the hill on the other side, going backwards. I spun the wheel and tried to drive out of the skid, but it all happened in seconds and I was no Grand Prix driver. Backwards, we sailed, and off the edge of the road, turning over and over, rolling down a slope until we came to rest, with the wagon on its side, in a field of snow. I was unharmed, lying on my back on the passenger door with the sky framed above me in the driver's window and a polythene bag of hash hanging out of the roof lining above my head. 'Everyone cool?' I called out, jumping up fast, remembering the police on the road. 'Yeah, OK!' 'OK.' 'OK.' 'What the fuck happened?' and so on. That all three answered was a great relief for me – but, at any second, the cops would show up.

'Stash the hash, Carlo!' I yelled. As I stood and pushed the door open above me, I heard Mrs. Christmas scream 'Oh, my Gawd!' as she saw the bag.

I climbed out and jumped down into the snow, which was thigh-high. The cops were coming down the slope into the field, floundering in a deep drift at the bottom and heading towards us. I plodded towards them as fast as I could and stopped them just a few yards from the truck. 'Accident!' I cried, playing for time. 'Van turned over!' They nodded and shouted and tried to get past me, but I held my arms wide and acted like a fuckin' loon. 'We turned over,' I cried, again, working my arms roly-poly. Then, I heard Carlo call out, loud and clear, 'OK, man, it's cool!' I turned to see him emerging from the sky-facing door, followed by the two others, like disorientated crewmen climbing from the turret of a capsized tank.

As we examined the wagon, ourselves and the cops, we saw that it was in a sorry state indeed. We all stood there looking at it like a corpse at a removal. Carlo had stashed the half kilo of dope in a hold-all, and the Christmases were staying sthum – although Mrs. Christmas sure wasn't happy with me and made it plain to see.

Before long, the cops brought along a woman, a teacher at a local school, who spoke some English. She said the police had arranged to get the wagon out of the field. How this was to be accomplished I couldn't guess, but soon afterwards an army unit turned up with a couple of big, high-wheel-base trucks and a lot of young soldiers. Together, we plunged down through the snow and, with all of us lifting together, we managed to get the wagon back on its feet. The Christmases, by this time, had gone, and who could blame them? A cop car had driven them to the nearest station where, the school-teacher said, they could catch a train to Sofia, and on into western Europe from there. They'd forgotten to ask for their gas money back.

As we heaved and pushed the wagon, there was a great *espirit de corps* amongst the soldiers, the cops and Carlo and me. The fog had lifted by this time, and the yellow sun glinted off the snowfield under a clear, blue sky. It was good to be still alive, and Carlo and I were chirpy – half out of nervousness, half out of the joy of having survived. Miraculously, no other panels had broken open, and Carlo had the half-kilo in his bag, which he carried with him. Nobody seemed to be interested in shaking us down; the cops had taken the details of our passports, and handed them back. What would happen next, we had no idea. We really had to just keep smiling and go with the flow.

Our hope was that the old bus, which had been through so much and had served us so well, would be able to continue the journey but when she was upright again, she looked a total wreck. All the windows in the rear compartment, down both sides, had been smashed. The double doors in the side were bent back, one hinge ripped right out of the metal. The passenger door was also sprung and there was a wide crack across the windscreen. But what state was the engine in? And if it was alright, could the doors and windows be repaired?

A huge, green army truck with wheels nearly as high as ourselves backed into the field. Somebody hitched a derrick onto our old bus and with her front lifted off the ground, the truck began to haul her like she was a Matchbox toy. When we got back onto the road, the teacher directed us to a car, a big Russian Volga, and climbed in beside us. We set off in a motorcade, a truckfull of soldiers in front, then the truck with our wagon suspended behind it, and then ourselves in the Volga. She said we were going to the 'mechanik' – said in a German sort-of-way. After a ten-minute drive, we arrived at tall gates with barbed wire and a big red star over them – a Russian Army camp, the teacher explained – and the motorcade proceeded past some armed sentries. This was all getting a little hairy now, especially when the gates closed behind us.

As the wagon was unhitched from the truck, a couple of guys with greasy overalls came out of a garage like an aircraft hangar and began looking it over. I gave one of them the keys and he tried to start it but it wouldn't go. Don't worry about that, he signed, that'll be OK. His mate signalled that he'd hammer the door a bit to get it straight and then smacked one of the panels with his hammer. I wanted to say don't worry about the panels but thought it better not to. The teacher said they'd look it over and let us know their thoughts by and by.

We subsequently had a nervous thirty minutes sitting in the camp canteen, smoking cigarettes, drinking coffee and exchanging inanities with the teacher about the cost of cigarettes in England and the price of pigs in China and so on. It was lunchtime, and we queued for a meal at the self-service canteen but it was hard to keep smiling at everybody in the muggy, smoke-filled refectory, given that any minute some military cop might come through the door with a couple of kilos of dope in one hand and two pairs of hand-cuffs in the other. I don't know how we survived it, but we stayed cool. I almost fell in love with the teacher, a heavy smoker and coffee-drinker, even though she was twice my age; she was the only friend we had in a world where we were total strangers.

The time came when she said she had to be going back to her classroom but first she would go and check out what was happening. She came back to say that the guys would repair the bus; it would take them two or maybe three days. We could leave it, and go spend some time in Sofia and come back for it, or even go back to Spain and return later! There was no hotel locally, but there was a woman who could put us up. Carlo and I had a quick word, and said OK to that.

The house where we were to stay was a simple dwelling and the woman, in bits of German and sign language, told us her son, a policeman, also lived there – which was a further piece of hairy news. However, we settled in and slept for a while. We woke in the dead of night and took a look at the situation. To flee, or not to flee, that was the question. We had our bags now, our passports and our basic possessions. We could high-tail it the fuck outta there the next day and leave the stash to the soldiers, and let them get high.

When I went to take a leak, I found that the woman had left a tray with milk and bread and pickles outside the door. In the room, there was a big wood stove, which we fed with logs, and on top of which, using the cello-phane sleeve from a fag packet, we baked up some pollen from Carlo's bag in the Turkish manner, more or less.

We smoked a joint and threw the *I Ching*, Carlo having the good book and the Chinese coins in his hold-all . . . along with the half-kilo of dope. The hexagram we threw was entitled 'Do not cross the Great Water, Do not see The Great Man'. We looked at one another, over the candle flame, and shrugged agreement. There was no discussion of pros and cons. We had the dope in the wagon; we'd gone through who knows how many thousand kilo-metres of road-work and how many howling blizzards to get it. We'd stay. It wasn't the *I Ching* that decided it, but the hexagram was a good omen. We went back to our beds. Fortune had smiled on us so far.

There wasn't a lot to do in that village – not in the depths of winter anyway. It got dark at four in the afternoon; in fact, apart from that first morning in the snowfield with the soldiers, the sun never seemed to shine. We decided to go on an outing to Sofia; it was about an hour by train. We found our way to the British Council; there would have been no Irish or American diplomatic mission in Bulgaria then. We were told there was an English-language movie to be shown that night and given an address and a map. It was all *Third Man* stuff, Soviet Bulgaria in the snow, dark streets with small streets lights – you could almost hear the Harry Lime theme. A second-rate black-and-white movie was shown on a flickering screen for the expatriate community. We were politely received but nobody talked to us much – which was a relief. Nobody we knew anywhere in the world was aware of where we were right then.

A week before, I'd sent a postcard to the boys from Istanbul and had written to Hanna to say all was well and I figured to be home for Christmas but that we were still waiting for Jacey's money to arrive. As we'd finally left town, I'd sent her a card to say we were on our way. I knew, of course, that absence raises the threshold of desire and makes the heart want to share its natural affection but I was sure that I loved her now, not like I had Nancy but with a kind of love new to me. I told her I loved her. I decided that when I got back I would tell her about my affair with Fran, in London. It would hurt her but I hoped she would forgive me. We would begin with a clean slate. Carlo had also written to Nicole, and so both women – and, by now, everyone on Formentera – would be expecting us. But, owing to the recent turn of events, nothing was certain.

We had spent three days in that bleak, grey-skied, snowbound landscape before the summons came. Apart from the riveting visit to the British Council movie in Sofia, we'd trudged out once or twice, got high and threw a few snowballs at one another. There was nothing to see; it was a flat, featureless world. There weren't even birds and there was little of interest in nature, although I do remember one morning when it was bright and clear and icicles sparkled on the silver birch trees as if some mad admirer had hung diamond earrings on the boughs. I wished Hanna was there to see them and I wrote to her about them, knowing I'd be home before the letter arrived.

Carlo developed some sort of flu and started sweating and shivering. We had some aspirin, so he started taking these, but he was in bad shape from then on. I could see he felt lousy, but he didn't complain. Americans travelling in Europe or the East seem to get sick more than Europeans; why I don't know.

And then the morning came when there was a loud rap-rap-rap on our door and we woke and pulled on our jeans and it's a guy in police uniform who, to our relief, we recognise as the son of the house, not a cop sent to arrest us! 'Kom, kom!', he says, and indicates we should bring along our bags. We want to pay his mother but he says no and he whisks us out into the smoky air and into a pokey little car. Five minutes later, we're going through the gates of the Army camp and they're closing behind us. It's scary but, of course, we knew this was going to happen; sooner or later, we'd either get the wagon back or be arrested and sent to a gulag. But everyone seemed benign. We pulled up outside the garage like an aircraft hangar and there stood the van, transformed. We could hardly believe our eyes. As we got out of the little Trabant, three or four mechanics came out of the garage looking right proud of the job they'd done. And, indeed, they deserved to be. They'd turned the VW van into an armoured car. Never before was there a VW van like it. They'd had no glass, they explained, but plenty of steel, because they were a tank regiment – so all down the sides they'd welded steel plate over the windows to keep out the wind and the cold. They'd hammered the bent barn doors back to where they should have been and welded them into place, similarly, the passenger door, so now the only way in and out was through the driver's door or the back window. This was sort of awkward, but who the hell cared; they hadn't found the dope. How they didn't find it, I wonder to this day. It was a miracle that the welding torches didn't melt the plastic bags inside the panels and make the van smell like a mobile hash factory. Maybe they ripped off a percentage. If there were Kazakhs or Uzbeks or Turkomen amongst the soldiers, they'd have known all about dope.

Anyway, next minute, we were being handed the keys and were throwing our bags aboard and shaking hands with everyone. Nobody was asking for payment. It was all smiles, pats on the back, and good luck now, and a cheer when I turned the key in the ignition and she started and, with a wave through the only window that opened – the driver's window – we pulled away. The gods were with us! It was good Karma.

We'd lost a few days and had to make up time. It wasn't just about getting to Barcelona; we had to catch the boat to Ibiza and then the boat to Formentera. I'd sent a letter to Hanna telling her we'd had a breakdown but that all would be cool; we'd be a few days late but we'd make it for Christmas. For Hanna, family togetherness at Christmas was important; my not showing up would have made her think I didn't care.

Carlo was ill – sweating and yellow. He was too sick to drive but sometimes he sat up front beside me, wrapped in a blanket and coughing, with the camping-gas stove alight on the bench seat between us as we tried to keep warm against the wind whistling in the crack in the windscreen, and every other aperture, of which there were many in our armoured minibus, which must have been carrying almost her own weight in steel.

We'd both arrive home flat broke but after Jacey paid some of our expenses as promised, Rick, Bruno, Black William, even Longini – whoever was on Formentera – would be happy to chip in, in exchange for some of the hash. I told Carlo that we owned the dope equally and that he should have half of any expenses we got back. He insisted that any expenses recovered should go to me – I'd ended up financing everything and my van was now an un-saleable wreck. I didn't listen. While we would take no profit – we had agreed on that from the start: in Formentera we gave to one another, we didn't sell – these would be our small but rightful wages for the trip.

The back part of the wagon, where Carlo spent most of the time, was in semi-darkness now. It was a pit, with stuff thrown all over the place, pebbles of broken glass, pieces of rubber seal and bits of roof-stuffing underfoot, and the presents we'd bought for Formentera slung around in torn packages. We had no time to clean up; I hardly had the heart to look at it. With the side doors welded shut, it was impossible to sweep it out and, besides, we didn't have a brush. It would be clear to Customs that we'd had an accident and the darkness and mess would discourage them from searching us. Plus the only way into the back was to get in through the driver's door and climb over the bulkhead – no easy job.

We crossed from Bulgaria into Yugoslavia on 16 December. By now, we'd been six weeks on the road, and we looked it. We would re-enter Spain at La Junquera two days later on 18 December. That was a hell of a lot of driving between Niš and the Spanish border, through snow, ice and rain, but I remember almost none of it, just Carlo bringing me coffee from the back now and then, and the various border guards staring in amazement at the armoured wagon. In Italy, they laughed at it – which was fine. Through all the borders, nobody ever bothered to look inside. They could see we'd had some massive accident and it was a miracle that we were moving at all.

We stopped only to fill up with gasoline and take a piss. No wash, no shave. We bought biscuits and lived on them; I had the boat fares from Barcelona to the islands stuffed down my boot – pesetas we'd kept aside all the way – and no money for anything else. We just plugged on, trying to make time, with me trying to push the old 1100cc engine to carry us past the big trucks before another approached out of the distance and I was forced to drop back and wait and try all over again, sludge and melt-water from the truck wheels thrown onto the windscreen so I could hardly see. The engine just didn't have the balls, and the armour plating made it slower still. To get past a long truck without a head-on, the next corner had better be half a mile away.

We passed through Yugoslavia in the dark and Italy passed in a blur, snow along the roadside and a cold rain falling all the way across the north, from Venice to Milan. France, the Riviera coast, was grey. Then we turned south, for Spain.

At the French border post, we showed our passports and were waved through. As we climbed the Pyrenees towards Spain, the sun shone out of a blue sky, the first sun we'd seen for a week, and we felt better already and praised España in loud voices. We'd decided that before we hit Spanish customs we'd check out the load, just to make sure all the panels were screwed down right and showed no signs of having been opened.

We pulled in on the side of a hill in no man's land between the borders, and I climbed into the back and held a flashlight while Carlo checked the screws. Everything was fine until we came to a place where two panels met low down over the back nearside wheel. Christ! One of the panels was all green and furry, coated with sticky pollen like flock wallpaper in an Indian restaurant! A small pyramid of pollen, like a miniature Mount Fuji, sat on the floor! Thanking our stars that we'd taken the trouble to check, we scooped it onto a piece of cardboard and threw it out. After unscrewing the panel, we saw what had happened. The wheel arch was rusted: a stone had been thrown up and split the bag. The space behind the panel was coated with pollen and some had been blown between the panels into the van. We'd have to clean up, re-wrap the burst bag, re-stash it and screw the panel back down. This was easier said than done. The pollen was sticky as fuck, making it hard to scrape off the dirty, tin floor. We did our best. A sniffer dog, would, of course, suss the dope right away, but that wasn't a worry back then.

When we were finished, we stood outside in the sun and smoked a cigarette. It was now or never. In a few minutes' time, we'd be at Spanish Customs. Funny, we hadn't thought twice about running the other borders – and yet who knows how long that green pyramid of pollen had sat in the back, all plain to see . . .

Standing beside the wagon, we looked raunchy and rough in the sun, blinking at the intensity of the light. Carlo was very pale, his unshaven jowls dark and his skin jaundiced, with layers of sweaters and shirts and a donkey-jacket on top. Having taken off my jacket, I was wearing a maroon, round-neck sweater a size too small, frayed at the neck and with holes in the sleeves, and manky blue jeans, stained with dirt and mud and oil, and my Turkish fur-lined boots. We'd had nowhere to clean up; even in the house in Bulgaria, there was no place to wash clothes. Our hair was long, and we hadn't shaved for days. I can still see the two of us, standing there like troglodytes, blinking in the sunlight beside the van.

We set off from the top of the hill through no man's land and came down the winding road into La Junquera, a good road of sweeping curves. We turned the corners, gently easing down, letting the gears do the braking. And then, there was a sudden, sharp corner before the Customs post and, whatever reception committee might await, there was no way we could turn back. No way, in any case, in a lumbering, armoured VW van that would climb back up hill so slowly a fast runner could catch it.

'A las cinco de la tarde' goes a poem by Garcia Lorca; it was at five in the afternoon when his friend, Mejias, died in the Plaza de Toros at Manzanares, poor bastard, although I also pity the bull. It happened to us at three o'clock in the afternoon. Mejias was gored to death; I was lucky I wasn't shot.

Chapter 16

THE BORDER POST AND CUSTOMS offices at La Junquera were then oval, one-storey buildings, with windows running all along the sides, situated in the centre of an empty area of asphalt half as big as a football pitch. Each side had a channel, on the left for cars leaving Spain, on the right for cars entering. But on the right, that day, there were two lanes of queued cars because it was seven days before Christmas and Spanish migrant workers were coming home from the restaurants and factories of Europe with goods piled high – packages, boxes, TV sets – on top of their bangers, presents from as far away as Scandinavia for the families at home. And, because they were carrying such items, on which duty might be payable, the Customs were going through every car.

At the end of one lane nearest to us, an old guy was hauling the back seats out of his jalopy, with Customs officers inspecting them as his wife and children stood amongst the scattered contents of their car. If they were doing that to respectable people, what would they do to us? We knew we were in trouble but we didn't talk about it. I think we'd gone numb.

Elsewhere, there was similar shit going down; the Spanish Customs were nit-picking everything. Around the perimeter of the asphalt apron, trucks were parked, facing the building, some being searched, and some waiting to be searched. Soon our turn would come. All we could do was sit there and try to look unworried.

A couple of Customs guys came to my window. '*Pasaportes,*' they asked. I handed them over and they leafed through them and handed them back. All the felonious stamps were there, not only Turkish stamps in both but, in Carlo's, stamps from Afghanistan, Pakistan, India, Nepal. '*¡Fuera!*', they said – 'Out!' – like we were shit. I climbed out, and Carlo after me. I tried to make some joke about having only one door because we'd had an accident. It sank like a lead balloon. One of the guys tried the cargo door, although it was clear it was welded shut, while the other, an overweight guy of about fifty, climbed into the cab. He turned and shone his torch into the back. '*¿Que tiene en las paquetas?*' he demanded. '*Regalos,*' I said: presents. He grunted and – I could hardly believe my eyes – knelt up on the seat and set about swinging his overweight leg, ass and belly into the back. There, he shone his torch about while I craned my neck in, trying to look helpful rather than anxious. Meanwhile his mate was kneeling down outside, looking under the wagon. '*¿Que son estos?*' the guy inside growled. '*Más regalos . . .*' I said, '*Una jaqueta para mi niña pequeña*': a jacket for my little girl. My voice faded off; he wasn't really listening. My heart had fallen to the bottom of my ridiculous, fur-lined boots and my guts were churning like I urgently needed a john.

Now, as I watched, he knelt down and started shining his flashlight beam along the panels. And when he came to the one the hash had blown up through, he stopped. Was it Customs-man instinct or did the screws look newly opened, was the metal in the screw heads scratched? He leant closer and peered at the panel, then took out a screwdriver and began to unscrew. I knew that the minute he stuck his hand down inside it, it would come out green.

I stepped back from the door. Carlo was standing directly behind me, looking pale as a ghost.

'What's happenin'?' he asked.

'We're gettin' busted,' I answered. The guy with the screwdriver was inside the wagon and wouldn't be back out for a few minutes. The other guy was nowhere to be seen. 'OK,' I said, 'Let's go . . .'

Holding up the passports in front of me, I weaved my way through the nearby cars, confidently, unhesitatingly, heading for the offices where I'd seen other drivers taking their papers for stamping. I was trying to look as if I was on a mission, acting on instructions. I rounded the corner at the nose of the oval blockhouse, the end pointing towards Spain. I put down the two passports at a window and the guy inside stamped them, asking no questions. I turned to Carlo. But he wasn't there. Now, I was out of sight of the van and the guys examining it, but no Carlo. And I couldn't dare go back.

I crossed through the short line of cars leaving Spain and walked, unhesitatingly, towards the trucks parked along the periphery of the asphalt. I got in amongst the trucks and, now hidden from the office, stopped to catch my breath. Why hadn't Carlo followed me? Why wasn't he behind me when I'd turned?

Later, he said he had been rooted to the spot; he couldn't move. People react differently; there is no praise or blame involved. I was electrified into action; he was paralysed into inaction. Poor fucker, he was sick anyway, and hardly had the energy to move.

Now I was away from the Customs men but I wasn't going any farther until I'd found out what had happened to Carlo. I'd wait; he'd see me and we'd escape together. I was not going gently into a Spanish jail.

I sneaked around behind the trucks. If the entrance and exit roads were at twelve o'clock and six o'clock respectively, I was at three o'clock now, and the van was at nine. Thing was, to reach a viewpoint of the van, I had to cross the twelve o'clock road leading in from France, or the six o'clock road leading out into Spain. Either way I'd be exposed and be fucked if I was seen. I picked the road coming in from France and lay underneath a truck and watched and waited. Then, I made a dash across it. Unseen, I made it to the trucks parked on the other side. Working my way along behind them, I reached a place where, lying on my belly under a truck, I could see the wheels of the van.

A whole lot of green trouser legs had converged around it, with legs coming and going. We were sussed – there was no doubt about that. Who I was looking for was Carlo. Where the fuck was Carlo? I couldn't go without him. Maybe he'd also walked away, but in a different direction. I had to find out.

I dashed back again across the open mouth of the road; once more I wasn't spotted. I split along behind the trucks which were backed up towards a rough slope that rose behind them: the border post was in a sort of bowl. I clambered up this to get a better view. Dodging from rock to rock, staying low, I got high enough to see over the top of the building to the van. Customs men were coming and going but there was no sign of Carlo. I stayed there three minutes, maybe five; minutes seemed like hours. What would I do? The world had changed in a second. Hanna, Aoife, the boys, Christmas: when would I see them again now? I had only what I stood up in: the old sweater, the stained jeans, the passports stuffed down my belt and, in my boot, the price of two tickets to Ibiza. The furry jacket for Aoife, the wooden animals for the boys, all lost now; never mind the van, never mind the dope. And, the photos – the photos I'd shown Cesar. How could I have been so dumb as to bring photos on this trip? Now, the fuzz would have my mugshot – and my name which was on the envelope from Hanna's letter. In the letter, she'd talked about Formentera; they'd have enough to track me down, alright. What should I do? Where was Carlo? Suddenly, I spotted a group of maybe four Guardia moving through the cars and Carlo was walking amongst them, held by the arm, his hands held out before him, handcuffed, his eyes to the ground. He looked defeated. He looked like he was in shock. If I split, he'd understand. But what would everybody in Formentera think? That I'd abandoned him, betrayed him? Maybe. Let them think what they wanted. My getting busted wouldn't help Carlo. The van was mine – it said so on the letter of exchange the Aussie had given me, like the one I'd given him; my passport number was on it too. Carlo could claim he was an unknowing passenger, an innocent man.

If I escaped, I could quickly inform the American Embassy that I was solely responsible, that I was coming from Afghanistan on a dope run when I picked up Carlo hitchhiking in Turkey. They'd be duty bound to tell this to the Spanish fuzz, and to get him legal representation. But would I be abandoning a friend? Carlo wouldn't see it that way. He'd see it as crazy to do otherwise. So would Rick – so would anybody. But still, but still . . . What I needed was time to think, to evaluate the implications. I scrambled down onto the asphalt. I had to get out of there now. I would head into Spain; if I felt I had to, I could always turn myself in.

Bent double, I dodged from truck to truck, my heart racing, my thoughts in chaos, heading for the road into Spain. Once I reached it, I didn't hide myself. It was as if I wanted the gods to make the decision. I walked away from the Customs post, imagining eyes upon me, thinking that at any moment the police would arrive. I was on the right-hand side of the road and, as I heard cars coming from behind me, I tensed, waiting for that moment, but they all passed me by.

I headed into Spain led by an instinct to keep going, to finish the journey, to get home, as near as I could, and to seek the help of friends in a time of need. It was madness; I should have gone north and crossed the French border. Once I got out of sight of the frontier post, I could have taken to the hills. In France, I would be free; nobody would try to find me or extradite me. But I hardly knew what I was doing; I'd been driving for forty-eight hours and hadn't slept or had a proper meal during that time.

I walked like an automaton into Spain. There were rushes in my head, like an acid trip. I shouldn't be going south, I knew, but I wanted to see my friends, I wanted to see Hanna, I wanted to see Rick. I wanted to tell Hanna everything would be OK; I wanted to tell her that I loved her. Even if I was caught, it would be worth it. I could tell her that before the cops took me away.

Anyone who has had someone suddenly die on them wishes they'd had a few minutes to talk with them before they went. I believe prisoners must feel the same when they're seized, wishing, above all, that they had even the briefest time with the one they love before being taken away.

The road into Spain was a long straight road stretching away from the border, with no pedestrians and no houses; bamboo cane lined it on both sides. Behind the bamboos were fields, hidden from the road. Once I got to the bend some four hundred metres along it, I'd be out of sight of the Customs. While I feared every car coming from behind me, I also feared that drivers coming towards me could be asked if they'd seen anyone suspicious. I certainly looked suspicious. Nevertheless, I stayed on the road. The gods would decide whether I would reach that corner of not. If I reached it, I wasn't meant to be with Carlo.

I reached the corner. That was it; it was time to take control! I snapped out of the dream and went into escape mode. I stuck my thumb out to hitch a lift. No luck; today, cars would be full of families or luggage. Then I saw a vehicle approaching out of the distance. It didn't look like an ordinary car: I sensed danger and dodged into the bamboos. I waited for it to pass but it didn't. Stepping out, using the bamboos for cover, I could see it without being seen myself. Jesus! It was a jeep and two guys in uniform were heading away from it, walking up the road towards me. They were Guardia; they would have guns. One was leading a dog on a leash; it looked like an Alsatian. They were no more than two hundred metres away. The second cop was crossing to my side of the road; he disappeared through the bamboos below me. I jumped back.

Behind me was a big ploughed field, devoid of cover, falling away at the end, and then rising again into some scrub. There was a concrete blockhouse in the middle, like an electricity sub-station or an outside jacks. Out of the bamboos below me emerged the second policeman, heading for it; he wasn't looking my way. The cop on the road, with the dog, would be upon me at any moment. Maybe fifteen yards from where I stood, a ditch ran across the field at right angles to the bamboos; it was just deep enough to hide me if I could get to it unseen. But if I tried this, the cop walking across the field only had to turn his head and I was done for. But I had no other hope: taking off like an Olympic sprinter in my fur boots, I ran the distance and dived into the trench and started crawling like fuck – like a US Marine in a movie – to get as far away as I could from the road. The cop in the field hadn't seen me; if he had he'd have come after me. The ditch was full of briars and tares but I didn't feel them. The end of the field fell away out of sight; soon, I wouldn't be seen even if the cop with the dog came in off the road.

The ditch followed the slope down to a river, a wide, shallow watercourse. OK, I tell myself, rip off the boots and cross it, lose the scent, Hungarian-refugee style. I stand into the water. It is so fucking freezing it takes my breath away, and the stream bed is all broken rocks. I slip and nearly fall and it takes me two minutes of pussyfooting and high-stepping to get across. On the other side, I sit and pull on the boots; my tender white feet, which haven't been exposed to the outside air for two months now, have no feeling. I get up and plunge into the scrub, where I stop and turn to see if I can spot the cops. The cop in the field is heading back to the road; maybe there was a telephone in the hut. The stream I've crossed is between me and him, with a big ass-mark in the sand where I'd sat to pull on the boots and my footprints leading away from it. Some Hungarian refugee me!

I decide the best thing is to stay in the fields, heading south and staying parallel to the road for a mile or two before getting back onto it and hitch-hiking. It's for sure I'm not going to walk to Barcelona; it's one hundred and fifty kilometres away. First thing, when I arrive there – if I make it – I'll go to the US Embassy and put Carlo's passport through the letterbox with a note from myself taking all the blame, saying he was an innocent party and didn't even know the dope was in the van.

I started out through the fields, with thick hedges between me and the road, and I didn't see a soul, and any farmhouse I saw was far away. I hurried along. I came to a tall but scrawny hedge and heard something coming towards me on the other side. I realised there was a narrow farm track below me, and someone was approaching. I heard the snort of an animal. It was a mule, with a guy leading it. I froze. What happened next was like a scene from a B movie. As I stood there, I looked down at my feet and there was a snake crawling across them. I stood stock still; I had no option, with the guy only a few yards away. The snake was about two foot long: I have no idea if it was venomous. But in that minute, it was like a slow-motion film but not the kind my old lag pal, FM, said was so great to be in when a dope deal was going well. This was a horror film; and I could do without dope deals from now on.

When the guy passed, and the snake had slithered away, I set off again and, when I was a couple of miles into Spain, headed back to the road. I was still super-paranoid as I hobbled along in my overheated, uncomfortable boots, trying to look normal as I hitched passing cars. I rounded a corner and there was a sort of picnic spot with tall trees and grass and wooden tables under them. A minibus was parked up and sitting at the tables were two Sikh men, with brightly coloured turbans, two women in saris, and right on the verge, only yards from me, two dark children whose brown eyes followed me as I passed. This was pure Fellini. In another world, I walked by.

At last, a car stopped to pick me up. They were a relaxed Spanish couple in their early thirties. Where was I going?, the man asked. Barcelona, I said.

OK. I climbed into the back. He tried to make conversation, asking me where I was from. I pretended to speak no Spanish. Inglanda, I answered – or some such bullshit. He tried again and I gave an equally inane answer. We lapsed into silence. I felt bad about it; they were good people, but what could I do? The next question would be why I had no luggage. It was safer not to talk at all.

Then, up ahead, I saw a tailback of cars. As we got closer, I saw that there was a roadblock. Police were checking vehicles. Were they looking for me? Maybe they'd be pissed off that I'd escaped. Even if the roadblock was routine, if I was questioned I was in trouble. We were fifty metres back in the line. We moved forward slowly. I thought about saying I had to get out, that I felt sick. I'd hop over the hedge and get into the fields. But the cops were too close. Now we were only ten cars back from the checkpoint with a big queue building up behind us, then nine cars, then eight. I sank low in the rear seat and tried to angle myself so my friend the driver wouldn't notice me in the mirror. I closed my eyes, pretending to be asleep.

But I had one eye open and, through the windscreen, I saw a cop come towards us, a tall guy, with a moustache and a flat hat, not a Guardia Civil. We moved forward and, suddenly, he was turning and another cop farther along was waving to him. He started walking more deliberately towards us, then hit the roof of the car in front and then the roof of our car with the palm of his hand. '¡Vete, vete!', he cried. I could only see his uniformed midriff, with his *pistola* in its holster, and his arm as he waved it in front of the windscreen signalling go – '¡Rápido, rápido!' – because the queue was building up behind us. My friend, the driver, eased into gear and pulled away. He and his wife exchanged a few words and that was the last thing I knew until I was in Barcelona; out of sheer physical and nervous exhaustion, I slept.

They dropped me well into town and I made my way to the American Embassy. I knew it would be closed; it was about six o'clock and a Saturday evening. I got a piece of paper and a plastic bag from somewhere, leant on a wall and wrote a letter saying that I hereby testified that Mr. Carlo Kominski, a US citizen – find passport enclosed – had come with me to Turkey (the story about picking him up hitchhiking would never work; the cops would trace us both to Formentera) where I had bought illegal drugs, the which I had concealed in the panels of my VW van, registration number XYZ123, without his knowledge or consent, and that the drugs had been apprehended at La Junquera, where Mr Kominski had wrongfully been detained and that it was the duty of the American consular service to inform the Spanish authorities that he was innocent of any offence and was a victim of circumstances and to ensure his release from custody upon sight of my enclosed confession of guilt, signed 19 December 1964.

Would I append my correct passport number? Yeah, why not? By now, the Spanish fuzz knew who I was anyway, and I wasn't going to be trying to leave Spain on my own passport, for sure. So, I would claim responsibility. I owed it to Carlo, *mi compañero, mi amigo*. He was taking the rap but the van was mine and we couldn't have done it without the van – though the idea was flaky Jacey's in the first place.

This done, I headed for the port to catch the night boat to Ibiza. I had a great feeling of freedom, there in the pre-Christmas bustling streets of Barcelona, under the flashing lights and Santa Clauses and cribs in the big shop windows. People turned to look at me as I passed, a foreign vagabond who should maybe be locked up under the *Ley de Vagos* that put vagabonds in jail. I walked past Guardia Civil, patrolling in pairs, and they paid me no notice. Anyway, would the authorities have put out a nationwide order to apprehend the smuggler of a mere five kilos of dope? They might well have. Nowadays, busts of a tonne, one thousand kilos, happen regularly. But, then, dope wasn't commercial. It was for 'own use' and, even in Formentera, we couldn't have smoked a thousand kilos. Five would have lasted us a year!

At the Trasmediterrania office at the end of the Cristobal Colón, I waited for the windows to open, to buy a ticket. I did have some paranoia now. It was just possible that the fuzz would have already gone through my papers, or Carlo's, and found that I had family in Formentera; they might have figured that I would be headed for there. The only way to Formentera was via Ibiza, so it would be routine procedure to watch the Ibiza boats.

The windows opened and I was standing back a little to see if there was any sign of fuzz or if the clerk was asking to see people's ID, when I spotted Lise De Graff, my old friend from Ibiza. Few faces would I have preferred to see than Lise's. He was not only an old friend but a soul brother; he wasn't an acid-head but he was a dope smoker, therefore an outlaw like me.

'Hey, baby!' he said, looking at me closely, 'What happened to you?'

I steered him away from the queue and told him.

Lise reacted as I thought he would; what could he do to help? My first problem might be getting a ticket; the second might be getting on board the boat. For sure, there'd be cops near the gangplank; there always were. In case the ticket clerks were asking for ID, Lise said he'd buy my ticket along with his own and tell them I had gone to the jacks if asked. He'd lend me some clothes and give me cover when it came to walking up the gangplank. Like most of the Ibiza crowd, Lise didn't have much time for the law.

I changed in the toilets. As we approached the boat, Lise was walking in front of me with the tickets and I was keeping my head down under a beret, carrying one of Lise's framed canvases wrapped in brown paper and wearing a big, leather army-surplus jerkin with knitted sleeves like I think motorcycle dispatch riders wore during the war. We made it on board without being stopped. Lise was on his way home from selling some paintings in Amsterdam and had some bread, so he'd booked us a twin-berth cabin. I went straight to the cabin, and stayed there; sometimes, there were plainclothes police on the boat.

Lise brought down some coffee, *bocadillos* and booze. I told him the whole sorry tale. He said he'd hide me at his farmhouse out near Playa D'en Bossa, beyond Ibiza town, and get in touch with Rick and Hanna. I couldn't risk the crossing to Formentera. The boatman would immediately recognise me and would for sure be questioned by the fuzz – with luck, they might think I had escaped into France but they would certainly check Formentera anyway. I had to lie low; nobody except a few friends should know that I was back. After we stopped talking and turned out the cabin lights, I lay in the dark and listened to the ship's engines and tossed and turned, not with fear but with the loss of the world I loved besetting me in waves.

So suddenly, everything had changed! I was no longer free to go where I wanted or do what I wanted – no longer free to see Hanna, to hold Aoife, to see my friends, to sit by the fire, to swim in the sea. The island was gone and the world that was the island. The future was gone. If only I could reverse it all, if I could go back up the hill that had carried us down to La Junquera, where our fate was sealed in that instant . . . We were already in the west; we had already succeeded! But of course we knew nobody in France who'd take the dope – and nobody in England, for that matter. And anyway, it wasn't for sale. We just wanted to bring it home to friends; that was all we ever wanted to do.

And what about Hanna now? What about Aoife? What had I done to them? Why had I been so crazy, why hadn't I been cool like Jacey, like Bill Hesse, like Bruno and Desiree? Why hadn't enough been enough? I always thought I'd never get busted. I hadn't been caught – so far; at least there was that. I thought about Carlo, in jail. If I got out of Spain and was free, I'd get him out, whatever it took. I'd get lawyers, I'd take the blame and he'd be exonerated and set free. If that didn't work, I'd raise the money to buy him out. In Spain it was possible to buy a prisoner's freedom, as long as it wasn't a political offence.

Soon I'd be seeing Hanna, seeing Rick. Rick would organise my escape – he'd get me out of this jam, like I'd saved his ass in London. Once I was back in England, I'd send money for Hanna to come. I'd work every hour of every day until I could buy Carlo out and buy my own way back into Spain. I'd see the boys again, as before. How long I took to sleep that night, I can't remember. Perhaps I prayed.

In the morning, it was best that I disembarked alone because Lise would be met by friends who would know me. Foreigners gossiped and Franco's Spain was full of narks and informers, and many Ibicencos, although there were anti-Franco, could be compromised: they had brothers, fathers, husbands, sons still in jail from the civil war, and might give up a foreigner in exchange for those they loved – and who could blame them? It was a dangerous place, a small island, a dumb place to come to on the run. Because I'd lived there when foreigners were still a novelty and stood out, many locals knew me.

From the time I set foot on Ibiza, I'd be relying upon the help of others. But I was fortunate; I had my friends in Formentera and they would come over; nowhere could one find better friends. I desperately wanted to tell Hanna I loved her and to be reassured of her love for me.

Painted Deserts

Chapter 17

NEXT MORNING, WHEN THE BOAT docked in Ibiza and the straight passengers swarmed onto the deck, I stayed below. When I knew they'd be disembarking and there'd be a lot of distraction, I came up a back companionway, reached the railings near the stern and jumped ten feet onto the dock. Heading away, I crossed the open space of the dock and slipped into the narrow alleyways that led off it and would take me to the Vara de Rey, the edge of town and the road to Lise's. It was weird to be dodging from corner to corner in this town which had been my home. It was a Sunday; the streets were all but empty. I made it to the San José road and headed west, taking paths that ran through the scrubby *matorral*, where possible. I didn't want to be seen, even if the people I met didn't know me.

I reached Lise's house. He was already there, with Joanka, his wife, Steelbaum's mistress, whom I'd always liked. She showed me to a room at the back; it was small, with only a very small window, but it was perfect. I reckoned it was better to avoid talking about the bust; it might only make Joanka paranoid. We had Dutch coffee and then I went to my room where I wrote a note for Rick, half-coded, telling him where I was and asking him to come over as soon as he could. Lise went to the evening ferry to Formentera and found a guy who knew Rick and said he'd deliver it. Rick didn't come the next day – because he hadn't got the note – but he came the day after.

As we sat on a low wall behind the house, I told him all that had happened in Turkey and about the bust, how Carlo just didn't walk away with me. Rick was very warm and familiar, sitting there in a new but battered hat, old jacket and the desert boots we'd bought in London, half-shaven, nodding, looking at his feet, smiling now and then or meeting my eyes in sympathy. When I'd finished, he grinned and said that at least it was good that I'd made a run for it; he wouldn't be trying to get both Carlo and me out of jail!

I asked him who was around in Formentera. Bruno would have helped me but he and Desiree were gone, Bill was gone, John Walker from Tangier had been and gone. Jacey was there and Marvin, a good guy, did I remember him? I took out a piece of the Turkish hash I'd had in my fob pocket since Bulgaria, the last piece left, enough for two joints. Rick looked at it ruefully, and smiled. He burnt it to get the smell and we talked about what a pity it was we didn't have the five kilos. We didn't smoke the piece; he said to keep it until next day, and smoke it with Hanna.

She'd be coming over; he'd broken the news to her when he got my note. How was she? I asked. OK, he said, she's OK, and Aoife, too, and Nicole. Nicole would also like to see me; she wanted to hear about Carlo, of course. It was a pity I couldn't come to Formentera, but it would be crazy to try. The bad news was that some cops had asked Pepe, who ran the boat, about an *estranjero* who sounded awful like me. Longini, who spoke good Spanish, had heard him talking about it. It mightn't have been me at all but, nevertheless, we'd better take it that the cops were on my case and the word would be out in Ibiza soon too. I'd better lay low and get off the island and out of Spain *rápido*.

Rick told me about his trip. He'd never made it to India. After bussing and hitching across the Middle East, he found the Iran-Afghan border closed because of some war. He spent three weeks hanging out in a manky village smoking opium and when the border still didn't open and he was almost out of money, he headed back. He'd carried with him two hundred grams of boss opium, half of which he'd off'ed to this guy Marvin in Formentera and got a bit of bread for it – which was a good thing because he didn't have a pot to piss in at the time and, indeed, had barely a pot left to piss in now. He'd hoped Carlo and me would be there when he got back, so we could all smoke the O together. It was all smoked and gone now – at least what he'd kept of it – although Marvin still had a bit left and might turn me on.

I didn't say it, but what I knew of Marvin hadn't impressed me. Anyway, the last thing I was worried about was getting turned on to opium. I'd only ever done opium once before, when a guy in Paris had given me a ball as big as a pea and said put that inside your lower lip and let it dissolve there. It tasted foul, and when I got on the Metro, I suddenly felt like I was going to heave up all over everybody. I made it to the next stop and then, to everybody's disgust, spewed my cookies onto the rails.

Rick and I talked and talked. It was like old times. I told him that I thought I could make it work with Hanna; that I would tell her about Fran and we would begin with a clean slate. It was my first opportunity to talk about such things since the bust. Lise and I had never been as close as Rick and myself had become in the six months we'd known one another. Rick and Carlo; I thought I'd never had friends as close, except women. Rapping with Rick brought back the island, and sitting on that stone wall in the Ibiza sun, I could have been again in the timeless Formentera world we were both part of. Rick would get me out of Spain and into freedom, he swore: 'I'll shoot our way out if I have to!' Although I was sure it wouldn't come to that, I remembered his previous life as a gun-totin' punk and was comforted by his passion. He would lay down his life for me, he as much as said.

Once we could put some money together for fares and expenses, we'd head north together, with him covering me on the way. Either I'd end up free, or he'd join me and Carlo in the slammer, the Three Musketeers.

Hanna would come over next day, he thought. I said that, what with the fuzz maybe watching the Formentera boat, he should tell her to hang out in town for a while and then walk out on the road to Figueretas as if heading for a day on the beach. However, she should go all the way to Playa D'en Bossa, where there'd be nobody, only the empty beach and flat land; I could watch her coming from a long way off and see that she wasn't being followed. I told Rick to tell her where to meet me; she'd know it from the time we'd lived in the breeze-block house where we'd taken the first acid trip. He grasped my arm before he left. 'Don't let fear take the best!' he said. His eyes locked on mine, and there was warmth and reassurance in them.

Yeah, it was a bad time now, but nothing had changed with the things that were really important: not with me and Carlo, not with me and Rick, and not with me and Hanna. From Col and Kilian there would be a new separation but Nancy could come to England now and then – I'd send her the fares – and, in time, maybe I could buy my way back into Spain. People were the important thing. The van; the dope? They meant nothing. I'd see Hanna next and then Nicole. I knew it would be OK with Hanna, despite my having wrecked our dreams. She loved me. She'd always wanted my love. Now I could give her that love, unconditionally, and we would be truly together from now on. Maybe the journey was meant to open my eyes. On those long Anatolian roads, with the world blotted out by snow, I had felt my love for Hanna. Like I'd said to Carlo: I'd never been a hundred percent with her but would be, always, from now on.

The meet with Rick left me feeling good. We already had a rough plan, and I was ready for action. Carlo had stashed an out-of-date British passport Lowery had given him in C'an Pujolet in Formentera and, with luck, I might be able to alter it and give myself a new ID. When everything was set up for me to make a break for the mainland, I'd ask Rick to bring over the passport. Until then, it was better not to have it with me. Meanwhile, we had to find money to go north. Hanna might still have some of the bread I'd left before I went away but Rick didn't know. If not, he said he'd try to raise the cash to cover our fares to France, plus he'd get me a better place to hide out; a guy he'd met had a flat in the Old Town and was leaving the island for a few weeks. The fuzz would have my picture, so I'd have to alter my appearance. I should begin to grow a beard. We'd dye my hair and Rick would borrow a camera and take my photo for me to put in the phoney passport, originally belonging to a dentist.

That evening some friends of Lise's came to the house and I had to stay in the back room with the door locked just in case someone going to the john might stumble in. I could hear voices and laughter – music from a further room I couldn't enter. I spent the time writing a letter to Carlo. The next day, I'd give it to Hanna to pass on to Nicole whom, Rick said, would go and see him as soon as the US Embassy found out where he was in jail. I told Carlo how Rick had sworn he'd help me escape and I promised that once I got to London, I'd do nothing, morning, noon and night, except raise the bread to get him free.

After their friends had gone, Joanka came with some food. She was a flirtatious kind of girl and she hung around, asking me about Hanna. I told her how I felt about Hanna now. After a while, Lise came in and said they were heading off to the Domino Bar. He left me a joint and when they were gone, I smoked it, standing in the darkness outside the house. I could see the lights of the town in the distance and, in the other direction, the lights of the Casas Baratas where my two sons would be asleep, little knowing I was so close. I wouldn't let Nancy know I was on the island; she wouldn't inform on me, of course, but she mightn't be able to resist telling someone. I stood in the dark for a long while, thinking about all that had happened and what it meant to me and Hanna. I felt ashamed about what I'd done to her, not only with this fuck-up but all along.

In the morning, Lise went to town to check the post and came back with bad tidings. Carlo and I had been a major story on local radio, with details about the bust, the biggest ever in Spain, the news that he was in jail in Gerona, north of Barcelona, and that I lived on Ibiza – this, of course, was wrong. Lise tried to be his usual cheerful self but I felt he was a little strained now. Nevertheless, when I set off to meet Hanna, he took me part of the way on his big motorbike. I had a share of worries on my mind.

I feared that the news would soon be published in the Spanish newspapers and then, maybe, in the Irish ones. The biggest bust? What with Morocco so close, I'd have thought bigger consignments would have been coming through. However, I knew that hash hadn't long been a product of Morocco and, besides, in 1964 there wasn't any market for hash in Europe, except amongst a few, largely penniless, smokers in London and Amsterdam. It would be two years yet before dope really took off, with Dylan singing 'Everybody Must Get Stoned', the Fab Four – later to be 'respectabilised' with MBEs or knighthoods – singing 'Lucy in the Sky with Diamonds' (which we all knew stood for LSD) and half the kids in Europe and America dropping out of college and turning on.

Chapter 18

I MET HANNA ON A dry flat behind the Playa D'en Bossa beach, where nobody went. She'd walked the mile from town with Aoife on her hip to meet me. I scared the living daylights out of her from the start. I didn't mean to, but as I crossed the bare ground towards the palm trees above the beach where we were to meet, a horse and racing trap suddenly appeared and started driving up and down between me and them. What with my jacket, beret and basket – my escape outfit in case something went wrong and I was cut off from Lise's – I looked weird and the driver might have heard the news on the radio. Also, after Lise's tidings I'd smoked a joint, thinking it would calm me. I wanted to be at my best for Hanna and thought having a smoke would bring me closer to her when we met. But instead of calming me, it made me agitated, and the guy driving up and down freaked me out.

I couldn't risk running for the palms – he might see me – so I jumped into a shallow pit on the dry flat, a sort of bunker where someone must have been digging sand. I waited there, watching for Hanna. When she appeared, coming from the direction of Figueretas, with Aoife hanging off her, she walked along the palms towards where I'd said we'd meet. I watched her over the edge of the bunker and, when the horse and buggy had passed and the driver had his back to me, I stood and waved to her, and she saw me and approached.

As the buggy turned and came back and she was in view of the driver, I signalled to her to stop, and sit, and wait. She did this, lowering herself to sit only a dozen feet away from where I was crouching. She was wearing her faded blue skirt and a white blouse. For a long couple of minutes, she looked at me and I at her, both of us unable to move, close but unable to touch. There was no joy in her face, nor in mine, only tension and fear as the horse clip-clopped past, its harness bells jingling and the driver's commands ringing clear and terse in the silence between us. When he'd passed, she came in a rush, sliding into the bunker, Aoife wriggling and trying to escape from her arms.

It was a hopeless, devastating meeting. Nothing got said. Crouched down, trying to keep Aoife from climbing over the edge, we talked in snatches. I was sorry, so sorry, I said, and I love you from the bottom of my heart and will never leave you again – but it was all scrambled and she snapped at me when I asked her to hold Aoife still. She'd found the British dentist's passport and had hidden it outside, in case the fuzz came and searched the house. But she had no money to give me – how did I expect her to have? I'd been away so long and she'd been feeding half the people on Formentera!

I tried to make peace. I asked her would she come over and stay the night when Rick got me the place in the Old Town. All right, all right! she said – she'd have said anything just to get away. Then she apologised for being so sharp. We kissed awkwardly. I tasted salt; I was shedding tears by then myself, tears of misery and contrition. What the fuck had I done to us? Now the child started crying too. 'Go!' I told Hanna, 'Go!', and she went. I watched her out of sight. Aoife had seemed hardly to know me. The meeting was a disaster. 'Don't worry about us. Just look after yourself!' she'd said. I dwelt on those words afterwards.

The following day, I met Rick, also at the Playa D'en Bossa. There was no horse and buggy but Rick was more than an hour late and I'd had to hide once or twice when people passed. By the time he arrived, I was angry that he'd left me there so long, exposed. He had Marvin, the guy who'd bought the opium from him, in tow. I didn't like that at all. The first thing Rick said when he arrived, puffing like he was dying, was 'Man, the things we go through for you!' It wasn't a reassuring start.

Marvin extended a hand for me to shake and I took it, 'Good to see you,' he said in a serious American voice. I got Rick aside, leaving Marvin rolling up a joint under a palm tree. I made a joke about my getting paranoid and how I'd thought of all sorts of heavy scenarios when he hadn't shown at the time we'd agreed. He understood and apologised; he shouldn't have let it happen. Marvin had had some business to do, so he'd been delayed. I talked about my meeting with Hanna. She'd already told him that it hadn't been good. Rick was warm, *simpático*; he said it was just the shock and the circumstances. Next time, she and I would meet in a better place and it would be OK.

I figured I could be up-front with him about Marvin and say what I had to say. I told him I thought it'd be better if Marvin wasn't with him when we met; it was our thing and there was no need for an outsider to be there. Half-joking, he said, 'Hey, c'mon, I have to have someone to smoke with!' Carlo was in the slammer and I was on the run and what was he to do? Marvin was cool; Jacey said he'd been a 'big dealer' in America. I was surprised: Marvin had told Longini that he worked in his father's garment business in New Jersey. Anyway, since when did we hang out with 'big dealers', I asked. But Hanna likes Marvin too, Rick protested. 'Oh yeah?' I said, and there must have been something in my voice because Rick immediately sussed it and told me not to even think what I was thinking; when he was in jail, such fears were typical of guys who had chicks on the outside. Look, he said, finally, Marvin would help him get me out of Spain and he needed all the help he could get, OK? He'd help raise money to buy out Carlo as well; was there anything wrong with that? Yes, there was, I told him; we could trust one another but we knew nothing about Marvin. As soon as I was out of Spain, we'd raise the money to spring Carlo; we didn't need the help of any Johnny-come-lately so-called 'big dealer'.

Rick can't have been too pleased. I didn't care who he hung out with but I didn't want people I hardly knew introduced to me when I was on the run. One good thing that did come out of the meeting was the news that Rick had arranged to see the guy who had the pad in the Old Town and that he was looking for someone to live there for a few weeks to feed his cat. He was leaving the island the next day; Rick figured he could get the key from him and I could hide out there. It wasn't much of a place, he said, but it sounded great to me.

We talked about money. Hanna had none to spare; nobody on Formentera had cash beyond what they needed for rent and food, with nothing left over to contribute to my escape fund. We'd talked before about my writing begging letters to friends in London, Amsterdam, Paris. Now, Rick suggested I should tell them to send any contributions c/o Marvin at the Lista de Correos, Ibiza; there was no connection between Marvin and me and there'd be no danger to him. The fuzz might be watching letters coming to Formentera to Hanna or himself or people they'd know I knew. I didn't much like it, but I had to agree.

We parted warmly, having arranged to get together again the following night: it would be safer for me to move into the new place under the cover of darkness. Rick laid a small lump of Moroccan hash on me, which was great because I could give it to Lise and Joanka as a token of my appreciation. They hadn't complained about my extended stay – unquestionably, it was putting them in some danger. The original offer was that Lise would hide me for a night or two before I'd move on, but it was turning out that I'd be there four nights. When I arrived back, I was able to tell them the good news that Rick had found a place for me and I'd soon be moving out.

The following night, as I left to meet Rick, I said goodbye and thanks to Lise and Joanka. They wished me luck, and I set off with my basket and an old briefcase Lise had laid on me, along with a spare shirt and jeans and a few books he'd given me, too. I met Rick on the sea wall near Es Vive. He was an hour late and, worse, pain-in-the-arse-Marvin was with him again. It wasn't a good meeting. First thing they told me was they'd blown the pad I was supposed to get.

They'd missed the meet with the guy. When they'd arrived at his place, he had already gone, flown off home to Italy. They'd gotten stoned and forgotten, they said, like it was some sort of joke. When I said that was a fuckin' drag, Marvin grinned and said, 'Hey, man, we're into drug-time, not clock-time, OK?'

It was the opium, of course; it was the fuckin' opium! Jesus Christ, it shouldn't have been hard to do: meet the guy and get the key from him! I was really pissed off with Rick. What was he doing with this fucking clown, this would-be comedian, with a big fat grin on his fat fucking face? I felt like telling him that in different circumstances I'd soon wipe it off for him, but I said nothing. I knew it wouldn't go down well with Rick; I had to keep my friends.

I was even more incensed when he turned to Rick and, as if I wasn't there, began to talk about why the Spanish fly he'd given to some chick down town had made her go to sleep instead of feeling sexy. Did he think I had come out in the night, a wanted man, to hear this shit? Spanish fly? Did it really exist? It sounded like something out of the French Foreign Legion. And laying it on some chick, dropping it in her drink when she wasn't looking? Hey, c'mon! We did not lay drugs on people without them knowing. Where was Rick's head at anyway? Now, the prick Marvin was saying that maybe they should hurry back there before the chick went off somewhere and, this time, drop some Nembutal on her. She was freaked out in any case – her old man had been busted at Tarifa bringing in a bag of grass from Morocco and she would-n't be seeing him again for some time.

Marvin sounded like a walking fuckin' pharmacy: opium, Spanish fly, Nembutal. I wanted to take Rick aside; I wanted to ask him what the fuck was happening. But I was supremely hip that putting them down would do me no good. They'd say I was some sort of spoilsport and, for sure, they wouldn't be very open with me from then on. So, whatever about the when-just-men-hold-their-peace-the-bad-guys-thrive syndrome, I kept my counsel and, for once, shut up. They felt my vibe, though; I could only pretend so much.

We parted quickly. Apart from not being outdoors longer than necessary, all the crap I was hearing was turning me off. Before the possibility of the Italian's cat-sitting gig had come up, Rick had mentioned another place that was available; the big difference was, it would have to be paid for. We didn't need it then but we sure needed it now. I'd have to use my bread, the four hundred pips I hadn't had to spend for Carlo's ferry fare and meals. The rent would be one hundred and twenty pesetas a week and we'd have to put up a month in advance. Rick said he'd raise the balance. But next day was Christmas, so there'd be no business done; he'd see me at the same place in two nights' time.

'I guess I'll have to go back to Lise's,' I said, half to myself, ending the conversation. It was a lame thing to say and Marvin overheard it.

'You could sleep out!' he suggested.

'I'd freeze to death.'

'Why ask then? You know the answer . . .' He shot Rick a smart-ass grin.

That was Marvin. It confirmed my first impressions, Longini's too. Marvin was a self-appointed teacher, a guru from the garment district, and this was the kind of lesson he specialised in: wisdom in one line. It was hit and run: having scored a hit, he walked away, smiling. I just stood there, struck dumb. When I looked at Rick, all he did was look lamely back, and say, 'Remember what I said, man. Don't let fear take the best!' Then he turned to follow Marvin back to town.

If I'd bitched to Rick, he'd have defended the prick, and said I had no right to attack him. Hanna, who told me the next time I met her that Marvin was a 'beautiful' guy, would have given me the same answer. So Marvin got himself a licence to put me down, and I could do fuck all about it. He had the ear of my friends on Formentera. Hanna told me, when I cast some doubt on him, that he'd read 'all of Ouspensky when he was on acid'; she told me this in some awe. Now what do you say to that? Where do you begin?

That, of course, was my problem; it was beyond me to listen to Marvin's gimcrack homilies like he was some sort of oracle. I knew what he was doing. He had Rick and Hanna enthralled, but I wasn't fooled.

As I headed back to Lise's, I was sick with worry. Sick about Rick, my main man, and what was going down with him. Where was he at, since he'd come back from Iran and got tight with Marvin? They were too fuckin' cool to be cool, the pair of them. I was no angel, but the sort of shit they were into now was too heavy for me.

I'd lost a safe hiding-place because they'd gotten stoned; and it was Marvin who had the opium. As I walked back to Lise's, asking myself how I could face him, I wondered if I could make it out of Spain alone. Cross to the mainland, walk at night, hide by day, cross the Pyrenees at night into France or walk maybe five hundred miles to Portugal? But I had no money now; I'd just foreclosed that option by handing all I had over to Rick. No bread, no phoney passport, no photo of myself to put in it even if I had – how could I leave? But more important than all that, before I went anywhere I had to know where Hanna was at; I had to restore her faith in me. I'd always been in control but I'd terrified her. 'Just look after *yourself*!' she'd said. Everything was different now. I had to see Nicole, and find out what she thought about it all.

Chapter 19

MY ARRIVAL BACK AT LISE and Joanka's was no picnic for them or for me. They had a fire going and were sitting very laid back when I loomed in out of the night. Lise cried out 'Kom!' when I knocked, thinking it was some friend stopping by. They went through some changes when they saw me, but tried not to show it. I said what had happened and that I was sorry and that I needed to stay another day or maybe two. 'OK, two days,' Lise shrugged; he wasn't heavy but it was a time limit, nevertheless. 'Your bed's still made up,' said Joanka. I refused the drink they offered and split to my room where I sat and smoked a jay and thought about what had happened with Rick, going over every word that had been said.

From now on, what had been said in conversations constantly preyed on my thoughts. I would replay the words and analyse the vibes, the tone and subtle inferences, whether they revealed a change in the way I was regarded and what that change meant to my future.

On Christmas Day, Lise had his brother and family from Amsterdam to stay and the house was full. I spent the day in my room. I think the visitors knew I was there but, clearly, it was best I didn't join them. Lise came and had a private drink with me, and Joanka brought me some Christmas dinner. Naturally, I thought of Hanna, my three children, my parents, brother and sister around the table at home. I figured the bad trip I'd had with Rick at Es

Vive was a one-off; they were stoned, that was all. I'd make no big deal of it. It would be OK next time.

I wrote letters to Bill Hesse in Copenhagen, Bernard in London and Zelda in Paris, asking if they could send me some escape money; also, with less hope, to wandering Bruno and Mel. I asked them to write back care of Marvin at the Lista in Ibiza. When I met Rick two nights later, I had the letters all addressed and ready to go. He was alone, and that was a mighty relief. The vibe was like the first time we'd met, that day behind Lise's. He'd scored the rented apartment he'd talked about. We headed for the town, him leading the way so he could watch out for fuzz.

We went via the dark, narrow tunnel leading up through the old walls west of the Vara de Rey. It started at a big, dusty square. In 1960 or 1961 a Guardia Civil had insisted on driving me around it on the back of a 300cc Vespa scooter because I'd almost knocked him down with it and he thought I needed to learn how to drive. When he'd asked to see my driving licence, I'd shown him an Irish blood donor card with the symbol of a pelican embossed on front and he'd laboriously written down my name and number and 'Group A'. Many of the streets I passed through had memories for me of Nancy or of Rainer, my Canadian pal, on our night-owl trips. I knew the town better than Rick and following him was yet another strange experience.

At the top of the tunnel, we came out at an open space of dust and bedrock. Two adjoining houses stood facing the parapets which overlooked the new town and the sea. They were two-storey and run-down, with flaking whitewash fronts. Rick crossed to one of them and I followed; I noticed that it had once had a shop on the ground floor. He opened the door with a big iron key and we went up a narrow, musty staircase to a door on the first floor which he unlocked. The Old Town pad, as I came to call it, was cold; it never got the sun in winter. It was utilitarian and bare, but none of this mattered to me: it was an ideal refuge. It had been empty for a long time and nobody lived downstairs. Nevertheless, I was careful not to draw attention to my tenancy.

The floors were tiled and the walls whitewashed, decorated with a few faded pictures cut from magazines. There was a kitchen sink, a cold water tap and an old-fashioned charcoal stove set into the wall, with a butane gas bottle with two rings standing on top of it. There was a frying pan and a few saucepans. The toilet and shower worked, but it was cold water. The furniture was a Formica-topped table and four wooden chairs. Doors led off the living-room/kitchen to the shower/toilet, the stairs, a small balcony and two bed-rooms, one of which was entirely empty and windowless, while the other contained a double bed and a lot of dead flies on the floor.

As Rick said, it wasn't four-star, but I had no complaints. I was on a high after the walk from Lise's and the rush of having made it safely into town. Rick had come through for me and, as far as I was concerned, the fuck-ups were forgiven and forgotten. He'd even brought me a few groceries.

When I thanked him for his trouble, he'd just shrugged and said, 'Hey, man, c'mon . . .' Clearly, he was pleased that I was pleased; it was like old times between us.

Although there was electric light, we lit the candle I had in my basket and sat down at the table and rolled a joint. I assumed he would stay the night; the bed could be split and the mattress laid on the floor of the other room. The mattress would also be fine overnight for Nicole, and for Aoife when Hanna came to stay. Rick said he and Marvin might even keep the place when I had gone: they'd met a guy in Figueretas who'd said he could get them some smack and the place would be useful when they came over from Formentera. I thought it was strange, the smack, and strange that they'd want to spend time in Ibiza, but I didn't remark on it.

Most of the bread Rick had used to pay the first month's rent had come from me. It would've been enough, in any case, to get us to Barcelona and pay train tickets to France. Every time we'd talked about it, we'd decided the train was the safest way to get me across the Spanish border. The plan was we'd take a night sleeper and find a carriage with other foreigners. When the Immigration guys came aboard, I'd pretend to be asleep and Rick would search for my passport in my bag. By the time he'd found it, he'd have created so much confusion and delay that they wouldn't take a good look.

We've barely finished the joint when he gets to his feet and says he's gotta hit the street; he and Marvin are going to meet the Figueretas guy. After that, Marvin planned to lay ten drops of Spanish fly on the chick they'd talked about to see if the increased dose would work. Rick smiled a little uncomfort-ably as he told me this, like it wasn't something he'd have done himself.

Maybe the chick didn't want to ball Marvin, I suggested; she sounded pretty fucked up and, besides, laying all that stuff on her – they didn't want to kill her, right? Rick shrugged: Marvin was into drugs and into balling the chick so who was he to tell him what he should or shouldn't do? Marvin was convinced she was coming on to him anyway and just didn't know her own mind – but, yeah, Rick told me, he'd look after her and make sure things didn't get out of hand. Before he left, he said he'd tell Hanna where the apartment was when he got back and that she'd be over in a couple of days to bring me more food and stuff.

'So, motherfucker,' he said, standing and smiling warmly, 'all's well with the world, right? I'll see you in a few days.'

I heard the door close after him, and went down and locked it from the inside, pulling the bolt across. Back upstairs, I decided I wasn't going to let Rick's quick departure bring me down. Alone in the empty rooms, I was thankful for the silence. It was the first time since I'd arrived on the island that there was nobody but myself to think of. At Lise's, I'd always been conscious of the danger I posed to them and of not getting in their way.

I whistled as I set myself up: my cans of sardines, and a can of meat balls and spaghetti, two bread rolls, the half-jar of coffee Joanka had given me, a tin of sugar, a box of matches, a few packets of fags. All was well with the world, as Rick had said. No more ducking behind bushes with a pounding heart. It would take five days for my letters to reach Bill and the others, and five days for them to write back. Give it two weeks at most and I should have the money to get moving. Meantime, I just had to lie low and stay cool. If I let it, my heart ached to be with Hanna, to see Aoife and Col and Kilian, to be with everyone. But things weren't so bad; Hanna'd be coming next day and old Rick a few days later. I was blessed to have such friends!

The balcony over the dusty street had the usual double doors, half-paned, with a thin view through the shutters out over the street and the sea. I would keep them open a slit during the day but at night I could open them a smidgen wider if I was burning no lights inside. That night, I opened them and stood inside, in darkness. The rooms behind me were simple and cell-like but they suited me, in this hidden corner of the Old Town. I went to bed a happier man.

Chapter 20

THE SECOND TIME I SAW Hanna was no better than the first. Nothing was as I'd hoped it would be. Rick had told her where to find me. She had come alone, having left Aoife with Lorna, Jacey's wife, in the town. She'd brought groceries for me; as she unpacked them, I went to hug her, but she moved away. I talked to her back as she filled the coffee pot and put things on shelves. I tried to tell her about the Turkey trip, upbeat things about Venice, how I thought she'd love it and we might live there one day, about Titov Veles, the town perched on the gorge-side, and about Carlo and how cool he was. Suddenly, she turned and said, 'I'm sorry, but this is your thing. I wasn't there and I'm really not interested.'

I was taken aback. 'I'm just trying to tell you the news, honey,' I said. I sounded a bit irked, I suppose, and there was a silence. Then she told me that Nicole had had a letter from Carlo; he sent his love to me and hoped I was OK. But there was no warmth in her voice. I said that if anyone could cope with jail, Carlo could, but I wasn't so sure how I'd get on if it was me. She said that I'd created the situation and I'd have to deal with it. It didn't concern her. Christ, I thought, whatever's happening with her, I'd better handle it gently. So I said I understood, and shut up.

It was strange sitting at the table with her, drinking coffee, not knowing what to say to this woman with whom I thought I was so close, closer than to Rick or Carlo or Bruno or anybody. I asked her how Aoife was. Fine, she said. Did she miss me? Yes; what did I expect? How were things in Formentera? All was fine, she answered, and no more.

I had thought her visit would give me a chance to tell her how my feelings had changed, to tell her about Fran and how it was going to be different from now on. But the silences and the coldness of the room – we were holding the coffee mugs in our hands for warmth – came between us. I had the shutters closed and the light from the bulb overhead was stark. It was like we were strangers, and yet we hadn't been apart for more than eight weeks.

I told her that when I had escaped I'd headed for Ibiza because I knew I'd get help but mainly because I wanted to see her. It was good to see me too, she said, but I should please get out of Spain, just go. Go as soon as possible. There was an edge of desperation in her voice. Rick and Marvin would help me, she said; they were beautiful guys and I was lucky to have them as friends. I hoped she was right, but as soon as I mentioned that they were being a little casual, she got uptight and told me I had no right to complain, especially about Marvin. He owed me nothing and was helping me only because he was a beautiful person. I should realise I was turning him off by making demands.

She was lecturing me; she was on their side, not mine. I was bewildered: what 'demands'? Where had she heard this? Surely she should be worried if Rick and Marvin were putting me in danger? I didn't expect her to help me physically, but what did she think? Marvin said they were 'on drug-time': Rick had missed a vital appointment. Were they reliable? She was seeing them every day. She was in the real world and I would trust her reading; she was the closest person to me. But clearly, she didn't even want to hear what I had to say.

Realising that there was no point, I dropped the subject. If they'd been putting me down back in Formentera, saying I'd been uncool when they were late at Es Vive – making 'demands' that they be on time?– there was nothing I could do about it. I couldn't go to Formentera and defend myself; I couldn't go the fuck anywhere! And now here was my darling Hanna siding with them. Yeah, she was pissed off with me – I should never have brought her home this grief – but my concerns about Rick and Marvin were legitimate. She'd be concerned too if she knew the weird bag they were in, into scoring smack, laying Spanish fly on some chick, forgetting appointments that could fuck me up. But I wasn't going to tell tales out of school.

Instead, I said I wanted to get out of Spain just as urgently as she wanted me to. I told her that although I'd been there only a couple of days, the apartment was driving me spare and if I had some money I'd make a break for it, right there and then, alone. I'd get to London and when I'd found us a place, send money for her to join me. We'd begin again from there. I asked her wasn't there any way she could raise some bread? What about Longini? With this, she turned on me as if I was accusing her of blowing the cash I'd given her before I left. She'd had people at the house, she cried; she'd had to feed them! If I'd come back sooner – if only I'd come back sooner, like I'd said in my letter from Istanbul . . . She'd expected me day after day but I hadn't come. Why had I ever gone?

I had no idea of what all this anger was about. I had never expected it; I put it down to stress. All I knew was that we were having a row, and that was the last thing we needed. I apologised and tried to calm her down. I thought I was succeeding when, out of nowhere, she said she had to leave.

This, coming so suddenly, knocked me sideways, and it made me hopping mad, too. Couldn't she give a single hour of her precious time to the guy she'd been living with for three years, the father of her child? It was because of Aoife, she said; she had to get back to her, she couldn't leave her 'like this'.

I stood dumbfounded as she picked up her basket. She was sorry, she said, she was just upset. She'd come again on the Saturday; she'd cross on the evening boat and see me then. When I heard this, my heart skipped a beat: if she came in the evening, there'd be no boat back and she'd stay overnight. There would be reconciliation: I had a mental flash of us having dinner together at the Formica table. We'd be talking and making plans for London and a brighter future. I just needed a chance and I could make her feel better, I knew. I'd tell her how I'd be back on my feet in no time; that we'd buy Carlo out of jail; that we could save and go to the Greek islands next.

Just before she left, I kissed her and she let it happen. It was one-sided, a buss of the lips; she didn't embrace me, but she didn't draw away. In some sort of euphoria, I asked her if she'd help me if I really had to go alone, if it didn't work out with Rick. I meant only that she might get someone else to bring me over the passport and she might borrow some bread so I could get to the mainland; I'd take my chances from there. But it was bad timing. Before I knew it, she was back telling me how I already had two good friends to help me and that I should stop 'trying to rule them'. They were 'on their high' and they were 'coming down' for my sake.

Jesus, I thought, 'on their high'! Did she mean so stoned out on opium they couldn't get their asses in gear to come and meet me at the time they said? What had Rick and fucking Marvin been telling her? I asked her what they'd said. She wouldn't tell me. She didn't want to discuss it – she didn't want to get involved, she had to think of Aoife. And then she said something lethal like, 'But, of course, you didn't think of her!'

After she left, I was pretty fucked up – fucked up, and also mad with her. Stupid bitch, I thought, believing those guys! But I felt more sorry for her than angry. She was right. She had Aoife to think of; there were more important things in the world than the problems I'd made for myself and into which she was now drawn. The paradise we'd found had turned into a nightmare, thanks to me. We'd have to leave Spain. Before I'd taken off, we'd had enough money for months, maybe for a year, but I'd gone and blown it on an adventure. She had a right to be mad.

I spent the rest of the day in my head, smoking a joint now and then, staring out the sliver of the window at faraway Talamanca, trying to take stock of what Hanna had said. I figured it was Marvin who'd been putting me down; Rick wouldn't do that. Nobody wanted me in Ibiza, and the sooner I was gone, the better. If Rick let me down, she wouldn't help. I wouldn't ask her, anyway. I'd done enough damage already, but I'd make it up to her as soon as I was free.

The next time she came, I'd woo her and romance her, as I'd dreamt of romancing her on the long, dark roads of Turkey, conjuring up pictures of the nights we'd have together by the fire when I came home. I'd promise her a better future, where nothing like this would ever happen to us again.

In my inner-directed mind, her Saturday visit would be the panacea for all my ills. In hindsight, it's easy to see that I was spending too much time in my head, in solitary confinement, smoking too much dope alone. But, of course, we all thought that dope was a door to perception. However, once things started to go wrong, smoking didn't lift me up; it brought me down. Timothy Leary wrote about the positive or negative effects of 'Environment and mood' on the stoned psyche; I should have paid more attention to that. Smoking dope made me less able to cope with the deterioration of my relationship with the others, less able to distinguish the reality from the illusions; it fucked me up. The breakdown with Rick and the others was gradual but inexorable; I remember it step-by-step, blow-by-blow.

It's bullshit, the cliché that says if you can remember the Sixties, you weren't there. I remember no decade more vividly. As for that Saturday night which I so looked forward to spending with Hanna, I remember it like yesterday, every minute of it and every word that was said.

When Saturday afternoon came, I was full of excitement and expectation. The fact that I'd had no sight of Rick for four days bothered me a bit but it wasn't like he lived around the corner and Hanna would bring news of him, good news, I was sure. I was going to cook her dinner – I was no chef but I could manage a corn beef hash. There was no hashish in it like in Alice B. Toklas's famous hash brown recipe; it was made by mashing a can of corn beef into a saucepan of spuds mixed up with Tulipan margarine. For drinks, I had a half bottle of Bacardi which Lise had given me before I'd split his place – 'For the road,' he'd said. By the time the Formentera boat was due in, I was wearing a clean shirt, had made the bed up nicely and put a candle on the table. Through a slit in the shutters, I watched the red glow in the sky fade and thought the boat would surely have docked by now. But dusk began to gather outside and Hanna still hadn't shown.

Time ticked slowly by. The apartment was silent, and there were no footsteps outside. Had she been stopped by the cops? Had she decided to cut loose and wasn't going to see me again? Not Hanna, I told myself. But it was a fearful thought; that I could lose her and, therefore, Aoife, like I'd lost my sons.

While I refused to let paranoia get hold of me, I became more distressed as darkness fell and the distress began turning to a sort of desperation, a crying need to assuage my fears. I thought of going out and looking for her, but that was impossible. She mightn't even be in Ibiza, she might have simply missed the boat or the boat mightn't have made the crossing. I couldn't know and, what was worse, I couldn't find out.

It was an hour after the time the boat usually docked and I was finding it hard to keep my fears at bay when a loud knock sounded at the street door. I stood up, not making a sound. It wasn't a Hanna knock; she wouldn't bang so loudly. It was more like Rick. I ran down the stairs. 'Comin', comin',' I called, pulling across the bolt and fumbling with the key; there was no light there and I had to find the keyhole by touch. I found it, opened the door a sliver and peered out.

Rick and Marvin stood outside. 'Open the fuck up, man, it's us!' Rick grinned at me, all friendly. They were all lit up like they were going to a party. OK! I thought; make the change, make the change, forget Hanna for a minute, join the spirit. You'll find out soon enough what happened with Hanna; there's probably a good reason she isn't here. Don't make a big deal of it. Be light-hearted. *Do not bring them down!*

Chapter 21

THEY HAD SCORED SOME SMACK, they said, and had come to share it with me. Now, that was nice. I wasn't into smack but I wasn't going to refuse it if they'd come especially to turn me on. In fact, maybe getting high with Rick would bring us back to normal together and I might even see Marvin in a different light. I welcomed them and said nothing at all about Hanna. I put out another glass, opened the Bacardi and was going to pour. Marvin looked at Rick like I was doing something stupid. He put his hand over his glass. 'We're not into alcohol,' he said. I just smiled and shrugged. I poured a small hit for myself. I wasn't going to be intimidated.

Without further ado, they cleared the dinner plates off the table and laid out a spike and syringe. They produced the smack – a neat packet of brown powder – and a small packet of white powder, which they said was coke. They were into mixing speedballs. They were whooping with the anticipation and were soon making a collar for the spike and cooking up in a spoon. Marvin was laying the needle on Rick's vein, and sucking in a wisp of blood and then giving him the hit, and drawing up the blood again to follow with the boot. Once again, I was fascinated by the language. It was like that they were making love to one another. It's strange that so evil a drug as smack can engender a feeling like love, but in the first rush through the body that's what it does to you.

When they'd each given the other a fix with love and care, they found there wasn't enough left to make a hit for me. I didn't give a fuck about that, but now Marvin, sitting back and smiling away, began to tell me how unhip it was to drink alcohol and what he thought of the people he saw in the Domino Bar, all of whom, he reckoned, were old friends of mine. He was needling me but not in a friendly way. I asked him why didn't he say it to them, and he said he had better things to do with his time. Yeah, I thought, I'd sure like to see Marvin try to tell old Steelbaum, or Brunswick, or the Flying Tiger, or my ex-wife, Nancy, about the error of their ways. Lushes, some of them might be, but they'd chew him up and blow him out in bubbles.

While he was talking, Rick was getting together a joint. When it was ready, he passed it to Marvin to light. 'Give it to The Fugitive!' said Marvin. I didn't like it, but I laughed, 'Yeah, like I'm an IRA man on the run!' As it turned out, Marvin's comment wasn't intended as a joke. As I smoked the jay, I looked at the bent spoon and the syringe and I remembered what Rick had said about him and Marvin wanting a place in Ibiza: they were already turning the pad into a fuckin' shooting gallery, and I was paying the rent.

As the joint passed around, Marvin told me that they'd come to hang out with me, so why didn't I seem at ease in their company? He could feel my paranoia; it was in the air. I didn't know what to say to that; it sure was in the air after he'd said it. And, of course, the joint hadn't helped: 'The long grey wolf of paranoia stalks the pot-head's heels . . . '

Marvin said he could see I had problems but I should know from taking acid that there was no problem unless I made one; that it was all in my head. I was clearly fucked up and was imposing myself on others like, for instance, on Hanna when she'd come to see me. I needed to take a look at myself and my attitude towards people.

As I listened, I could hardly believe what I was hearing. The prick hardly knew me. Meantime, Rick was nodding to everything he said and looking at me with concern, like a visitor at a sick bed. I said, half-joking-all-in-earnest, 'Hey, Marvin, none of us are perfect but I don't need a fuckin' sermon!'

This was not a good move. Rick looked up, his eyes suddenly cold. 'You got a problem?' he asked me. 'C'mon, spit it out . . .'

I shrugged. 'Who's he to tell me all this, Rick? You hear what he's sayin'!

Who does he think he is? Some sort of LSD God?'

Silence fell. My words were left hanging. Marvin sighed and shook his head like I was so uncool, I wasn't worth his time. But Rick didn't let it go. He told me I should be listening to Marvin, not insulting him, because Marvin loved me and was trying to straighten me out, straighten me out because I was fucked up and didn't realise it.

'Fucked up?' I said, 'Who says so, Rick?' But it was true – what with the shit they were laying on me, I was getting fucked up alright!

I had got the wrong idea, Rick said, and a lot of stuff needed straightening out before they'd go another step to help me.

Firstly, I should be grateful, not critical. Like this thing about being late: they didn't have to come at all. Secondly, what I'd said to him about Marvin when we were alone, about him laying Spanish fly on the chick: Marvin knew what he was doing and it wasn't anybody's business to question it. Thirdly, I should stop making assumptions, such as that when we reached the north he and I would get together to do travellers cheque scams to raise Carlo's bread. Marvin thought cheque scams were penny-ante bullshit; they'd have some serious deals going and my help wouldn't be needed to look after Carlo, did I understand that?

My ears were ringing with the hardness in his voice, the implications of what he was saying. 'OK, Rick, OK, OK.' I said, just wanting to stop the bombardment. But then Marvin chipped in to say that, by the way, I should also forget any ideas about getting a place in London where everybody could stay. He and Rick would be getting an apartment: Carlo and Nicole would be staying there when Carlo got out of the slammer. It would be a big place; if Hanna wanted, she could stay there as well. The best thing for me would be to find myself a room somewhere and get a job.

I was stunned. Turning my back on Marvin, I looked Rick in the eye and said 'Rick, this isn't how it should be. You know that!' He did know it, too; I could see it in his face. But then, suddenly, something else possessed him and he was like I'd never seen him before or imagined he could be, full of dishonesty and lies. It had to be down to the weeks of smoking O – the itch it leaves when it runs out, the irritability, the yen for smack, then the rush of the cocaine in the speedball.

He'd been lonely, alone with his opium in Formentera while Carlo and I were in Turkey. Then Marvin had showed up and they'd begun to smoke together, Marvin filling their skulls with euphoric dreams of opulence from big dope deals. With the drugs they had done that night, they were riding high, Marvin, an LSD guru, and Rick, a cocaine superman. I was dismayed and heart-sore at the treatment I was getting from my friend. He had rushed to Marvin's defence. Rick was fiercely loyal to friends; and Marvin was his friend now.

He jumped to his feet, eyes cold, jaws tight, nostrils dilated, 'You don't listen to Marvin!' he yelled. 'You're too fuckin' smart, right? Smart enough to get yourself into this fuckin' situation!'

'He's on an ego trip,' Marvin interjected, lighting another joint. I ignored him, as if he wasn't there.

'You're fuckin' paranoid,' Rick went on. 'It brings us down!' From the minute they'd come in, he said, they'd felt my paranoia: pouring them the booze when I knew they didn't drink, all that shit, and then I attack Marvin when he's trying to straighten me out.

I attempted to interrupt. 'Shut up!', Rick told me. 'You disgust me!' They'd come to turn me on, they hadn't come for this and they were going now. It was my fault, not theirs and they weren't going to go through this again!

As the diatribe went on, Marvin sat there, looking at the table, nodding, like Right, Right, Right-on! At last, Rick stopped. In the silence, he turned his back on me and walked to the sink and started to wash out the syringe and spike under the tap. Now, Marvin took over. He told me that, after tonight, the only reason they'd be helping me get out of Spain would be for Hanna's sake, and after I was out, I'd be on my own. 'On your own!' Rick said from the sink, did I get that? Did I get that now? Then, he turned and said, 'We're goin'!'

Marvin rose; it was like choreography. I was in shock – I was like a child, I suppose, standing there. I desperately wanted to wind back the clock; I saw them slipping away from me, taking Carlo and Nicole with them, maybe Hanna too. They were the movers now, not me; I was pathetic – what would Hanna want with me? 'Wait, Rick,' I said, talking to his back, 'I'm sorry. I'm fucked up, man. I'll be OK next time . . .' But without meeting my eyes he pushed past me and disappeared down the stairs.

'You've fucked yourself up. We didn't do it,' Marvin told me as he picked up their things from the table. 'Remember what I said, "There's no problem unless we make one,"' and then he was out the door, off down the stairs. 'You're your own worst enemy!' Rick shouted from below, viciousness in his voice, and the street door slammed behind them. Off they went into the Ibiza night of friends and music. I could hear them, as they went, talking in loud and careless voices; hardly a cool thing to do outside the door of the fugitive they'd left behind.

In the room, the debris of their visit was everywhere – not least in my head. There was half a joint left in the ashtray; I sat down and smoked it, and poured myself a Bacardi too. I tried to recover, to take stock.

Some time after they'd gone and I was still staring into space, a light knock sounded at the door. It sort of spooked me because I wasn't sure it was even a knock at first. Who could it be? The knock sounded again and suddenly I knew who it was. It was Hanna!

I must have looked kind of freaked as I stood aside to let her past me up the stairs. She didn't smile and she didn't buss me on the lips or anything. The table was a mess, with a burnt spoon, a burnt-down candle, a gutted cigarette, torn cardboard from the collar they'd made for the needle, and the ashtray filled with fag ends and roaches. I wanted to ask her where she'd been, why she hadn't come when she'd said she would, but I was so pleased to see her that I was prepared to forget all that. She looked good, as if she'd dressed to meet me. She had some make-up on. I saw her coming as a beam of light in the darkness after Rick, and conceived of her as some sort of angel come to lift me out of my despair.

The first news she gave me was that the fuzz had been to the house in Formentera; two plainclothes cops with the trousers of their suits rolled up because they'd lost their way on the *camino* and come across the fields. Their shiny shoes were all dusty and they were hot and heavy, going through the three rooms to see if I was hiding out, and demanding photographs (which Hanna didn't have). They flashed the photograph left behind by me in the wagon at the border, saying: '*¿Su marido, sí? ¡Ya sabemos!*'

They'd found nothing incriminating in C'an Pujolet because there was nothing to find; Hanna had already stashed the old dentist passport outside and there was no dope on the premises. Nicole had been there with her at the time; even when the cops had started acting friendly, she and Nicole had given nothing away. They admitted that they knew Carlo was in the nick in Gerona but they had no idea where I was, they said. There were no telephones, they hadn't heard from me since Hanna had got a postcard from Bulgaria. The cops left, none the wiser, but their visit had scared her. And she was spooked more than ever, I suppose, as she sat and told me.

I was about to offer her a hit of the Bacardi or a cup of maté, and to say I'd make some food, but it didn't get to that. She told me she wouldn't be staying long; there were things she wanted to talk to me about and then she'd go.

My heart fell; one minute I'm up, next minute down. My dreams of a candle-lit corned-beef hash dinner and my fond hope that I could make things right between us dissolved. She said she'd left Nicole looking after Aoife at the place they'd be staying – it was in Figueretas; it belonged to some guy Rick knew – and she'd have to get back there soon. Nicole would be catching the Barcelona ferry the next day, to go to Gerona to see Carlo. I tried not to show my disappointment, to play it cool, when another piece of news stopped me short. She said she'd met Rick and Marvin in the town and they'd warned her that I was very fucked up and paranoid and I'd been very heavy with them. She hoped she could talk to me about it, that I wasn't going to make another scene.

I must stop being paranoid with them, she told me; I was alienating them and if I wasn't careful, they'd stop helping me. The problem was in my head. I was my own worst enemy. She said it with genuine concern but to me it sounded like an echo of the holy Marvin's homilies and Rick's bad vibes. I had no answer to this, only a huge fatigue. Why did she have to stay at this place in Figueretas? I asked her. There was room for her and Aoife here – there didn't have to be sex or anything. No, she said, I can't. I asked her to tell me why and then, in tears, it all came out, what she'd come to tell me. She had been sleeping with Marvin. It was my fault; I'd stayed away too long.

Soon after Carlo and I left, Marvin had started turning up at the house offering to do things, like mending Bruno's old bike, getting firewood and so on. At first, she and Nicole had laughed at him, but he'd kept showing up every day and turning them on and then crashing out in the living room at night. Hanna had hoped and prayed I'd come back because she missed me, and day by day it was clearer that he was slowly moving in, making himself the man around the place and she couldn't send him away because his help had put her under an obligation. She knew what he was after but – and this was how she put it – he'd 'worn her down'.

The night it happened, he'd brought three acid trips on sugar cubes and he and she and Nicole had each taken one. Later, when she went to the bedroom to be alone, he'd come and lain down beside her, saying that a few days before he had read Ouspensky when he was on a trip and that he would guide her trip now. He started talking. At first, she hardly listened, but slowly she began to realise that we – she and I – had been wrong about Marvin; that he was an enlightened person, but we had been too blind and unenlightened to see. When he started to make love, it happened naturally; it had been right, and it was beautiful, she said.

I wanted to say, 'Bullshit, his Ouspensky – he's a Creepin' Jesus, he took over your mind because he wanted your body and your soul. It was my fault, not yours, because I left you to the mercy of charlatans. I was profligate with your love and it was me who was to blame for this, not you.' That's what I wanted to say, but I didn't. I knew that to attack Marvin would make her defend him all the more, because it would be attacking her judgement too; this much I knew from experience, from Nancy-time. As she stood by the window sobbing, I said to her, 'I love you,' but she wept all the louder and said 'No. No,' and turned away.

'Hanna,' I said, 'You weren't the only one. When I was in London, I had a scene with this friend of Nicole's. It was nothing and—'

'I know,' she interrupted, 'Nicole told me. It doesn't matter now.'

I believed that she still loved me, that this was not the end. If I didn't drive her away, that love could be rekindled. Aoife was a bond between us, precious to us both, and we were precious to her. Hanna would think of that. Whatever was happening now, we would remain in contact, and there would be a second chance.

I could understand what had happened while I was absent. It was my fault, her distress; I felt no anger or hate towards her, only a greater love. I wouldn't lose her; I would not give her up. I would play it calmly and I would win back her love.

The place she was staying that night was where Marvin and Rick were staying too. I figured that was where they'd scored the smack and it was probably through this guy in Figueretas that they planned to get into the big-time deals they boasted about. They were welcome to them. If I'd ever wanted to do such deals, I could have put them together through guys like Bobby G. I couldn't believe what had happened to Rick; I couldn't believe where his head was at now.

I asked Hanna to stay a little longer. She said no. Why she was in such a hurry, I couldn't understand; I'd promised her I'd say nothing more about Marvin or Rick. I wanted to hear about Aoife and to tell her about the journey. But she wouldn't stay.

As I said goodbye, I thought she was probably going to meet Marvin downtown. I had done my best to lay no guilt on her. It was a replay of how I'd let Nancy go to Vern, hoping that by doing so she'd get over him and come back, but of course she hadn't; she'd just got involved with someone else.

With Hanna, whatever happened, I'd keep the doors open; she would have no recrimination to fear. Marvin wouldn't last long; he was an asshole and she'd see through him, all his Ouspensky-on-acid bullshit. Poor Hanna. If she only knew it, I'd never really left her. There was Fran, yes, but '*that was in another country*', in a city already synonymous with free sex and free love, the nostrum of a generation. Poor Fran, in truth, had only been a recreation, and that she had engaged me no more than that had made me realise, all the more, my love for Hanna. Even at times when Hanna and I were at war and I'd wanted to leave her, I'd never been able to. She was so vulnerable, so sincere and good. Now, I'd driven her into the arms of Marvin and she was confused, inconsolable. I should have been a pair of ragged claws, scuttling across the floors of silent seas . . . !

Chapter 22

UP TO HERE, THE NARRATIVE has been tales of journeys, road trips and acid trips, of love lost, found, and lost again. Now, it becomes a journey to Hades, a trip to the edge of the mind. To escape my difficulties would have been easy, given the opportunity; hide and run, hide and run. On the road to Hades, however, there's nowhere to hide, no place to run to. You're on a downhill spiral and you can't get off. The ground you think is solid sucks you down, the slope is slippery and the walls impossibly high. As you reach out for footholds, they fall away beneath you and the dreams that once inspired you call after you like plaintive ghosts. I had been on such a downhill spiral once before, after Nancy.

For Carlo, in jail, it was different, he told me later in a letter; all decisions were taken away from him. He knew how long he was in for – four years – and that there was a brighter future sometime ahead. In Hades, you don't know if you'll ever be released. It's '*Une saison en enfer*' – a poem by Rimbaud I'd read in a library in Glasgow – and how long the seasons last in hell, or if they ever end, I couldn't know. However, as Carlo might have said, with a wry grin: 'Hey, life's a journey of self-knowledge; the farther it brings you down, the more you pull yourself up, and the more you learn.'

I remember isolated incidents on the downward journey as if they were incised on the retina of my mind's eye. I see them as they took place, and my ear is true for the get-out clauses dredged up by Rick and Marvin and others as they distanced themselves from me as if I was the carrier of a disease: 'We love you, man, but we can't be with you, you're bringin' us down . . .', and 'There is no problem unless you make one . . .' I can remember each blow of the Four Hundred Blows.

Smack, not love, was what my flaky amigos, Rick and Marv, brought that night to my lonely rooms, that night I remember so clearly. In the rush and glow they smiled at one another as I watched from a cold place, afar. They were feeling good, holidaying in Ibiza, the next best thing to living free in my house on the Barbary Cape. Old C'an Pujolet had become the throbbing centre of a Nowhere, and Marvin the Good presided there. How this all worked for my beloved Aoife, I couldn't guess, but I knew, of course, that Hanna would protect her; no tigress ever guarded her child more fiercely.

I'd been in fear of the fuzz since arriving on the island; after what Rick had said about my making them feel paranoid, I was suddenly more fearful of my friends. Every meeting was fraught; the last thing I wanted was to say or do something that would make them reject me, and the sad but inevitable result was that I became *paranoid of being paranoid* in case they would feel it and back off. Being paranoid of being paranoid sounds like a conundrum but anyone who's been there will know what I mean. You're afraid you'll drive them away before they even arrive. You blame yourself for every rejection, hard glance or slight you suffer, real or imagined. The paranoid is like a leper with a bell, only it's got no clapper. No matter; folk can feel the disturbance in the air. Therefore I made a vow that next time visitors came, *I'd try hard not to try too hard.*

And so madness beset me; it was a private madness and I didn't want people to know. I fought against it, always trying to remain positive, always believing that everything would turn out all right in the end, and I tried desperately to hide it. The more I tried, the more it stood revealed. Marvin accused me of deceitfulness, of attempting to put on an act that I was relaxed when I wasn't really. I couldn't win. My vibes disturbed them; they couldn't be around me. *I brought them down.*

It was weird when Nicole came for the first time a couple of days later, strange that she was so strange with me, so uptight from the start. I tried to be supremely relaxed; I tried not to try – and I was relatively relaxed because I knew we had our love for Carlo in common and this would be a bond. But she had changed. There was no talking to her, no reaching her. I wondered if she felt guilty about having told Hanna about my scene with Fran, but it wasn't that. Neither was it anything Carlo had said about me. No, he'd sent his love; he'd explained what had happened at the border; that he'd frozen and had been so glad to know I'd got away. In a letter he'd sent me, he said he knew I'd make it out of Spain; that I'd get to London, somehow. He wasn't panicked. He figured I'd buy him out before he'd done six months. What he said confirmed what Longini had told Rick: you could buy a jailbird out almost by the day. The *multa* was two hundred thousand pesetas, twelve hundred pounds. Pay a quarter of this fine and Carlo would get off a quarter of the time. Meanwhile, he'd become the prison barber at the *carcel* in Gerona, and he was learning Spanish, and the food wasn't great, but they could spend all day in the yard and he was cool. His finishing words were, 'Get yourself out of Spain and worry about me later.'

When I tried to ask Nicole about how things were with Rick and Marvin, she stiffened and said she knew nothing about that, nothing about what had gone down between me and them, but she clearly did. She was the same about Hanna and Marvin, when I brought that up. Her reticence was a drag. I had figured I could talk to her, but she clammed up. It was survival, I guess: go with the flow.

Rick, the last man on the loose from the former Formentera Hole-in-the-Wall Gang, had endorsed Marvin. Marvin was next best thing to the Messiah, and Nicole gave me the feeling that I was wrong for questioning it. Yet Nicole and I had been close. *Et tu*, Nicole? I thought, but I didn't accuse her. I didn't lay any blame on her. It would have made things worse.

Soon afterwards, she began screwing Rick, although I didn't know that then and she didn't tell me. But it figured. Carlo was in the slammer and she was living with Hanna, whose bed Marvin had already gotten into while Carlo and I were on our way home. Rick was regularly hanging out at C'an

Pujolet and, in this time of crisis, why should he and this unhappy girl sleep on separate mattresses on the floor when they could sleep together? Comfort she needed, and I guess comfort she got, although it was hard to imagine Ratbag Rick as a lover.

I understood in my heart more than in my mind what was happening, but there wasn't a lot I could do about it. Everything I tried to do made matters worse. I realise now that what happened amongst that small, isolated group on that small, isolated island in those early days of 1960s' freedom wasn't so unique. But it sure was heartbreaking at the time. Was it them, or was it me, who was distorting the sacred duty friends owe one another? I concluded that it was them, but I began to lose trust in my own perception. I had only their viewpoint on everything. I had nobody to ask. Hanna and Nicole concurred with them, and I couldn't meet people from any other world. I spent days and nights wrestling with the question, getting stoned and thinking, analysing. There was nothing to take my mind off these thoughts. If my perception was wrong, I wanted to correct my attitude and behaviour. I had always valued truth and integrity, even if it meant going against convention and society, as I had when I was a kid in holy Ireland.

Was I on an ego trip, I wondered, thinking I was right and they were all mistaken? If so, that was the worst! Objectively, what Marvin said was true: I was deceitful and hypocritical. For reasons of survival, I didn't attack them and castigate their values, which I saw as false, their actions, which I saw as wrong – as I would have in other circumstances. I couldn't afford to alienate them. I sacrificed integrity for survival.

What, then, was the truth about their behaviour? The more I considered it, the more I became enmeshed in my own dialogue. I couldn't escape my mind. It was like when you wake at some noise in the night and you're dog-tired but thoughts begin and you think: '*Oh God, let me stay in sweet oblivion, let me not start thinking!*' But the minute you think '*I mustn't think!*' you are already thinking, and you can't stop, and you can't go back to the dream.

You wake out of the comforting dream and your mind starts to dissect everything, and you can't get it back to sleep. Thinking becomes the self. You are awake and cannot sleep again. But that wakefulness, that awareness, as we know, is OK; it's what we strive for, to be awake always and to find our way to peace and comfort with our thoughts. Our hope is that they may, at last, lead us past the painted deserts and take us to the oasis where the girls bring sherbet, and love never faileth for the rest of our days.

Now, however, for me, the fugitive in that fucked-up time, those I loved came and told me I was wrong in my expectations of them, in how I behaved with them and in how I saw the world. Should I have humbly accepted what they said? But what if *they* were wrong, not me? (But there you go again, the voice said, not trusting them!) Maybe I should let go, surrender: let what would happen, happen. Sometimes, in the twilight zones, I thought that maybe I should just walk out into the street, try to stow away on the Barcelona boat and, if I got busted, I got busted and so be it. But I couldn't leave it to chance; it wasn't in me. It was my responsibility to try every way I could to deliver myself from tribulation. That belief, of course, was ego; it was an attempt to control my own destiny. Maybe that was why – as Brunswick, with his tattered Korean War manuscript, would have put it – I was convicted of the crime of Rampant Ego by my peers.

Sometimes, in these disturbed nights, the Turkish roads unwound before my eyes and I saw that everything Carlo and I had hoped for had been lost. Sometimes I would wake on the iron bed, the deep dark around me and the damp wall beside, and pencil on the flaking whitewash the things about love I'd say to Hanna the next time we met.

I was amazed when, one morning, some time later, I found Marvin at the front door. The knocks had been loud, insistent raps and I'd woken out of a disturbed sleep to be seized by the fear of God – or the fuzz – and dashed about the place like a rat in a trap, trying to look out the balcony window to see who was knocking at the door below. I could see nobody, but it continued, rap, rap, rap, demanding and incessant, and I had to go down. When I opened the door, I found Marvin standing outside, eyeing me with a smile. I didn't know what to make of it. Nobody had come since Nicole – no word and no fresh food for days. Now here was Marvin, the last person I wanted to see, smiling beatifically, inviting himself in. But who was I to harbour grudges, to reject overtures of friendship?, I thought.

I should have guessed that he'd come to give me further edifying lectures and to play more games. At other times, when not on my road halfway to Hades, I would have shut him up or thrown him out, but survival advised against it. Do that, and I might never again see Rick. And so Marvin sat down, as if the place was his, saying nothing except grinning as he produced a glass jar of yogurt from his basket, and took the rubber band and the butter-paper off the top. A blanket on my shoulders, not knowing what to do, I waited to see what next.

'A spoon, man, you got a spoon? You got sugar?,' he asked, and I supplied both. He settled down to eat.

Maybe I was ungrateful; after all, he was there and had taken the trouble to come. 'Hey, sorry about the other night . . .' I ventured, 'I was on a bad trip, y'know.'

'Yeah, you're paranoid. You're a classic paranoid, man.'

While I digested this, he slurped up the yogurt with great gusto, and I wished I had one too. He went on, 'The other night, you thought we were putting you down. That's clinical, casebook paranoia. I've read Freud. We want to help you. We love you, man. We love Hanna, too.'

'Love', the way he used it, was such a bullshit word, so cheapened; but I had loved Rick, the way he had talked about his life, his self-effacing honesty. Rick, who had betrayed me. I had loved him as I loved Carlo, as I loved Bruno and Bill and Desiree, and Hanna too.

He finished the yogurt, and took out another. Again he pulled off the rubber band and the butter-paper, spooned a centimetre deep of sugar on top and dug in. He talked between mouthfuls. 'Hanna's a great chick. I don't know if you appreciate her.' I told him I did but I hadn't always in the past because I'd been hung-up on my ex-wife and sometimes I'd even wanted to leave her.

'Why didn't you?' he asked.

I told him how it was. That I didn't want to hurt her; that she was very screwed up when I'd met her, that I was, too. And then, as she grew stronger, what could I do? Destroy her again? Of course, it might have been that, subconsciously, I needed her but, anyway, I didn't want to damage her again, that was the thing.

'If people are damaged, it's their own fault.' he told me. 'Remember, you're nothing to me; I'm nothing to you, except you make me something. Do you understand that?'

I said yes, I understood, but what if she *did* damage herself, *and you knew she would*, you knew she wouldn't be able to detach herself, that she would suffer, that her heart would be broken?

'That's speculation,' he answered. 'Who are you to pre-judge what she might or might not feel?'

'But I should try,' I said. 'I should try to judge what my actions will do to her.'

'Why?' he asked.

'Because I love her . . .'

I was dismayed that he should ask; the answer was self-evident surely. If you loved someone – even platonically, even in the wider sense of love – and knew the hurt you could cause, surely you would try to protect them, even if their hurt was self-inflicted.

'But you said earlier that you didn't understand her,' he countered.

'No. I said I didn't understand why she didn't stay longer last night.'

He pushed the empty yogurt glass away from him. 'You said you didn't understand her, and now you're judging her.' There was triumph in his voice. 'There's a lot of things you need to learn, my friend. Other people are free. Hanna's free.'

'I know this, I know this already.'

'You don't,' he said, and his voice took on a monotone, and it was Instruction Time again.

Before he got started, I interrupted to ask if he might have another yogurt. He didn't. He started to roll a joint however and as he did so, he began the homily. I would have liked to tell him to go fuck himself with his hip aphorisms and cool clichés but I stayed silent. If he turned Rick against me, I was in deep shit, and clearly he could do that. So I shut up and let him talk. There was so much in my heart that I shouldn't say, that would be dangerous to say.

'Maybe Hanna didn't want to stay longer last night. She told you she was having a scene with me now. Maybe she doesn't need you any more. If you get fucked up about that, it's because you want to get fucked up . . .' He lit the joint and passed it to me. I took a toke and said nothing. I took the toke because I didn't want to be unfriendly.

The lecture went on. 'You're a fugitive. Do you know what that means? You're in no position to take or ask. You're given to. Rick agrees with me about that. And this stuff you told me, just now, about you and Hanna – does this concern the here-and-now we exist in?'

I shrugged, 'I guess not.'

He continued, 'Because if it doesn't, we don't want to hear it. That's another thing, my friend. Hanna may not want to hear about what happened to you in Turkey, or anywhere. People are experiencing their own things. They may not want to listen to you, right?' He smiled and took out a packet of biscuits. 'You're not paranoid of me, are you?' he asked. 'I'm just telling you these things to help you, do you understand that?'

He reminded me of a smug school kid, with his tuck box of goodies. Nevertheless, when he offered me a biscuit, I took it; I'd been peckish before but watching him I was suddenly ravenous. He put the biscuits away, washed out the yogurt glasses so as to return them for the deposit, and left.

Chapter 23

NEXT MORNING, THERE WAS A knock on the door below and I went down to find a bag of groceries and a note from Nicole saying that Hanna had sent them. She was sorry she couldn't stop to stay hello. Hanna sent her love, so did Rick and Marvin. 'Love, Peace, Nicole.' It really wasn't cool to leave groceries outside my door. It would draw attention to the fact that the apartment, long empty, was now occupied.

Next one up was tall, laconic Jacey, as usual the epitome of California dreamin', with his tasselled, somewhat greasy, buckskin shirt. Jacey, who had started the whole trip that led to this, Carlo in jail and me a fugitive from justice. Nevertheless, I thought it was good of him to call. He didn't need to, and he wasn't there to score points. He had his home, his own attractive wife and Maria-Juana, his daughter, Formentera born. It was easier with him but, ultimately, it came down to the same. My reputation had gone before me; it had been put out that I was demented and ungrateful, demanding, mendacious and paranoid. I was fighting a losing battle trying to prove otherwise, as evidenced by Nicole's attitude – and, in fact, I was becoming all those things by then.

Tall Jacey must have felt the vibe as soon as he came in. I hadn't seen anybody for a couple of days and talking to myself was only the half of it. I'd been hungry too. I'd even have risked going out to score some food, but I had no money. I kept thinking the money from Bill or Zelda or Bruno should be through soon but Rick hadn't come and there was no news of it.

Jacey must have noticed that I was weird. I tried to act laid-back, but my words were detached from me and it was all sort of jangly, like a voice somewhere else, or an image in a broken mirror. He said he'd missed the boat back to Formentera. It was a Sunday afternoon, the town was dead and he'd dropped in to say hello. He was relaxed, that was for sure. He might have been on the beach at Cala Sohona.

He was friendly too, genuinely friendly. I'd never been quite sure about Jacey, what with the haiku book he'd so readily taken when Hanna had offered it to him, and I'd been pissed off by the way he'd proposed the Turkish trip, then dropped out and persuaded easygoing, unsuspecting Carlo to do it for him. Then, it had been his promises that had kept us waiting for his money in Istanbul – money that never came. If I'd been back a couple of weeks sooner, Hanna's scene with Marvin wouldn't have happened; that was down to Jacey. Furthermore, but for his promises, we'd have been through and home a week before the Christmas rush and the universal shake-down on the border.

I asked him about the money. He just hadn't had it, he said; it hadn't come through from California. He was still expecting it and, if it arrived, he'd try to help me out. I left it at that. He was pleasant and I appreciated his visit. He bugged me a bit with some stuff about all the foreigners in Ibiza being lushes and deadbeats, but I let it go. He said he'd heard my ex-wife sometimes worked in the Domino. I guessed she was short of money – I'd never been able to give her as much as I'd have liked, especially since I'd had another child to support. Now, I could give her nothing at all. He drew as he talked, pencil sketches on the tabletop, his speech slow and casual. He pointed at his basket, 'Couple of bananas there, a couple of shop yogurts, a bar of chocolate. You're welcome, man.'

I asked how was Lorna, how was Maria-Juana, how was Hanna.

'Hanna? Oh, y'know, beautiful. She's having a hard time. You gotta stop puttin' it on her, man.'

I didn't react. I just let him meander on, watching him as he drew. There was a sense of peace about Jacey, a sense of having another human being around me who didn't have any edge, who wasn't feeling guilty, who didn't feel he had to teach me anything. But he was trying to do that, too, in a way.

'Yeah, man, everybody's groovin', y'know. Everybody's groovin'. It's the way to be. It's all about where you're at in your head, baby. Geographical location is of no importance.'

Before he left, he said, 'I hear you bin' a bit freaked out, man. Just be cool. Rick and Marv, they're takin' care of business. Relax, man, go with the flow.'

When Hanna next came, I hadn't slept well for days and I looked it; she said so. There was concern in her voice. Like Jacey, she said I should relax, go with the flow. She sat opposite me at the table. It was night and, with no lights on, I opened the balcony windows a few centimetres and I could see the port and the Barcelona ferry steaming out.

She'd brought some groceries. We drank maté, and sat with not much to say. We talked about Aoife, and she told me she had seen Kilian and Col with their mother that evening. They hadn't seen her.

Later, somehow, I was sitting on the bed, my back against the bed head, and she was sitting at the end. I don't know how we got there; I don't know what I had in mind. It can't have been sex; she was, after all, screwing Marvin. I knew her: Marvin couldn't have got into her body if he hadn't first of all got into her mind and it'd be more than sex for her, it'd be a relationship and, meanwhile, she wouldn't make it with anyone else, certainly not me. Making a relationship of her thing with Marvin was, maybe, to legitimise her need for comfort – which was understandable, given the scene – or simply her sexual need. The act of love, I knew, was important to her.

Anyway, we were sitting on the bed in the cold bedroom with the white-washed walls and the clear light bulb with a paper shade. She was crying and I was saying. 'C'mon, baby, c'mon. It's OK. Look, you're happy. You deserve happiness. My problems are my problems; if I love you, I should want you to be happy. And I do. I'm not going to make you feel bad about it. It's your right, Hanna, if it's what you want to do . . . '

I took her in my arms. There were tears in my eyes too but I wasn't going to let her see them; I didn't want a sympathy vote. I meant what I said. I'd screwed her around, had scenes with other women. Now it was her turn. Bad luck, man, but you deserved it! What else did you think would happen; leaving your chick alone like that, fuck your fuckin' arrogance!

'Are you in love with him?' I asked. It was the same question I'd asked Nancy, years before, and she gave me the same answer, with the same tears, 'I don't know, I don't know.' She buried her face in my chest, and my shirt was wet with her tears and I felt so devastated, so fucking sorry, so fucking sorry! 'He's really *there*, you know – I could see this when we were on acid. He just came and lay beside me. I was all screwed up, I just wanted warmth. You hadn't come, I didn't know if you'd ever come. It just happened. It was spiritual, a sort of unifying on another level—'

'So that's what Marvin calls getting his dick into you – unifying on another level! He's a fucking Creeping Jesus, that's all—'

'No,' she cried, and now she's defending him. 'He's beautiful, he's not like he seems! Try to see that, try, please. Don't blame him . . .'

What, so I should blame her instead?! 'I'm sorry.' I told her. 'I'm just bitter. I love you, you know? Do you know that? I love you.'

And then she commenced to weep again, and her whole, small body shook against me, and fitted so closely against me, and my face was wet with my own tears.

Crazily, as she gathered her things to leave, I decided to go with her, to walk her a-ways towards the tunnel, to see her down to the barrack square below. No, she said, no, don't come – but I went anyway. I couldn't care – I really couldn't care if I got busted. I'd be better off with Carlo in jail. Better off than here, losing her and everything.

At the edge of the Vara de Rey, I got sense and stopped. 'Hanna, I love you,' I said. 'If you're happier with someone else, you should be with him, not with me. If I truly love you, I want you to be happy, and if I ever say otherwise, I'm a liar.'

She smiled up at me, a tearful smile, with the kohl running down her cheeks as so many times before.

We kissed, and it was a real kiss, and I left her. 'Just don't be afraid of me,'

I said and I was gone, sneaking off into the night, seeking the shadows, back to the four walls of my cold rooms.

How the following days passed, I'm not sure. I slept and woke – not much else. One night, I heard the door below being thumped like someone was putting a battering ram to it and I sat up in bed, terrified, thinking I was fucked, that this was it, the raid in the night, but then it stopped and I opened the shutters a sliver and looked out and there was nothing in the street except a cat sitting on the parapet opposite and the dust in the square as white as snow under a full moon.

On a night like this, I thought, there'd be a full-moon party in Formentera for sure. I could imagine a fire on the beach at Cala Sohona and everyone sitting around passing a chillum, and Aoife asleep, and the dogs curled up and someone maybe playing a guitar. I remembered the night of my birthday a few months before when everything had been so different and I'd been celebrating my first quarter-century on earth. But I tried to put that sort of thing out of my head because it only brought me down and the thing was to stay positive.

There'd be other birthday parties in other farmhouses on other islands and, OK, once I'd escaped, I couldn't ever go back to Formentera or Ibiza or Spain again, but there was no point dwelling on it. Maybe, someday, I could pay a fine – after all, we knew Carlo could be bought out, that it was only a question of money. It might take a year or two, or three, but so long as I knew I could come back, it would change everything. While I was saving up for the fine, I'd somehow sneak back to Ibiza to see the boys, if Nancy didn't come to England. Maybe I could go in disguise, with a phoney passport – but people would talk once they knew I was on the island. Maybe I would stay in San Antonio. Yes, that was it, I could buy a holiday in Ibiza and go straight to San Antonio Abad, where nobody would know me, and sit around a swimming pool, pretending I was like the other tourists and had never been on the island before. I would turn up at Nancy's house one day out without notice and say hello to the boys and stay a couple of hours – maybe on the last day of the holiday, or a few hours before taking the plane home – and never tell Nancy where I was staying or what name I was staying under. She wouldn't give me up, of course, but it would be safer for her not to know.

Figuring out how I could get things like that together in the future, running such movies through my head, took my mind off my troubles. I fully believed that such an option would be possible once I got out of the rat-trap of the apartment, once I got out of Spain and had time to regroup. As soon as I was in London, I could get myself together again real fast. From the minute I arrived, I'd teach every hour I could get and raise fifty or sixty quid – maybe even a hundred – and send thirty or so to Hanna so that she could come up to London, and lay out the rest as deposit and rent for a flat. Then I'd earn another hundred and do a few travellers cheque scams to raise money to get Carlo out and, sometime, maybe in the late summer, I'd buy myself a British Visitor's Passport from a post office under a phoney name, organise a package holiday to Ibiza and go and see the boys.

Sometime in between all that, I'd go and see my parents in Ireland, if I hadn't already disgraced them – which I wouldn't have wanted to do. First, I'd suss out from my brother if the bust had been reported in the Irish papers; even if it had, they mightn't have read it. Having said that, an Irish guy being busted for dope in Spain would have been a big deal in 1964 and, because my name was distinctive, others might have spotted it and told them. Up to that time, I'd met only one other guy in Ireland with the same first name. I really didn't want to cause my father grief or break my mother's heart.

For now, however, the thing was not to let the fucking cold and privation of the place and my situation get me down. It would all be alright in the end, I knew. It was tough, yeah, but, hey, what was wrong with spending a few weeks alone and being confined to a few rooms? Things could be much worse and it wouldn't amount to weeks, anyway. It wasn't nice but it was no big deal.

I smoked the black hash Jacey had left and took a Romilar trip which I'd never before done alone, carefully counting out twenty of the pills, as greeny-blue as a hedge sparrow's eggs. I thought that maybe I'd break through my confusion and see everything and understand everything and throw off all the illusions that were fucking me up. I'd see that geographical location is of no importance, like Jacey had said.

My big worry, besides getting Hanna back, was that I could no longer talk to Rick, Marvin and Nicole. When they came, I tried to be relaxed but it never worked. Rick wasn't interested in talking about the good times in the past or my optimistic scenarios for the future. Here-and-Now was where it was at, they said. I knew they wouldn't want to hear about my problems; that would bring them down and, if I brought them down, they'd leave. So when they came, the cool thing was to say nothing at all as much as possible, which was sort of strange and made for a weird atmosphere.

They talked to one another, affably smoking joints at the table but they were never very affable when I chipped in. A cautious silence would suddenly fall. For example, when I asked them if any money had arrived in the mail yet, they told me to stop asking, they'd tell me when it came. Marvin made a cheerful couple of jokes about how the friends I'd written to overseas might be pissed off with me, like everybody else was – maybe I'd said they should send me the money on time: I didn't seem to realise that Time had no meaning in the Ultimate Reality. Yeah, Marvin the fuckin' philosopher knew all about Time, and he spoke in capital letters. I wanted to ask him would he prefer to do two years or ten years in jail, but I didn't. I had to keep Rick sweet. 'Remember, you're The Fugitive!' Marvin would regularly say, and grin. Same tired joke, not funny. Rick was uncomfortable with some of this. Once, he told Marvin to leave me alone but Marvin said he was just 'breakin' my balls', just trying to keep me on my toes.

When I was alone, I wrote to Hanna a lot but I'd end up burning the letters because I didn't want to give them to the others in case they'd open them, read them, and say I was trying to manipulate her; I couldn't communicate with her without their help. I didn't keep the letters in case I was busted and the fuzz would figure out that Hanna knew I was in Ibiza and they'd bust her too. I guess I was getting weirder and more paranoid by the day.

I began to prefer it when nobody came. The only one I really wanted to see was Hanna, or Rick if he would come alone and brought good news. But he never came alone and, day after day, there was no news.

Each room was like a separate world, and I spent time in each. Hanna sent food; once or twice I heard a knock on the door and found it outside. I didn't know who'd brought it. There were figs from our tree that we'd dried in the summer, and *sobrasada* from our landlord's pig. There was spaghetti and potatoes. I made a doll for Aoife out of a potato, with carrot eyes, meaning to give it to Hanna to give to her but Hanna didn't come and it dried up and went grey and looked like something dead.

I was living in my head. I was hearing what they said, even when they weren't there; in fact, sometimes I thought they were there, that they had got in somehow with another key, but when I pulled on some clothes and went into the living room to greet them, I found I was wrong, that I'd been dreaming.

It was very cold. The apartment got no sun. I was going a little crazy and I knew it.

Time passed with no visitors and no food delivered. Perhaps the police were watching them and they couldn't come: perhaps they'd agreed to leave me to find my own salvation. I considered this outcome with equanimity. After days and nights of introversion, I'd decided that we live and die alone but delude ourselves that we are at one with others. You are you, and I am me, and we live in separate universes, as remote from one another and as incapable of merging as rocks in the coldness of space. This truth was, I thought, my first step on the road to enlightenment. Now, all illusions of kinship became dust before my eyes and in my crazed mind I walked across a bleak but comforting desert.

I had understood this truth by being cast out and I was grateful for it. Nothing is earned without pain. I had been living in the illusion that others had a part to play in my life and I in theirs. But like Marvin had said, he was nothing to me unless I made him something. This was the problem: I had been making something of them that they didn't want to be. I was putting Rick on a pedestal, as I had once put Nancy on one. She had said 'I'm not what you think I am.' I had thought she was a loving and faithful wife, but I'd been wrong. Now I was making the same mistake again; cases of mistaken identity. I was making them important, giving them power over my well-being and self-esteem. It was my fault if I was disappointed; they didn't ask to be important to me, and it was an ego-trip on my part to expect them to be as I saw them. If they tried to be like this, my demands, however benign, would rule their lives. Letting others rule our lives flew in the face of all we, in Formentera, believed in. We had escaped the rule of being what society thought we should be, of leading acceptable lives, of pursuing careers and selling our lives for economic security.

The rule on Formentera was 'If you don't dig it, don't do it'. *Mea culpa*: I'd broken that rule again and again. However much I'd wanted to at times, I'd not left Hanna. I'd enslaved myself to her; I wasn't free. As Marvin said, if you did something that you didn't want to do, for any reason, and it brought you down, you had only yourself to blame. That was why Rick didn't want to come near me, and Nicole too, and even Hanna. They'd listened to Marvin and stayed away; they weren't going to allow me to bring them down. They weren't going to allow themselves to be enslaved.

I realised that I should stop blaming them, that it was their right to leave me to solve my own problems and they were justified in doing so. I was alone, that was the reality. I would slough off my illusions. I would escape alone. I'd escaped from the border; I could cross fields and rivers. When my brother and I were kids in Ireland, it was what we did all the time. I'd forget Hanna for now; I'd have nobody to worry about but myself. Better to be free and moving than be imprisoned in those cold rooms, haunted by the reality.

Such thoughts of action, born of despair, I would entertain; but then I would return to hope. Rick, after all, hadn't said he was abandoning me. At no point had he said that. There could be many reasons why he hadn't come – the police might be watching him or he was simply too stoned. I was letting my fears run away with me. 'Don't let fear take the best!' he'd said. I would wait and keep faith. Anyway, Hanna wouldn't let them abandon me.

Chapter 24

IN THE ROOMS, DAYS MERGED into days. I tried to keep a routine and buoy up my hopes. I tried to think warmly of my friends. I understood that, in Formentera, they were living on a higher plane and to come down to my level would be a sin against the light. In relating to me or sympathising with me, they would be endorsing my misery, and my misery was wrong, arising, as it did, from false premises and distorted expectations, from errors of attitude and thought.

I wrote a lot about my conclusions, the logic of them, analysing them on paper, with diagrams, figuring them out. I realised that I should surmount any residual bitterness and see that my friends' actions were motivated by love. Hanna, who wouldn't tell me lies, had told me to listen to Rick and Marvin, that I should stop laying my trip on them, that I should let my ego go. She was sincere; it wasn't in her nature to be otherwise. I thought of how, in my blindness and stupidity, I had hung on to things of the past, things that had never been real – like my dream of Nancy – and I had failed to understand that I deeply loved her. I realised now how much I had lost and how I deserved this lesson. Worst of all, it now dawned on me that Hanna might somehow stay on in Spain, with Aoife, like Nancy had done with the boys. That even when it was over between her and Marvin, she might not return to me, but find someone else, like Nancy had after Mel. She might not come to London. She might disappear and I would never see her or Aoife again.

The afternoon that Chris Longley came 'out of the blue' – I opened the door in the darkness of the stairwell and he was standing there against a brilliant, blue sky – I had been lost, as usual, in the labyrinth of my mind, and I didn't know who he was for a second. 'Good afternoon, *estimado señor mio*,' he said, in his English voice, 'Are you receiving visitors?'

'Chris!'

He stepped forward, good humour, irony, warmth in his face; it was like my old world rushing through the door and engulfing me. But where had he come from? How did he know I was there? He had nothing to do with us in Formentera; he wasn't one of the crowd. We hadn't met since I'd brought the paints to his house on Brunswick's bike, with Col and Kilian both dressed as Superman.

The main room was dark, so I went to flip on the light.

'Why not open the shutters?' he asked.

'Don't want people to know anyone lives here,' I said.

'It's all right,' he smiled. 'They're all asleep. Siesta time, right? *Con permiso* . . .' and he walked across and opened the shutters a few inches, and stood there in the sunlight, a big, grave grin on his face.

In the sunlight, he took a look at me and at the room. It can't have been a pretty sight, me with a half-grown beard, mad eyes and tousled hair, and the flies that I should have exterminated or expelled waking up and buzzing all over the unwashed dishes in the sink. Chris didn't remark on it however, just reached into his basket and said, 'I thought you might like a beer and a bit of company. How about that?' And he stood there, smiling.

I nodded. Something suddenly welled up inside me and there were tears in my eyes. I hid them from him by turning to the sink and washing a couple of glasses. I handed him an opener with my back half-turned and I heard him open the bottles; he told me he'd brought some food too. A minute or two later, we were sitting opposite one another at the table, the light behind him. It all seemed unreal.

He began by saying he'd heard from Lise that I was on the run. How was I?, he asked, how were things working out? I told him I was fine; no problem;

friends were helping me. It was hard to keep my voice steady. I said I was just waiting for money, and then they'd help me get out of Spain. I asked him would he like a joint. He said no. He told me I'd become a notorious character on the island. '*El contrabandista irlandés*', his neighbours called me. My mugshot was posted at the cop shop and it had been on the news that I'd escaped from the border after a big bust.

Soon after he'd heard about it, he'd bumped into Lise. We'd been friends, the three of us, back in the early days, so Lise told him I was on the island and hiding out and that Rick, a Formentera friend, was organising to get me out. He'd found Rick hard to contact. When he'd eventually met him, Rick told him that everything was under control, that I was OK and there was no need for him to be involved: Rick was trying to protect me, I'm sure. However, Chris asked if he could see me and Rick, not very willingly, told him where I was.

Sitting opposite me, he must have been able to see I was a wreck, although I tried to put a good face on it. For sure, I wouldn't have looked my usual on-top-of-it-all self. I could read in his face that he was surprised. I could see that he was treading lightly, skirting around things, choosing his words carefully as he asked me a bit about how my 'escape plans' were progressing. The last thing I wanted to do was tell him the truth. By now, the feeling that I should keep my problems to myself was deeply implanted in me. If I told him, he might be sorry he'd ever asked and start telling me he had an urgent appointment elsewhere. But I was beyond pretence; maybe it was exhaustion. I had nothing to lose. I told him the whole story, from escaping at the border, to arriving in Ibiza, to now. I didn't tell him the bad bits. I didn't sigh or moan: I was beyond self-pity; I was into self-blame. I had no compassion for The Fugitive; it was his own fault. He'd fucked up with Hanna, had got his friend put in jail, had pissed off his friends with his demands and had alienated the people who loved him. What Rick and the others had said was right; I should fuck off to London and leave Hanna to get on with her life and stop bothering her.

All I revealed to Chris, however, was that I'd had a disagreement with Rick and a guy called Marvin, Rick's friend – but that I was responsible and they were, as they said, only trying to get me to take a look at myself because

I was my own worst enemy and not acting in a very enlightened way. Chris simply laughed and said it sounded to him like one of those soup kitchens where sinners have to listen to a sermon before they get their supper.

He asked me about the Turkey trip and the bust, and sat listening, sipping his beer. I was halfway through when he suddenly interrupted and said why didn't I continue the story at his place? Nobody ever came out there – he had a spare room and I could get some sun while I waiting for my escape money to arrive. I was taken aback, filled with relief and yet with anxiety. I didn't know what to say. What would Rick think? Suppose he saw it as ingratitude; if I moved out he might say, 'OK, so fuck you, you're on your own now!' and maybe I'd lose contact with him, and with Hanna.

Playing for time, I mumbled something about if the money came Rick mightn't know where to find me and it was a long way out of town and he didn't like walking. Chris laughed; 'I'll tell him where you are – and if he wants, I'll lend him a bloody bike!'

I left for Chris's house half reluctantly, half-expecting to see Rick arriving even as I walked away. It was still siesta time and, as Chris predicted, we cleared the town without seeing a soul.

Half an hour later, I was tramping the yellow dust of a *camino* a mile beyond the town, leaving the walls and the apartment far behind me. Chris walked ahead, pushing his bicycle. Between us and Figueretas beach lay the Casa Baratas, where Nancy and the boys would be taking a siesta. It felt extraordinary to be out under the blue, bright sky, amongst the scent of thyme, with the sounds of the earth and the scrub crackling in the heat and the grasshoppers singing. It was as if the inside of my head had expanded from three rooms to the infinite blue dome of sky, with all its possibilities and its lessons of my own irrelevance and the irrelevance of all I'd worried about in the prison of my mind.

The house was two miles from the town off a *camino* that had been the old road to San José. It was beautiful. The German couple who owned it, two guys, had used every native artefact to enhance the setting. I had never seen a *finca* so beautifully restored before. The aura of it, the relaxation of Chris as he showed me a room where I could sleep, was almost overwhelming. He told me to take my time, he was making dinner. When the door was closed, I sat on the bed with my face in my hands and it was as if I could hear the angels singing. But even as relief swept over me, hovering in my heart was the great worry that Rick would be pissed off. I quelled that fear and had a shower and left the room.

In the kitchen, I said to Chris, 'I hope I don't get in your way.'

He stopped cooking and looked at me. 'I have no way,' he said. His eyes, shone, humorous, twinkling. I can remember his expression to this day.

Chris had helped restore the *finca* for the Germans. He got free rent in return. His girlfriend worked for a Paris publisher and came down for weeks at a time when she had editing to do. His accent was English public school, but he was no Hooray Henry. He'd studied art briefly before throwing it in, concluding that art couldn't be taught. He was my age, tall and slim, with the taciturn face of a hanging judge, as I once told him. His personality was reflective, but not taciturn, and his face lit up when he smiled. Chris was his own man – one of the few foreigners who lived amongst the Ibicinks and spoke Catalan well. Like me, he'd decided that, great fun though it was, there was more to life than getting smashed in the Domino Bar. However, rather than migrating to esoteric Formentera, he had found a quiet life in the Ibiza countryside. I don't think he followed any particular school of thought. He wasn't a Buddhist or anything; he just did his own thing. Most days he drew and painted in a studio separate from the house, walked his Podenco bitch in the hills or visited neighbours.

The first night at the house, I could hardly sleep for worrying about Rick and the others but I felt better when I woke. Chris wasn't around. I messed about in the house and sat outside in the sun. The house was entirely isolated, reached only by the mule track winding between the scrub, and nobody could approach unseen. Chris, I assumed, had gone to town and would look out for Rick and tell him where I was, in case he'd suddenly got the money. I couldn't believe the freedom I had now; I sat on the patio, and drew and read. I watched ants in a column dismantle a thistle top and carry the little seeds away, like flags. Sometimes, when the breeze caught them, the flag-bearers were blown over, but they got up and went on. I smiled to myself, feeling I was like Robert the Fucking Bruce sitting there, getting a lesson in fortitude! I was strengthening a bit, unquestionably, in the sun. I wasn't seeing clearly yet, but there was much to distract me from my thoughts.

Apart from the crack about the sermons at the soup kitchen, Chris made no comment or criticism of Rick and the Formentera crowd. I made no complaint to him about them, and kept my conflict with them to myself. I had arrived at the conclusion that I owed them gratitude, and I was still of this view. Neither did I talk to Chris about my scene with Hanna. I believed that I deserved what had happened. Hanna had good cause for splitting from me.

The day after I arrived at the *finca*, Chris ran into Rick in town and he was bugged alright, like I thought he might be. No money had shown up yet, he said; however, he'd come out if he had news. I'd decided that whatever Marvin had said, Bill or Bruno or Zelda wouldn't be pissed because I'd asked them to send me some bread in a hurry. But, as I told Chris, the only address I'd really been sure of was Bill's, and that was c/o The Blue Note Jazz Club in Copenhagen; I had no street name. Meanwhile, Zelda might by now have given up her flat in Paris and be in California, and Bruno, God knows where he was; the only address I had was the name of the French village where his father, with whom he was persona non grata, was the local *grand seigneur*.

Chris and I chatted sometimes but, because I didn't want to talk about the things in the forefront of my mind, I didn't have a lot to say. On one or two evenings, we sat by the fire and drank a glass of wine and rapped about seeking truth, about the destructiveness and ignorance our flesh is heir to, about how to make a better and a more equal world.

We talked about the effects of LSD. Chris had taken a trip once. I said how I thought acid could sweep us into a beautiful and transcendent reality where we could reach God – the God being within ourselves, a reality where the wonder of the world was revealed and all self-seeking was forgotten; where, stripped of our desires and hang-ups, we could be free.

He didn't go for that; he thought an LSD trip was no more than a glimpse of the vast expanses of the mind. If we were lucky, it showed us the best bits but afterwards the curtains closed and we were back in everyday reality. It was from there that we had to work on opening the mind – a task that we might, if fortunate, achieve in a lifetime's journey. Acid, he thought, was a vacation, not a transformation, and there was a danger that it could make us underestimate the true distance to be travelled, make us think we were far hipper than we were, and that we had already arrived.

I couldn't help thinking how this applied to the Guru Marvin with his Sermons from the Opium Mount, the Ouspensky and Tao and so on that he'd digested while tripping and then regurgitated for everyone's benefit. But I didn't talk about Marvin. I told Chris that the way I saw it, acid expanded the consciousness and left a residue, a seedbed for a beanstalk to the stars. It projected the cosmos against the cranial dome, and stardust fell and took root in the brain, and we could nurture this to outgrow the shell of thought we lived in, the earthbound cell of our subjective minds.

And so we spoke of hope and glory and how we might transform ourselves and do something truly useful with our lives. The old, dried-up olive logs burnt on the fire in the room lit by oil-light and firelight, but inside, I was heart-sore and pining for Hanna and Aoife and my home on the Barbary Cape.

Yet there were distractions too. The Germans had a record player that ran on batteries, and a small library of good jazz. When Chris went to get his mail, he brought back news from town. One day, he'd heard the latest developments in the case of Joan Briden, my Scottish friend who'd been involved in the 1962 murder with Bad Jack and afterwards had fled to Ibiza where she had been captured after police searched the island. How Joan had changed from an Argyllshire librarian to Bad Jack's jazz club moll was beyond me. She was again in the news in England, where a tabloid newspaper had taken up her case and was demanding her release from a Spanish jail.

Next day, remembering the Joan 'manhunt', I put all my worldly goods, including my passport, into the canvas briefcase and stashed it amongst the trees on the hill behind Chris's house. If the fuzz came to the house, I could make a getaway. I'd have my escape kit to hand.

Chris said he had something to do in San Antonio and he'd be away for one night or maybe two. He cycled there, about twenty kilometres. There was plenty of food in the house, and nobody was likely to come. He was right; nobody came, including nobody from Formentera. I read and drew, something I'd never done before. I made an illustrated storybook for

Aoife, but never gave it to her. I still have it somewhere.

But even as I drew, my mind was elsewhere. The birds of the air or the light on the Mediterranean – I didn't see them. I was immersed in my thoughts. The future was on hold, a mere glimmer, while the past and all I'd lost was in blinding light. The present was there only in episodes: when I had to eat; when I had a rendezvous; when someone came or didn't come. *They flee from me that sometime did me seek* – a line by a sixteenth-century poet which I found. I copied it out. I made a timetable of activities to distract me and stuck it on the wall: Feed dog – Listen to music – Clean house – Read – Draw. But it was hard to fight the anxiety and bitterness.

I got a hell of a fright the first morning Chris was away. It was my own fault – I was too jumpy for my own good. Out of the silence, I hear a click on the back-door latch and a voice, muffled, Spanish. The door is still locked from the night before. I dart through the house; the front door is closed but not locked. Keeping low under the windows, dodging beneath the shafts of sunlight crossing the room, I reach it. I hesitate, not sure whether I should lock it or rush out, grab my 'escape kit', take to the hills and watch until whoever it is goes away. I decide to turn the key. Now, I'm locked in, all doors secured.

Sure enough, I soon hear footsteps arrive at the front. I stand inside the door, holding my breath as whoever it is tries the latch. I wish they'd say something, so I could maybe figure out if they are friend or enemy, but they don't. I see their feet moving about, breaking the slab of light pouring under the door. Could it be Rick? No: he'd call out. I lower myself and put my cheek against the tiles, hoping I can maybe see the shoes. I can't. I lie there, breathless. After a few more clicks of the latch – I see it going up and down above me – the feet move off. The light seeping beneath the door is unbroken. I turn and lie on my back on the cool tiles in the half-dark, and breathe deep breaths.

A minute later, I peek through a window. I see an Ibicenco woman in black, with her headscarf and sombrero, limping off on a path into the scrub. She's old, I can tell. She must be Chris's neighbour; he's told me about her. So much for false alarms. But this time it wasn't paranoia so much as sensible fear.

Later that day, Hanna arrived on a bike, with Aoife strapped into a seat on the carrier. Perro, our dog from Formentera, was running alongside. Seeing me, he leaped up, paws on my chest. I shook him off and greeted Hanna. I didn't know whether to try to kiss her or not. I kissed Aoife instead; I'd almost have kissed the fucking dog I was so glad we were all together suddenly, for however long. But Hanna was distant, like a stranger, so much so that I thought she'd only come for Aoife's sake. I decided to act as if Marvin's shadow was not between us, as if it was just us three.

She sat on a wall and watched as I played with Aoife. I hadn't seen her since that miserable morning at the Playa D'en Bossa and I made a big fuss of her, swinging her in circles like I did with Kilian and Col, holding her up to the sky, tickling her. But my heart wasn't in it; I knew I had her love – it was her mother I wanted to hold. I went towards Hanna and sat beside her. I took her hand. It lay limp in mine. I turned to face her.

'You make me nervous,' she said.

I quietly said that it hadn't always been so.

She replied that she couldn't relax with me like she could with other people.

'Like Marvin?' I asked, and she said yes.

'He's so relaxed, he's almost asleep half the time!' I couldn't help but answer.

After that, things went from bad to worse. She said that Marvin wasn't asleep, he was meditating: he was into hatha yoga. I responded that I hadn't had a lot of time for yoga, given that since Aoife was born I'd been busy bringing in the money that looked after us. To this, she answered that there were things more important than money. And so we had a row.

It didn't last long. I shouldn't have let it happen.

'Look,' I said, 'Read this.' I handed her the love letter I had written. I walked off up the *camino* with Aoife and the dog.

She sat and read it. When I came back, she was crying. She didn't comment on the letter. She left almost right away and wouldn't explain why. I wondered if maybe she was beginning to find Marvin flaky, and if what I had written about the love we had was another blow. Anyway, she split immediately. By then, Aoife was crying too, reaching out for me. Hanna had to pull her hands away. She said she'd bring her to see me again before I left the island. I stood watching as she cycled away.

When Chris returned, the first thing he asked was if Rick had come out, and if the money had arrived. I had to say no – and there was no money yet, as far I knew. Well, he said, maybe it just wasn't meant to happen with Rick. Getting me off the island one way or the other was all that was important and he had good news. He'd found a guy with a yacht in San Antonio, a Dutch guy who was sailing to Gibraltar in a few days, and he'd asked him if he'd take me on board. The guy remembered me – I'd played poker with him once – and he'd said OK. Gibraltar would be freedom; I'd be out of Spain; it'd be like being in England. I could get some money somehow and fly from there straight to London. The Gibraltar authorities wouldn't be interested in me; the last thing they were into was helping the Spanish government or police. As far as getting aboard the boat was concerned, if there were police watching San Antonio port, it could pull around to Playa D'en Bossa and I could slip into the water after dark and swim out to it.

Chris's news was great, yes, but it was only half-welcome. If I went with the Dutchman, I would lose contact with my friends. I would not be part of the tribe when they set up camp in London – Carlo and Nicole would be there, Hanna too, if she wished, but I would not be welcome.

My hope had been that when money came and Rick and I travelled north together, without Marvin and the opium, our friendship would be restored. Now, if I left on the boat, not only would I lose that opportunity but my action might be like saying that I had no faith in Rick, and that would alienate him, and everybody else, all the more. Bruno, Desiree, Bill and Zelda and all the others would hear that I had rejected the help of my friends, that I'd been freaked out, that I'd been on an ego trip and trying to control them. Hanna would back them up and, therefore, it would be believed.

Troubled by such fears, my priority was to remain in contact with the circle and prove that their perception of me was wrong; this was more important to me than my liberty. I had nightmare flashes of Hanna moving away from me, as if she was part of a tribe in a desert, while I stood powerless, watching, not allowed to approach her or speak to her.

Before I made any move, I decided I needed to see Rick. I had to know if his promise to help me was still good. I had an offer of a ticket to freedom; now was the moment of truth, and I had to make up my mind. I was still on the island after the guts of four weeks and nothing was happening. Maybe if Rick and I could talk, he'd see the sense of me going to Gibraltar and be relieved that I could escape alone. Maybe with the tension gone, things might be all right between us. We might talk about meeting in London and combining our plans to buy Carlo out of jail.

I thanked Chris for the trouble he'd gone to. '*¡De nada!*' he smiled, 'You'd do it for me!' I told him that before taking up his offer, I had to check things out with Rick; he might have something already set up. He said to go ahead, of course. When he'd seen Rick in town, he'd been going into a half-finished apartment block on the waste ground between the Malaysian restaurant and Figueretas. I figured it might be the apartment where he and Marvin sometimes stayed, and I decided to go there that night. Even if he wasn't there, somebody might be able to get a message to him in Formentera.

Now that things were happening at last, I decided to write an optimistic it-will-all-be-OK letter to Hanna; I'd give it to Rick if I met him. If I went on the yacht, I might not see her or Aoife again. I said more or less what I'd said before, that the scene she'd had with Marvin didn't matter to me, that if it didn't work out, I'd be there and there'd be no recriminations. I wouldn't expect any instant reconciliation, but that, once I was in London, I'd send her the money to come north and maybe, in time, we might get back together again.

Chapter 25

AT SUNSET, I PICKED UP my bag from the woods behind Chris's house and, after dark, set off for town. It was extraordinary for me to be walking under the stars, the vast star-flecked space above my head, following the *caminos* inside the road, the headlights of the now-and-then cars passing a hundred yards away from me and the sea beyond the Playa D'en Bossa shimmering in the moonlight, cactus and scrub around me and even a white owl coming towards me and passing softly, and bats flying across the half-moon now and then.

I reached the outskirts of Figueretas forty minutes or so later and, crouching in the scrub across the road, surveyed the scene. There was nobody. I dodged across the road under a big arc light. With the beret and the jacket and the canvas briefcase, I must've looked like the Shadow-of-a-Gunman or Ill-Met-by-Moonlight. The scene resembled a movie set: the pools of light with darkness in between, and the big, unfinished apartment block with cement mixers and stacks of building material in the shadows. I didn't know which apartment Rick's friend was in, but there was only one that I could see with light in the window, maybe five floors up. I dodged in the door and skipped up the stairs. I arrived breathless outside the apartment: I could hear music inside. I knocked, not knowing what to expect but I had the beret off and a story ready in case it was answered by someone with nothing to do with me. I heard a voice call from inside, in English: 'Who is it?' It had to be the right pad.

I didn't want to announce my name so I called out 'Is Rick there?' There was a long silence and then the door opened, and standing there was Bobby G. I'd last seen him in Istanbul. 'Jesus!' I said.

He stared at me. 'No, man, I'm not Jesus, but step inside, you crazy fucker – you want to get us all busted, man?'

For a second I thought, *You too, Bobby?* – but he shot me a grin and I knew he was kidding. 'Come,' he said, 'There's people here who know nothin' about you, so be cool.'

I followed him. We passed through a room of people sitting around on sofas and on the floor, dim light, music playing, a lot of smoke in the air. I saw Hanna in a corner amongst some people; she had Aoife on her lap and a joint in her hand. She didn't see me or, if she did, she looked away. Rick saw me, though. He was sitting nearby and, as Bob led me into an empty room, he followed. Bobby quickly left, closing the door behind him.

'Hi, Rick. I thought I'd come and see you. Is everything OK?' I asked, as casually as I could.

'I'm alright,' he said, 'but you don't look too good . . .' Then, he smiled, and offered me a cigarette. 'It's good to see you, man, only it's not cool to come here, you know that.'

I nodded; I knew that, surely. He said he'd planned to come out to see me next day. He had news. A telegram had come from Bill in Copenhagen saying he'd wire me two hundred bucks when he got his pay cheque at the end of the week, which was tomorrow – how about that!

Bill, I thought, you are beautiful baby – Bill, with your 'axa phone and head full of sweet music, you are my best man! See now, Marvin, you're wrong that my friends have walked away from me – that's one thing you can no longer say!

Rick and I stood and smiled at one another. Aw-right, then, I thought – we'd soon be on the road! Now I told him about the yacht.

He shrugged, and pulled a face. 'It's up to you, man,' he said. But I'd already dismissed it. The money was coming: Rick and me – this was the way I'd always meant to go. We set about planning things.

The dentist passport was already in Ibiza – Black William had brought it over; I told Rick to tell him thanks. Rick said he could borrow a Land camera from Bobby and take a mugshot of me. A Polaroid was the only way: if he tried to get a roll of film developed with me on it, whoever did the developing might have seen my wanted picture in the *Ayuntamiento*; it had been moved from the cop shop to the town hall. So he'd come out to Chris's the next day, bring hair dye and the camera, and we'd trim my hair and I'd put on a collar and tie and try to look like an English dentist. These plans were music to my ears. Here we were, Rick and me again, putting a number together.

We didn't talk for long, maybe five minutes. Then it was time for me to go – Ill-Met-by-Moonlight exit right. I told Rick I'd seen Hanna as I came in and would like to talk to her for a minute before I left, given that there might be no further opportunity before I split the island. 'It's up to her,' he said, and went out, pulling the door behind him. It didn't shut fully. I looked through the gap. There were faces I'd seen before but didn't know: new people in Ibiza. I saw Marvin approaching the door and I drew back . . . 'You shouldn't be here,' he said, as he came in, 'You want to see Hanna ? I'll ask her. You shouldn't even be here!'

He left and a few seconds later Hanna came in. She left the door open a bit behind her and stood glaring at me. I reached around her and closed it. 'Why did you come here? Why are you hounding me?' she demanded, fast and angry.

'Don't be mad,' I said. 'I just want to talk to you. I'll soon be leaving.'

She said no, she couldn't talk to me, she couldn't leave Aoife. I asked why she couldn't go and fetch her, so that I could see her too.

She went out and fetched her. Again I had to close the door. 'I'm not hounding you, Hanna,' I told her.

'Nobody wants you here. Don't you know that?' she hissed.

'You bitch!' I said. 'Here you are, getting stoned out of your face with my friends, and now all you can tell me is nobody wants me here!'

'It's true,' she said. 'And what I do is my business. I'm staying here tonight, but I won't be welcome if you keep turning up!'

'Oh, stop it, Hanna,' I begged, 'For Christ's sake, stop it . . .' I sat on the bed and buried my face in my hands. Now Aoife started whingeing. I heard the door open. It was Nicole.

'Are you all right, Hanna?' she asked and threw me a hard look – what did she think, that I was beating her up or something? 'Hanna, everyone's waiting.' she said, and Hanna rose to go.

'Would you mind leaving us for a minute, Nicole?' I asked. She looked at Hanna, and Hanna nodded. She left.

'What's come over you, Hanna?' I asked.

She looked at me with her slit eyes. 'Nothing. It's you. You're all screwed up. I'm perfectly happy . . .'

'Oh, for Christ's sake,' I said, 'leave me alone.'

'*You're* the one who won't leave *me* alone.' she snapped back. She sat there, looking at me, stiff as a board, Aoife on her lap. 'It's your fault. You came here. I tried to avoid this.'

The door opened; again it was Nicole. 'Hanna, c'mon,' she said urgently. Hanna nodded. The door closed. 'Where are you going?' I asked.

'Down town,' she said. 'It's none of your business.'

'Aoife's my business. What are you going to do with her?'

'She'll be alright. You can't talk. You were always leaving us anyway!'

I rose. I was frantic now. 'For God's sake, Hanna, don't be like this,' I begged. 'Please don't be like this. I'm fucked up. I can't help it. You know how it is. You know!'

'Pull yourself together!' she told me. 'Pull yourself together, or I'll leave!'

I said nothing for a minute, just stood. 'Can I see you before I leave the island?' I asked. 'Just as a friend, Hanna, OK?'

'I'd prefer not to.'

'Won't I see you again?'

'No.'

'What about Aoife?'

'I'll write to you.'

'So that's it?'

'Yes.'

'You bitch!' I said, 'It's so easy for you to forget! You forget what it's like. When you were down and fucked up, I never—'

'I'm going now,' she said, her lips tight and hard. She opened the door, went through and slammed it behind her.

I stood there, my head reeling; I felt like I'd been on an acid trip or in a boxing ring. By Jesus, could Hanna, for all her sweetness and smallness, deliver knock-down blows.

Rick came in and sort of hustled me down the corridor, through the room, now empty but for a few strangers who silently stared at me, then down the stairs and outside. He shook his head sympathetically; he must've known what had gone down. He reached out and squeezed my arm in reassurance. 'You're near deliverance, man. Remember that.' Our eyes met, and the understanding between us was like before. 'We been thinking of you,' he said. 'You're over-anxious, man. I understand. It's all OK. Don't worry. We love you; you ain't forgotten. Don't let fear take the best.' He'd said that before, but I nevertheless appreciated it. He promised again that he'd come to Chris's the next day. He was biting his lower lip, and his eyes shone warmly, like the Rick I knew.

On that note, in the glow of that warmness, Ill-Met-By-Moonlight dodged across the road and into the darkness beyond. I found the path and headed westward, not feeling my feet touch the ground. Hanna, cold as ice, Rick, warm and heartfelt; deaths and entrances fast on one another. *'It's all jumping from illusion to illusion,'* I sang, to the beat of my footsteps. *'It's all jumping from illusion to illusion, It's just a matter of staying on one . . .'*

The night had turned wild and almost pitch black. Things leaped about; plate cactus rearing like horses, caught by the wind. Ahead, some orbs of light hovered in mid-air, disembodied and eerie. As I approached, I heard loud snorting and trampling. They were goats, held in a corral; they shied away in a panic as I passed. 'It's cool,' I told them aloud. I walked in a dream, footstep behind footstep. *Won't I see you again?*, I had asked her. *No*, she'd said. No. So simple for her. Suddenly, after all the time together, it's over: Hanna wants out! Now, pick up the pieces, start again alone. Hit the road, Jack! You're down, you're a drag and she can't love you.

'Nobody says I must be unhappy,' Hanna says. 'I'm me and I'm free, and all the rules are different now because *I want out!* Who are you to me, any-way? I'm free to leave you after three years, *yes*, and to take your child, *yes*, because *I want to*! And that's what's important. *To do what you want to do!'*

So you'd better split, Mr. Ill-Met-By-Moonlight; don't ask or beg or make her feel guilty. The more she sees of you, the more she'll hate you. You are the spectre in her bright world and she don't want no sad things mopin' there. Like you once wrote about Nancy, '*Last night she sailed/ I watched her from the walls / All white and beautiful / Sail out to sea . . .*' Now again you're alone, not alone like Chris is but aching for that part of you that's gone and for what you thought was real. And that's where you begin from, my friend, with the taste of the lie in your mouth, the lie that love is real when you know it is *convenience*. People love only as long as it suits them to love. They choose to love and they choose to stop loving, and you had better not be around when that change happens because everything you are will become a drag. '*How could I ever have been with you?!*' they ask.

At this point of his interior dialogue Ill-Met-by-Moonlight trips on a rock because he isn't watching his feet, only the darkness ahead, and falls on his face, smashing into the ground. He watches himself rise. He goes on as if it hasn't happened because, in truth, he doesn't feel it; he feels nothing. He marches on, talking to himself and others, to Hanna, Chris, Rick about when love flees and suddenly it's all different. He remembers reading it to Hanna: '*Love one another, but make not a bond of love.*'

When I get back to the house, wild-eyed and bloody, Chris produces some antiseptic and cleans the grit out of my kisser – which is somewhat meaty where it bit the dust. Meanwhile, I dab bright red Mercurochrome on the heel of one hand and one knee and try to tell him how beautiful it is, it truly is, the world of Formentera, how beautiful the people are – which is why, now that money will be arriving, I will go north with Rick. He doesn't argue. He may see me as a classic case of a victim in thrall to his tormentors, even unto defending their torments. If he does, he doesn't say so. He makes chamomile tea from leaves he's collected that day. I stoop over the fire, drinking it, watching the flames. Sometimes I forget what I'm saying. I get lost in the flames.

The ceramic bowl is full of black water as my head is pushed into it. 'Pushed' is the word; Jacey is doing the pushing. I can object, of course, but he's only trying to dye my hair and maybe doesn't realise that he's being a little rough and, anyway, who cares? He says, 'When we're finished, your best friend won't know you!'

I am sitting back and the sun is in my eyes as Rick tilts my chin and, clip-clip-clip, is trimming my beard, and then my head is lent forward and, clip-clip-clip, Jacey is clipping my hair. Formentera people, half of whom I don't know, are sitting around in the dust with their dogs, watching this. I'd glimpsed some of them at Bobby's the night before.

Now I'm standing up and Jacey, who is taller than me, is combing my hair flat across my head. Nicole hands me a towel to wipe away the dye, which is running down my forehead, and which I must not get on the white shirt I'm wearing, for the photo, with the tie that Rick had brought from somewhere and Chris's only jacket, my dentist outfit. I'm standing against a white wall, 'Chin up, man, chin up!' Click. Not good. Maybe we need another. We only have enough Polaroid film for two. Yes, this one's better, but still not good because my face is somewhat lopsided from hitting the *camino* the night before. Photo of Fugitive Looking Very Fucked up, San José road, Ibiza, 1965.

Chris is nowhere to be seen; he's gone to San Antonio to tell the yachtsman thanks, but no. Luckily, I hadn't put Mercurochrome on my forehead because if I had, we couldn't have taken the photo. An American girl who Rick says was a make-up artist covers the cuts with some paste, and on the black and white picture they don't show. The picture is blurred anyway and out of focus but it's the best we've got. I must cut it down to size and get it into the passport now, and neatly. Take out the real tooth-puller, put in me instead.

Rick has told me the telegram money-order has arrived from Bill, in Marvin's name, and they'll cash it the next day. I've already figured that, with two hundred bucks, I'll have enough to spare after fares for me and Rick to leave some bread behind with Hanna, maybe even enough to do the first small scam in London – a fifty-dollar double-our-money – and get the mojo working to buy out Carlo. But now he tells me that himself, Marv and Nicole will be travelling with me to the border. There's strength in numbers, he says; better cover. We might not find a train carriage of foreigners as planned; now we'll fill one up ourselves. I don't like it. I don't like it and I don't need it. It was to be Rick and me but once again it's fuckin' Marvin, and my money will be paying their fares. But it's too late for the yacht now, and what am I, ungrateful? So I keep quiet.

Hanna had come earlier. She'd simply said, 'Here's Aoife to say goodbye to. Goodbye. Trust Rick and Marvin—' and she'd left.

In a while, the Formentera people rise to go. They look at me like I'm some sort of exhibition piece; they're here for the freak show and I'm the freak. I feel nothing, say nothing, do what they tell me to do. Something happened last night. I went out of my mind, if I wasn't already: the smack against the rock on the *camino*, the hammer-blows of Hanna, the embrace of Rick, the illusions. I went out and I haven't come back.

Before they leave me, Rick tells me he and the others have come up with a plan to get me to the mainland. The Barcelona boat will be watched but the fuzz won't be paying attention to the inter-island ferry to Majorca and from there I can cross to the mainland. However, it's better I make the trip alone: for him, Marvin and Nicole to take the two ferries would cost too much, so they'll cross directly to Barcelona and will meet me there. They'll leave on the ferry the next night at eight; my ferry to Palma, Majorca, won't leave until ten o'clock, so they won't be around to see me aboard. When they cash the money order, he'll buy me a ticket and give it to Bobby, along with some bread. All I'll have to do is go to Bobby's. Bobby will see me to the boat. It will all be OK. It's the best way. In Barcelona, I can meet him at the statue of Cristobal Colon an hour after my boat from Palma gets in. We'll all travel north together. They'll make sure I'm OK.

That night, I began to do the passport. Not a good time: shaky hands; everything was shaky now. The photo was awful anyway and not easy to cut to size; the edge wasn't straight. So, I had to cut it smaller again, to get it right. It still wasn't square. It was a law of diminishing returns. If I cut it too often, it'd end up too small for the frame. And there was no other photo.

Sometimes, I thought, it was beautiful, so beautiful, everything, everyone in Formentera. Paulo, who read D'Annunzio, and Gianluca, who knew everything about art, and Blind George and his handmaiden girls. Bruno, so full of love for life and colour and the skies above and the rocks below, and Desiree, so zany and wild. Bill Hesse, quiet and self-effacing; Willi, the Dutchman, bringing us fish he'd caught in the sea. The crazy Aussie girl who came dancing through our house at night, with William, the posh black man from London; they blew our acid trip, but they were beautiful too. Beautiful, in our innocence, was everyone. I played with Aoife under the fig tree, in the shifting shadows: I carried her, salty, on my shoulders back from the beach. All that was over. But it was so glorious, the idea was so glorious! And it has come to this. I am leaving it; perhaps I am expelled from it forever? '*I have heard the mermaids singing . . .*' They do not sing to me.

I worked on the passport, my nose close to the page in the lamplight. I talked to Chris, although he wasn't there. Everyone had so much love, I told him. I want it to be like that; I want to believe in it. I believed in it over there, in Formentera, and as we drove north, too, Rick, Carlo and me. There was such camaraderie between us.

'Is it me, Chris?' I asked him. 'I don't know where to look from, now. Where is it real to look from? Tell me, tell me. So many possibilities of what's true.'

Keeping a steady hand, I inscribed the back of the photo with a square pen nib, following the pencil tracing I'd made, the quarter-circle of embossed stamp drawn with a compass to make it match up with the embossing on the page. But it wasn't good; the reverse embossing made by the nib wasn't sharp, the photo paper was too hard. Did I dare wet it? Would it dry sharp? As it was, anyone who took a good look at it wouldn't be fooled.

'But what is real, Chris?' I whispered. 'What is fair and just in the circumstances? How do you *try not to be* a drag? Watch yourself? Prepare a face to meet the faces that you meet?'

'But is it wrong in Formentera to be unhappy?' I hear him ask me. 'If so, you've put yourself in hell.'

'But they're beautiful people, Chris, the most beautiful I've ever met . . .'

'And the dope?' he asks.

'It's my world,' I tell him, 'The people in it smoke dope.'

I still have to do the '*Entrada*' stamp to Spain – the guy couldn't be in Spain unless he'd entered at some border. My hands are trembling, for fuck's sake. Better leave it until tomorrow. I'll draw it in, if I can get the right pen nib, the right ink: I'll dilute black ink, make it faint. I thumb through the pages of this English dentist's brief. 'There are other places,' I hear Chris say gently. In my mind, I see him talking to me across the fire, his smile reassuring me. 'Other places where you can belong, my friend.' Yes, Chris, now you've said it! *Other places, the only places I am fit for* – not Formentera: and the loss pierces my heart. I begin to draw a Spanish '*Entrada*' stamp on an eraser. It has to be written backwards if it's to come out right when I stamp it on the page.

Next evening, Chris sees me off from the house as it gets dark. The boat to Palma de Mallorca leaves in two hours. He says he'll walk with me into town, but I say no. I'm all kitted out. I leave my basket and old briefcase behind; now, I'm an English dentist on holiday, arrived in Spain ten days before – so my '*Entrada*' stamp, not too badly rendered in the event, confirms. I don't have much to carry, anyway. I have a small suitcase, scuffed, which Chris has given me. I am not a rich dentist; I'm a lonely Joe, travelling solo. I have one shirt, one pair of pants, a bird book, a tourist guide, no cigarette papers or dope, no dope paraphernalia, no hippie shit. I am Arthur Brown, dentist, lonely but intrepid traveller off-the-beaten-track in Spain.

When I arrive at Bobby's door, he greets me warmly, embraces me. He is a prince amongst men. He says 'Wait here, there's people inside', and returns with a tweed jacket for me, replacing the cardigan Chris has given me; it was OK but not quite right, a bit bizarre for a travelling dentist. He also has a matching 'necktie' for me, as he calls it.

We set off for the town together. Bobby's got no problem about talking to me. It's all jokes and reminiscence about our time in Istanbul and questions about the bust. I like Bobby but there's something that's been bothering me.

I ask him about Rick and the smack. I'm happy to hear it's not coming from him; a guy called Ben brings it from New York. There was a small market for smack now: Nico, a beautiful German singer, and others. That's a drag, we reckon. But as we get closer to the town, we concentrate on the business in hand.

We stand on a terrace that looks down directly on the waterfront, the con-crete *avenida* under the arc lights with the big ferry to Majorca moored along-side. There are a couple of Guardia Civil standing fifty yards away, smoking, chewing the fat. There's nobody, but nobody, getting on board the boat and it's due to sail in fifteen minutes. We stand and consider the scene. They'll either stop me, or they won't. If they stop me, and ask for the passport, it depends on how closely they look at it; it doesn't look good and you don't have to be a professional to see that. However, it's now or never. Go for it. Bobby hands me an envelope. It's from Rick, he says: my ticket. I open it. The ticket's there, but just a five hundred peseta note along with it. Five hundred? After I pay the onward Palma-Barcelona ticket, I'll have only pennies left and if anything goes wrong with our rendezvous, I'm up the creek! Bobby sees my face. 'They short-change you, man?' he asks, suspicious.

I shrug. 'It'll be tight but—' 'Here, man, I got a thousand and some change. Take it: if I'd known before I left the house, I could've given you more.'

Old Bobby, dear friend, straightens me up there in the shadows, looks at me, adjusts my necktie and the lapels of my jacket, and embraces me. He wishes me luck and I walk off alone.

On the broad, bare arc-light-lit apron of the dock, I approach the gang-plank of the Palma de Mallorca boat. My first step on it will be my first step towards freedom. The cops stand twenty yards to the side, the two of them talking, black plastic, lavatory pan hats shining in the light, guns in their big holsters. I pause, put down my suitcase, take my ticket from my pocket, squint at it through my round-framed bifocals, look up at the name of the boat on the prow. In truth, what with the spectacles, I can barely see it. They watch, casually – I'm just another foreign fool. I pick up my suitcase, reassured, and walk slowly towards the gangplank, ticket in hand. I pause to look back at the town; how interesting, how wonderfully fascinating is Spain! At the bottom of the gangplank, a smiling *mariñero* greets me. He checks my ticket, tears off a page, returns it to me. I ascend the first steps, trying to keep the lightness out of my stride.

Morning. Palma de Mallorca. I will have to stay overnight. I have an address. How I came to have it, I don't remember, but it is the address of Barbara Hughes, wife of Hole-in-the-Head Bart, she who first turned Hanna and me on to acid. She is living with Brunswick the Legend-Maker, with whom I played 'Bayonet Stretch' on the night I first arrived in Ibiza.

I don't remember much except her hospitality and the drinks. Barbara was easy to be with. She'd heard news of the bust but how I looked now, with my hair dyed and the beard, was a surprise. She asked me about Hanna and, in my demented state, I told her I'd get her back somehow. 'I'll look after her better, love her better – and make love to her better – than that prick ever could!'

Brunswick wasn't there all day. I think that maybe he was elsewhere in town, writing his nightmare story of the Korean War. I had to catch the night boat to Barcelona and he turned up not long before I left and hugged me hard, his rough, unshaven chin against my cheek, his eyes mad, as always.

He questioned me. 'What news of the island to the south, poet? How be The Holy Men? Do they yet seek Nirvana through the weed-smoke?' And then, aside, with a mad look and his face close to mine, 'That's what it is, you know, a weed!' But he continued, hospitable too. 'A drink, princess, another drink for the poet.' And then, wide-eyed, 'There's no quantity of the weed secreted about thy person, is there? No. Good! Nor of the acid that liquefies the mind? Good! A drink for the poet, woman!' And Barbara pours the drinks. And then, as we toasted, he continued his interrogation. 'And, poet, in the clear light of the Ultimate Reality, have you given the Sacred Unwashed all you possess? Lest possessions hang thee up? Have you given them your home, your woman and your mind?'

I tried to laugh at his crazy eyes, six inches from mine. Brunswick was as mad and paranoid as I was, and I wasn't able for him now. He lent back, hands folded across his stomach, smiling in sham holiness, and asked 'And did you thank them, my brother?' Then, in a feminine sing-song voice, nodding mock-wisely, he recited, 'For thanking shows the true enlightenment of the Giver.'

All this Brunswick said, while he was knocking back two or three beers. Like dope, booze can be inspiring too. It's arguable which is the more inspiring and which is the most likely to wreck you.

They took me to the boat that night in a taxi. Barbara kissed me on the cheek. Brunswick shoved five hundred pesetas into my hand.

Chapter 26

THE BOAT TO BARCELONA WAS another blur. I was moving, now, almost mindlessly. On the boat from Ibiza to Majorca, Rick had booked me a third-class cabin and I had gone there the minute I got aboard. Because of the bread I'd got from Bobby and from Brunswick, I could now afford a cabin ticket on the boat that would take me from Palma to Barcelona, and I did the same thing again: went below, watched the moonlight – and then the sunrise – through the porthole and kept out of the way.

Severely bothering my waking dreams was the matter of the money sent by Bill Hesse and now in Rick and Marvin's hands. The lousy five hundred pesetas Rick had left me to get from Palma to Barcelona would have been barely enough to pay for a berth in *cubierto* and a meal. I'd have arrived in Barcelona broke, and what if there was any kind of fuck-up about meeting him and the others?

Meanwhile, here I was travelling alone while my money paid for their fuckin' tickets – and they were holding the balance of my bread. However, I told myself to say nothing about it, to wait to see how it panned out. If they thought I was putting out bad vibes, they'd walk away, and that'd be the end of any hope of my reinstatement with Hanna or with them.

In the morning, I disembarked at Barcelona with no hassle. The three of them were waiting at the statue of Colón as planned. As I approached, Rick pointed towards a café on the pavement opposite, and they headed for it. I arrived. We took seats around a table outside.

There was something funny about the way they were walking, I'd noticed. Now I saw that they were wearing shiny, new boots. Rick and Marvin had bought themselves boots of Spanish leather; they were walkin' tall and acting tall and it was paid for by the bread sent in my name. 'You OK?' Rick said, noticing my glance, looking at me through narrowed eyes. I nodded, keeping my counsel. They ordered coffee, *ensemadas* and *bocadillos*, no expense spared.

Then Rick told me that they'd bought a car, and they all looked at me, as if daring me to make something of it. It'd been a real good buy, he said; they'd paid only forty bucks. They'd heard about it from an Argentinian guy they'd met at Bobby's and had bought it from his old lady who had a pad near the Plaza Real. Thing was, it would be useful for my escape. For starters, the train tickets to get us to northern France where I could take a boat to England would have cost almost as much. The car would be a cool way to get me out of Spain. Rick would drive us through the border. I could hide in the trunk, but it would be better if I snuggled down in the back seat and pretended to be asleep. Rick would hand over the passports and it was unlikely that the cops would look closely at them all. If they did and I was busted, I could say I was a hitchhiker they'd picked up, whereas if I was found in the trunk, they'd all obviously be implicated and be busted too.

The car would also be useful when he and Marvin met some friends of Bobby's in Amsterdam; they could use it to bring some Lebanese hash they'd get on credit up to Stockholm, where there was a small dope scene. They'd put aside some of the profits towards buying out Carlo. OK, so it was *my* money, he knew that, but it was for my escape in which they were all participating, and anyway, after Stockholm, they'd bring the car to London where they'd connect with Nicole and I could come around and collect it, OK?

What could I say? The three of them were looking at me like a panel of psychiatrists. Was I going to endanger them by demanding we all go by train? No – but, in fact, I'd never asked Marvin or Nicole along in the first place. Was I going to deny them the chance to make some bread for Carlo? No. I didn't know why they bothered even justifying the whole number; they were ripping me off anyway, and challenging me to object. Boots of Spanish fuckin' leather, stomping around like martinets, looking ridiculous. Back in Ibiza they'd said I was on an ego trip, because I defended myself; who was on the ego trip now?

I walked with them to see the car. It was an old Ford with Dutch plates, not worth more than forty bucks. It was parked outside their *pensión* in the Calle de la Ancha. They said they had the rooms until noon, and we'd leave town then. Meanwhile, they were going upstairs to cool out and smoke a joint. They didn't invite me but I followed them anyway. I caught Rick exchanging a glance with Nicole and then Marvin. Then, upstairs, Marvin said to me 'C'mon in here', while Rick and Nicole went to the room next door. That was when I realised Rick was sleeping with Nicole and it really made me think: Carlo in jail, and Rick's fucking Nicole, and Nicole's fucking Rick. Carlo would probably be cool about it, because he was never possessive about anything, but it didn't strike me as very kind or friendly. But, then, maybe I was old-fashioned in that way.

In Marvin's room, he indicated that I should sit on the chair; there was the chair, the bed, a bedside locker, a wardrobe and nothing else. I sat. He took out some kief and began to build a joint, saying nothing. A heavy silence hung. As he lit the joint and took a deep toke, he told me Hanna was pissed off when I'd shown up at Bobby's. However, that was my problem, not his. He was heading for Scandinavia, where they were a whole lot of chicks queuing up to be laid. 'Ever laid a Swede?' he asked me. 'They say they're something else!' He handed me the joint with a big grin. I took a toke; I wanted to keep my head clear but I also wanted to hear more of his plans. However, when I handed it back, he said he was bringing it next door. He didn't invite me. I sat alone, assuming he was coming back. I could hear the mumble of their conversation in the next room. After fifteen minutes or so, I went and knocked and, when they turned the key, went in. Immediately, whatever was under discussion was dropped. Rick and Nicole looked at me, as if to ask what I was doing there. They were sitting side by side on the bed; they looked awkward and uncomfortable. Marvin sat on the single chair, staring at the ceiling. I stood in the heavy silence. Obviously, they wanted me to leave. I said I'd go and walk around and come back. Rick warned me not to get hung up anywhere; they'd be leaving at noon. Marvin laughed, 'It's OK. If you're not back then, we'll report a missing fugitive.'

I left my suitcase and wandered out onto the Barcelona street. There was a sort of buzz in my head, a constant low-level-noise; I was in a world apart from the people swarming around me in the everyday of their lives – me, on the run from justice, an alien amongst them. What Rick had proposed for getting me across the border was crazy; it scared me, just listening to it. Me cowering in the corner of the car; that was bullshit, crazy for me, crazy for them. If the cops busted me, would they really believe that the others didn't know me? Fantasy land! They'd check with the cops in Ibiza. Under scrutiny, their story would never wash.

Also, the dentist's passport was a disaster. So far, it hadn't been looked at but the cops at the border would suss it for sure. Rick, Marvin and Nicole weren't impressing me now that we were on the mainland and the escape action was supposed to begin. Boots, cars, dope deals, joints at ten o'clock in the morning: fuck them and their Mickey Mouse fantasies. I was crazier than a fox now, thinking of myself, the main chance. They'd fuck up, for sure.

I still wanted to be with them, but staying with them suddenly had nothing to do with making my peace with Hanna. That had all changed. Marvin had finished with her, and there was no more talk of a communal pad in London. Scandinavian chicks? He'd be lucky, even with his Spanish fly!

I had fourteen hundred pesetas in my pocket, but I wasn't telling them. They'd lost touch with reality. For all the buzzing in my head, I was a lot more in the real world than they were. Free of the prison island which Ibiza had become, I was beginning to see straight a little. My head was ruling my heart. It was telling me that maybe I should have a back-up plan, just in case.

The first thing was to get a passport photo taken – a real one – and maybe replace the one that was fucked up. I should also replace the specs with ones I could actually see through. I found a photo studio and beside it was an oculist. I went in. Could they replace the bottle-bottoms with clear lenses? '*Sí. ¿Como no?*' It would cost me a hundred pesetas; they didn't seem to think it an exceptional request. Fifteen minutes later I came back and collected them and went into the photo studio next door. In the jacks, I scooped water from the hand basin on to my hair, combed it flat, and sat for the portrait of 'The

Fugitive, Studio Mayer, Pelayo 38, Barcelona, end of January 1965'. It was a nice shot. I looked like a total dickhead, with the owlish specs and slicked down hair: one sad, harmless fucker for sure. Nothing at all like the dashing *contrabandista irlandés*.

Next thing, I buy a map, then a compass in case I have to go on the run. Then, something weird happens, something with no sense or meaning. It makes one wonder about the magnetism of fate.

I'm on a pavement crowded with people going about their business. I see this old broad – maybe not so old but old to me at the time – well-dressed, heavily made-up, gesturing at me from a café window. She's smiling at me, beckoning me in. She's a foreigner, I can tell, at home in Spain. I go in. I don't know why. Maybe it's because she's picked me out of the crowd. If it was a man, I wouldn't have gone in.

The café is half-full. She indicates a seat at her table. I sit down. '*¡Camarero!*' she calls and claps her hands, '*¡Dos!*' and the waiter brings two drinks. They're cognacs: how does she know? We haven't spoken yet. I'm passive, trying to figure her out. She raises her drink in a toast and, as I go to lift my glass, she puts her hand on mine. '*¡Salud!*' she says. She smiles, conspiratorially and says in an upper-class English voice, 'You're in trouble, I can tell. I'll look after you.' For a moment, fear and then hope leap in my heart. Who is she? Does she have connections maybe? She drinks her drink. She calls the waiter again. I say I won't have another drink.

She takes my hand again. 'You're not English, I know.' But how does she know? Not from my accent. I've said very little, only refused the drink. Is she psychic? Can she see my green Irish passport, stuffed down the waistband of my pants. Has she been sent by fate, should I tell her everything? She looks like a woman who would have a house, have money and perhaps important friends, people in the embassies. Maybe she could get me out of Spain? These things I consider in my dementitude; such thoughts are swarming through my mind.

She's knocked back the second drink, and the *camarero*, without apparent bidding, is bringing her another. She takes my hand. She holds it to her breast. I can feel her breast. It's soft and she's pressing my hand against it, holding it tight; it's hard to pull it away without making a scene. She looks deep in my eyes. She's almost old enough to be my mother. 'I can help you . . .' Her gaze is salacious, and it seems to me many people are now watching. She's drawing attention to me. I draw back my hand. She grasps my sleeve.

I begin to get up, to make apologies: I have to go. 'No,' she says, 'don't go!' and she rises. I say I must. 'No!' she cries, 'I know about you!' She slams her palm on the table: her glass crashes to the floor. There's a guy at the counter, one guy in particular, watching all this, taking a special interest: a middle-aged guy with a pencil-moustache. He has the look of a cop about him but, of course, my paranoia is rampant. I turn towards the door. She's yelling something about knowing who I am. The buzz in my head has risen to a crescendo and suddenly I can hardly hear her. I feel the whack of her handbag on the back of my head and hear the waiter shouting, '¡Señora, señora!' This is all I need: to be pulled in by the cops as a victim of a drunken assault. Head down, expecting another blow, I make it to the door, and out onto the pavement. I walk off briskly, trying not to hurry, trying not to run.

'You bastard, I know who you are, you bastard!' She's outside the door, and screaming. I turn my head as I round the corner. The waiter is holding her by the arm as she stands staggering on the pavement, screaming after me at the top of her voice.

Some streets away, I catch my breath. I am frightened, unreasonably frightened. But that's what paranoia is: unreasonable fear.

Chapter 27

WE DROVE NORTH, THE THREE of them and me, heading for the French border. Things that happened in the car convinced me that I was riding with strangers. One after the other, things they did and said made me see them in a new light, 'the light of the Ultimate Reality', one might say. They didn't bother any longer to pretend love-and-peace; maybe they felt that, away from Formentera, there was no need for pretence.

They talked of deals and bad drugs and making big money. Whatever it was that had undermined them, had given them egos and boots, I didn't know. They were on a power trip; they seemed to be getting kicks out of walking over me. Something strange happened in that car. The Game of Enlightenment was over. I saw them for what they were – traitors to the dream.

They said I should do the driving, and that was OK by me. The steering wheel gave me a grip of something. But now I was a chauffeur for them. They slept, or gave me orders. 'Pull in here – I want to score some cookies. I got the munchies!' Rick said. The car had only two doors, and he was sitting behind me. I had to get out first and push my seat forward to let him out. When he got back in, I pushed the seat back too fast and caught his knees, no big deal, no great pain but he screamed 'I'll break your fuckin' head if you do that again!' I said sorry. I drove on.

I saw that the gas was running down and at a filling station I got out and half-filled the tank. Marvin handed me a handful of change and notes. I started counting the coins so as to pay with them because we couldn't exchange them in France. Marvin asked me what the fuck I was doing. When I told him, he flipped out, shouting at me that I was dishonest, that I couldn't do anything straight. I didn't know what he was talking about but the others obviously believed him. I let it pass and drove on.

With Nicole, it was an issue about whether we should take a left or a right turn. I read it as a left but she said it was right. They told me to do what she said. Five minutes later, it was clear that we were on the wrong road. As I turned to go back, Marvin said, 'You should have done like Nicole said, you fucking yo-yo!'

'She said a right!' I said, levelly.

'I didn't!' Nicole said. I looked at her in the rear view mirror and she must have felt my look because her eyes met mine. She knew she'd lied. She turned her face away and looked out the window. I drove on.

Sometime in the late afternoon, the jalopy breaks down. We've pulled over so that Rick can take a leak, but the battery's dead and she won't start up again. When I look under the bonnet, the fan belt is OK, so I'm pretty sure the alternator is gone. Somebody stops and says he'll send a mechanic. A guy turns up with a souped-up breakdown truck and hitches a chain to the front bumper. He is a mad bastard, I can tell. I ask does anyone want to take over at the wheel. They say no. Rick says 'You're our driver, OK?' That is my role.

The mad bastard takes off like a rocket. We're jerked along at the end of a short chain, and hurtle downhill on narrow roads at insane speeds. I try to keep the chain taut; the sheep-shagger, Jim Lowery, once told me that when you're being towed, you always do the braking. But the guy's driving like he's forgotten we're there. With the battery dead, I have no lights or horn to alert him to what's happening with us, dragged behind. All we can do is sit powerless in our metal box, thrown this way and that on every corner. I have the wheel to hold on to, but Marvin is thrown sideways on top of me, and Nicole on top of Rick and they're yelping in terror or sitting bolt upright. I can't believe it but I'm getting some sort of thrill out of it as we go into blind corners and he whips us across the road onto the other side and if there's anything coming, we're dead.

'Lost your ego yet, Marvin?' I yell and laugh. The zed bends and hairpins come up one after the other, obscured by the tow truck until the last second, and I am one crazy fucker now. They've said I'm crazy, they've said I can't let my ego go. They're right, I'm crazy, but I am egoless! I have nothing to lose but my life. I brake again, and the tyres scream and the mad bastard's exhaust pipe blasts smoke at me so that I can hardly see through the windscreen as he puts his foot down and accelerates once more. I have been towed too fast before, but now I am being hauled by a madman. My hands are like vices on the wheel. And then, his brake lights flash and we've reached the outskirts of a town, and he thunders down the main drag, us behind him, and with no warning whatsoever suddenly whips us onto a garage forecourt, and I hit the brakes before the jalopy slams into his arse.

As he steps out, he says something to a couple of guys standing by and they laugh. I don't catch it but I have a feeling it's about frightening the shit out of foreigners. 'Come back in an hour,' he tells me. We see a café down the street and head for it. As we sit down, Marvin says, 'You nearly killed us!' and the others nod in solidarity. 'I saved your fuckin' life!' I tell him.

I walk away, go to the counter, buy a hip-pocket bottle of Veterano brandy. I couldn't give a fuck about them. Lies, power trips and aberrations. They're a fuckin' liability and I'm going to look after myself, let them sink or swim.

When the car's fixed and we set off again, I've already scanned the map. It shows the back roads near the foothills of the Pyrenees. I've selected one; it's a dead end, stopping short before the mountains. Ten miles south of La Junquera, I turn off the main drag. They don't even notice. Marvin is dozing beside me and I see, in the rear view mirror, Rick with his head on Nicole's shoulder. Both have their eyes closed. I ask myself how people can waste their time sleeping as they pass through scenery – it's like I'm driving a fuckin' dormitory or a fuckin' hearse! Then Marvin notices the bumps, opens his eyes and asks, 'Where we goin', man?' I don't answer but I pull in under some trees on the narrow road; I want to check the map again. A few kilometres ahead is a village called La Vajol, where the road ends. I'll leave the car a kilometre before we reach it.

I tell him I think it's better that I walk across the mountains to France; it's safer than going by car. 'Hey, Rick,' he calls, 'wake up, man. You better hear this!' and Rick wakes. I can see he's grumpy. Fuck him!

I tell them I'm going to walk across the mountains. It'll be better for them; it will save them the risk of taking me in the car. 'You don't have to do that, man,' Rick says, some concern in his voice, almost alarm. 'It's what I'm going to do,' I say. I start the engine and set off driving. There's silence; they don't know what to say.

The road forks and I turn off and tell them how they'll find their way back to the main road after I leave them; in fact, they can have the map, I won't need it. It shows a village on the French side of the Pyrenees called Amélie-les-Bains. The road that passes through it runs parallel to the mountains so, one way or the other, if I get across, I'll come out on that road. I tell them I'll meet them in the village sometime in the early morning, if I make it. It's clearly a small place and I'll see the car.

When we stop below La Vajol, I step out and they step out too. It's getting dark, and a mist is coming down from the mountains off to our right; we're in a bright green clearing at the side of the road. I get my small suitcase from the trunk. 'OK,' I say. 'Wish me luck, I'm on my way.'

Nicole looks distracted. 'You don't have to do this,' she says.

Rick shrugs angrily, 'We come all this distance with him and then he goes his own fuckin' way! So let him go!'

He's pissed off alright; maybe his conscience is getting to him. They've gone too far and I'm not taking it any more.

I'm about to leave when Marvin says, 'Wait, I'm going with you!' He turns to the others, 'I'll walk ahead of him and if we meet the fuzz, he can split and I'll say I'm a birdwatcher. I'll be OK, with an American passport and all.'

I'm taken aback. I don't want this!

'You don't have to,' I say, my meaning clear, 'It's better I go alone.'

'Let him go then,' Rick snaps. He says the whole idea of crossing the mountains at night is crazy but, as far as he's concerned, let me go ahead and break my fuckin' neck if I want but, he, Marvin, shouldn't do the same.

'I'm not doing it for him,' Marvin says, 'I'm doing it for Hanna. He'll get lost. I'll lead him: I learned orienteering when I was a kid. I told Hanna I'd get him out of Spain and that's what I'm going to do.'

That's all I need, a fuckin' boy scout on a hero trip! I'm about to tell him this isn't the Catskills when Nicole chimes in, 'He's keeping you safe for the sake of Hanna, do you understand that? He wants you to be safe!'

'Safe?' I say, 'Safe? Jesus, you guys!'

The air is full of bitterness. When Rick pipes up, there's anger and reproval in his voice. 'What would Hanna think of this?' he demands. 'You got your head up your ass, my friend! The man makes you an offer and you throw it back in his face! You bring him all this way to help you and now he's helping. So have the grace to accept it, OK?'

Yeah. I see now that if I tell the heroic Marvin to go fuck himself, Hanna will hear how I threw his love back in his face, how I cut myself off from the love they offered me and she'll think Marvin all the more the saint and me an ungrateful, prideful bastard with no place in their beatific world. Marvin is playing mind games again, as he's being doing all along.

All three look at me, their eyes meeting mine in the green, still silence. The weight of their admonition infuses the air. Am I too small-minded and vengeful to accept a kindness, ingenuously offered? I think, why not? Let Marvin have his moment of glory. I'm free now, whatever happens, and Marvin, Rick, Nicole, they are of no interest to me.

'OK,' I say, agreeing. There is relief in their faces: it wouldn't look good if absent friends got to hear that I had turned them down and walked away. But now that it's said, I want to move on without delay. It's no place to be parked, a car full of foreigners on a back road by the border as night falls.

'We'll meet you at that village in France in the morning,' says Marvin. 'Don't worry, I'll get him there.' He's full of bullshit confidence; he's rarin' to rescue me. 'You got the compass?' he asks me, 'You haven't left your passport or anything in the car so they'll get busted for harbouring a fugitive?' He's laughing: it's a joke. They're all smiling benevolently, like we're suddenly friends again.

Rick steps forward and embraces me stiffly. 'Good luck, man. Trust Marvin, you'll be alright . . .'

Nicole smiles gauchely. 'See you in France,' she says, and does a little hop, as if it's a fun outing. Yeah, fun for them but fuckin' serious for me! I know that Spanish border guards, with their Tyrolean-looking uniforms and guns, will be patrolling these mountains. Bad Jack Hand told me all about them one time. The Civil War hasn't finished, twenty-five years later. There are people who want out of Spain, left-wing people, enemies of the state, people on the wrong side of Franco. So let Marvin go ahead and I'll hang back. If he's stopped, he's a birdwatcher: American passport, big idiot lost in the mountains. They won't bust him – unless he's caught with me. Let him walk a hundred yards ahead. If I see him getting stopped, I'll fade away like a shadow, quick and silent. That's the plan. But it doesn't turn out like that at all.

The mountains are somewhere to our right. There's a mist. We're in a field and the mist is amazingly thick, like a blanket of wet air, almost like foggy rain. We're part-way across – it's a big field and we can't see the other side for the mist – when we hear cowbells ringing: deep, dead chimes to one side of us, coming towards us, then louder and louder from every direction. As I crouch down, a cow looms out of the fog and looks at me with wide eyes. It veers off, and suddenly the bells are as loud as church bells all around us. I stay crouched on the spot, Marvin a few yards away, and my thought is, is there a cowherd behind them who will suddenly appear out of the gloom and see us? But it never happens. The cows, like the herd of dumb beasts they are, trudge past and tell nobody, and if there is a cowherd, I never see him. As the sounds recede, we rise cautiously. Marvin grins at me and I grin back.

As we walk, the fog is growing heavier by the minute. Soon, we can hardly see a metre ahead. We come to a stone wall. It's high, disappearing into the haze above us, and sheer, with no footholds – in any case, why climb it if we can go around? Go left, or right? We go left. The wall continues, and we follow it. It continues for a long time, taking us in a direction we don't want to go, not towards where the mountains were but blocking our way, sending us sideways, parallel to them, maybe. It's hard to know because we can see only the piece of wall immediately beside us as we walk. Finally, it comes to a sharp corner, and seems to continue. Now what? Go back? But where are we? Where are the mountains? I study the compass but it's the first time I've ever tried to use one and I don't know how it works. 'Marvin, you know how to use this thing?' I ask, holding it out to him. 'No,' he answers, 'Why should I? You bought it.' 'Yeah, I thought we'd be able to see the mountains and that'd be north.' 'Well, we can't.' He grins, 'It's your problem, not mine.' Some orienteerer, Marvin. He lied again; why should I be surprised? 'It's OK,' I nod, 'we'll find them.' And I set off walking straight ahead, along the wall again, and he follows. When I look around, he's smiling.

Five minutes later, we heard a cow moo pretty close to us and ducked down, and then we saw a light, very dim in the mist, and sneaked closer. It was a lantern, shining through the mist from an open-fronted run-down wooden barn. Near it, I could make out a guy with a beret sitting on a stool milking a cow. Other cows stood in the background. 'OK,' I said, 'you stay here. I'll find out where we are.'

I went and talked to the man. I stepped in out of the fog, coughing first to alert him and talking as I approached, saying 'Goodnight, please forgive the molestation, can you help me, please?' He looked up. He was a nice man, helpful. I told him I'd gone walking, left my car, couldn't find my way back to the road. He pointed out where it was, somewhere over his shoulder. 'No!' I said, in disbelief, 'God, I'm completely lost! So the mountains are there. That's north, right?' And he confirmed it, with the polite incredulity of a countryman. I thanked him sincerely and walked away.

As I walked out of the space of light, I glanced down at the compass cupped in my hand and saw which way the blue tip of the needle was pointing. I turned the 'N' on the dial to coincide with it and kept it there from then on.

We set off in a beeline, but there was no moon: mist at first, then just darkness. Rising ground, low walls, things ahead of us: rocks, trees, shapes. I would let nothing stop me. I had the taste of freedom on my lips, I was intoxicated with it, and my energy was boundless. I crashed through all that came before me, splashed through rushing streams, climbed rocks, sustained a thousand scratches, and never felt one. I was on my way, Marvin behind me, yelling now and then, 'Hey, man, slow down!'

A couple of hours out, maybe six or seven hundred metres up – looking at a map, I see that the mountains between La Vajol and Amélie-les-Bains rise to 1,449m, 5,000 feet – Marvin really started moaning, and I stopped. He sat back, panting. Me too. I was in a lather of sweat; sweat was gluing my clothes to my body. I took a swig of cognac. He said, 'Hey, I got a joint rolled. Let's smoke it and fall out here. This is heavy shit. Let's just cool out and cross in the morning.'

I said no. I had no interest in giving him reasons, or in talking either. I waited while he smoked the joint alone and got a bit mellow. When I stood up to go, he rose and followed.

An hour later, he was calling on me to slow down again and the next time we stopped, he said this was very uncool and what was my fuckin' hurry? There was no hurry, he said – chill out! But I had one idea only, which was to get out of Spain – and I wasn't stopping or chilling out until that was done. It was easier for me, in a way. I was driven; he was just tagging along. No drugs are more powerful than fear and adrenalin. All the dormant reserves in the body swing into action.

This time, I said to him, 'OK, so you stay here, Marvin. Tomorrow you can continue on your own. I'm going now. Have a good night.' And I picked up my small suitcase, to go.

'You're not leaving me here, with no compass?' he cried.

'You won't need one in daylight. What do you want me to do? Carry you? I'm crossing tonight, Marvin. You don't want to come, so stay. I didn't ask you to be here.'

But, in truth, I knew there was no way I could leave someone in the dark on the side of a dangerous mountain. He was a pain in the arse; he was slowing me down and putting me through all this persuading and cajoling and having to threaten him. But how could I leave him? He might fall down a hole and break his neck. We'd already almost walked over a cliff. At the last minute, as we pushed through heavy scrub, I'd sensed empty space in front of me. So, rather than abandon Marvin-the-Boy-Scout, I would have to practically drag him all the way. Every few hundred metres he stopped.

'C'mon, Marvin, it's not far,' I'd say.

'How much farther?' he'd ask. He was like a kid in the back of a car.

It wasn't as dark now; we were above the mist and here and there I could dimly make out paths or animal tracks through the scrub and there was some bare earth and widely spaced trees. 'Give me the compass,' he said. 'I'll walk ahead now.' I didn't like to give up possession of it but I realised it might be useful to have him walking in front. Up to now, nobody could have seen us, only heard us, but if there were patrols, they might see us moving in places where the scrub was low.

On a knoll of grass, we stopped. I had another swallow of cognac and caught my breath. It was light enough for us to half-see one another's faces. He lay on his back and was so silent that, after a few minutes, I thought he'd gone to sleep. Then, I roused him and we set off again.

A hundred metres along, there was a wide fork around some trees and I said, 'OK, Marvin, what's it say on the compass?' I'd stayed on a bearing as true north as possible all along, whatever had stood in the way.

'You have the compass,' he said.

'No,' I said. 'You had it, remember?'

Neither of us had it, so we walked back to the knoll, me telling him that he was the one who had had it when we stopped, him telling me that he hadn't, that I'd lost it, that I was drunk from the cognac. This wasn't true and we both knew it. Never in my life had my mind been clearer. Whether it was the mountain air or whatever did it, the chronic buzzing in my head had, at last, stopped. As we argued, tempers rose.

When we reached the knoll, I said 'Don't walk around too much . . . Easy does it . . .' I was down on my knees with my hands feeling the grass. Next thing, I heard a crunch and, yeah, it was the compass, Marvin had stood on it. It was where he'd put it down as he lay back. I said, 'Stay where you are, don't move . . .' and I lit a match and picked it up. Dead compass. The glass was broken and the needle was stuck. As we walked away, he maintained it was me who'd left it there. But that was Marvin. Marvin was a liar through and through.

In any case, we soon didn't need a compass any more. We came upon a path, a wide path running along the ridge at the top of the Pyrenees, white in the moonlight – white dust like the paths in Formentera, but smooth – and it wound ahead like a white ribbon with the moon and stars over it, bright in a clear sky. In my head I called it Freedom Road and, under my breath, I hummed Dylan's song, *'How many roads must a man walk down, before you can call him a man . . .'*, and I set out walking with a spring in my step, no more scrambling, and Marvin beside me. We passed a white-walled building sitting all silent and lightless but for the moonlight on its walls – maybe a monastery high on the ridge of those mountains but there wasn't a sound of life; it was all set in a hushed stillness, and we passed with silent footfalls, and no dogs barked.

As the sky grew brighter, we could make out the lower hills and the plain of France below us. I was near freedom now. The flat misty land stretched to the horizon. It would soon be lit by the rising sun.

We left the path, and started downhill. It was simple now, to pick out the way to go. Down, down. But again, no paths, and some cliffs, and tough going. And then, at an escarpment, we came upon winches and pulleys, and it was a sort of logging chute. In the clearing below, I saw a barrel; I thought this will say either *'Aceite'* or *'Huile'* and if it says *'Huile'*, I'll know I'm in France. However, the irony was that when I got close enough to read it, it said *'Pujols'*, which is a Catalan surname well known in Formentera; however, I was certain I was in France. 'I really got you through, man!' Marvin said. I laughed.

We followed a dirt track away from the logging camp, found a tarmac road and walked down it. As dawn broke, we walked into the village of Amélie-les-Bains.

Epilogue

ONCE I HAD REACHED FRANCE, the others no longer had a hold over me, the spell was broken, the illusion that I needed them dispelled.

In Paris, I left them. I let them keep the car: it wasn't worth bringing it with me to England. The last I heard of Rick or Marvin was that they'd got some LSD on credit in Amsterdam, lost it all in a bum deal and had been repatriated to America.

I arrived in London on 10 February 1965. By early August, with the help of American Express scams, the collusion of Nicole and a generous contribution from Zelda Bloom, I was able to send the money to a lawyer in Gerona to buy Carlo out of jail. He came to London and stayed with Hanna and me until he and Nicole found a room. Hanna had returned in March and she and I had gotten together again. We had two more kids. Six years later, we separated but my relationship with the children continued as before.

I have recently learned that others had crossed the Pyrenees where I did and with better reason. In La Vajol, there is a memorial to Lluis Companys, President of Catalonia, who escaped to France via La Vajol during the Civil War. He was later captured by the Germans, returned to Barcelona and executed by firing squad in 1940. It states 'In remembrance of Lluis Companys and the 500,000 Spanish, especially Catalan, who in this area tried to escape in 1939 to exile, but also all those who were victims of the dictatorship.' With no prior knowledge of this history, it was fortuitous that I chose La Vajol.